*When the doors of perception are cleansed,
man will see things as they truly are, infinite.*

William Blake

Contents

Section 1

Set-up and back story

'Buried' (1953), lithograph © Versus Entertainment/Kobal Collection

Preface

This book will teach you the advanced narrative techniques that will help you tell an original story in an original way. If that sounds a tall order, never fear. Screenwriting is a craft, as well as an art; and these techniques can be learned.

As a student of mine put it, once you understand these techniques, you understand that **Maverick** films are not complicated. They are just cleverly written.

Or as a teacher of mine once told me: everything is hard until you learn it; then it's easy.

All the classic principles of dramaturgy remain relevant. But **Maverick** techniques broaden your palette and give you tools that you never knew you had, buried deep inside you. Tools that allow you to play with time, logic and reality. Tools that set your imagination free.

In *Maverick Screenwriting,* all these tools find new and inventive use. We'll extract the techniques which have been successful in **Maverick** films, and I'll show you how you can use them yourself to create new and original stories.

But technique is only a means to an end. The aim is to learn to look at the world in a different way, and then to put that vision into words.

Once you succeed in doing that, you have found your voice, and can throw technique away.

This book is not a complete or definitive analysis of **Maverick** films. No doubt you will have your own lost or cult classic that you feel I have slighted or ignored. This causes me no lost sleep. On the contrary, it only proves that there will always be a need and a hunger for **Maverick** films.

It is the nature of the choices made by these films to be controversial. Great films (indeed all great art works) are made in spite of the system, not because of it.

I believe screenwriting is a craft. I am prepared to dig deep, but only to uncover techniques that can be applied, tools that can be put to use. I am not interested in analysis for its own sake – the academic need to define or label, to put something in a box.

The definitions of *Maverick Screenwriting* are by their nature slippery and elusive, but the techniques are practical and straightforward. With a little practice, they will greatly enhance the power of your writing.

I have always followed a simple approach to teaching this material. If something works, there must be a reason. It only remains to carve out the underlying principles, like an archeologist revealing the outlines of a lost, mythical city; then to dig a little deeper, to try to discover the source of its magic.

However, the tools of *Maverick Screenwriting* are not techniques in any conventional sense. They are not templates to be memorized and copied, like so many of the clones and franchises in cinemas today.

On the contrary, they will help you approach your screenwriting in a more intuitive way. You have far more creative options than you realize. This book will give you a greater palette to work from.

Introduction

I like all kinds of movies. Action, adventure, drama, arthouse – you name it. There is only one sin in movie-making I cannot abide. And that is: predictability.

The rising cost of international films, and in particular their marketing budgets, has created an aversion to risk-taking which has made movies boring and predictable.

Major movies are now "pre-sold" as a package wrapped round a familiar product: a toy you played with, a comic book you read, a TV show you remember with nostalgia. With so much at stake, why take a chance on something that doesn't have brand recognition?

This reliance on underlying material is a sign that we're losing faith in our own storytelling. It's as if nobody trusts screenwriters to write original stories any more.

Fortunately, movies aren't a science. William Goldman's dictum that "nobody knows anything"[1] is not a put-down of movie people – in fact, you'd be surprised how smart the executives who make dumb movies are.

Instead it's a recognition that, in spite of every attempt to turn movies into merchandise, nobody knows what audiences will decide to watch. For all the market testing, there are still plenty of expensive flops.

Then there are the films that have no right to be born at all – low-budget indie movies that only got made because someone's obsession made them happen. Films like *Memento, Amores Perros, Brick* and *Donnie Darko*.

As more and more movies have become salami-sliced franchises, adaptations of graphic novels or video games, many moviegoers have found themselves longing for something more. The problem is, we never know what we want till we see it. It drives Hollywood studios crazy.

But every so often they do get it right. In *Avatar*, James Cameron created a world that no one knew they wanted to see. Then it became a "must-see".

Orson Welles said: "Don't give them what they want – show them something they've never seen before." Great movies make us walk out and look at the rain-drenched sidewalk as though we've never seen anything so beautiful.

As Clint Eastwood's character in *Unforgiven* observes, after recuperating from a high fever which brought him near to death, he wouldn't normally notice the beautiful mountains all around him, but he's "sure noticing them now".

Great movies have that effect: they make the world seem a little more exciting, a little more vivid and alive. Suddenly, everything seems possible.

Increasingly, movies that do this for me have something in common. They use unusual narrative techniques to reveal a deeper truth about the world. These techniques of **Maverick** screenwriting play with **time**, **logic** and **reality** to change the way we look at the world.

You may wonder how much of this is down to the director. Some brilliant directors may create films in their camera, but few films can soar on visual inspiration alone. For the rest, the process begins with the screenwriter.

Maverick films are not born out of a desire to be fashionably different. They reflect a sense that the modern world is fractured, lacking in any overarching belief or faith.

Lacking that unity or consistent moral code, **Maverick** filmmakers are suspicious of conventional film structure, since this is apt to over-simplify the moral complexity of the world, its random tragedy, the impossibility of ever grasping or knowing it all.

Of course, great **Maverick** directors enhance this narrative off-kilteredness, expand it through image and sound; they find an expression for it through visual style. But as Bo Goldman explains:

> *When writing a screenplay, you have to imagine everything that's on the screen . . . what's between the words, between the sentences. The mortar, so to speak. You have to have a vision as a screenwriter.*[2]

As legendary screenwriter Robert Towne once said, you have to imagine you are describing a film that has already been shot. You cannot write it until you have fully imagined it. Before I explain how you can fulfill that vision by using the techniques explained here, I had better say first what **Maverick** screenwriting is not.

It is not an excuse for creating characters that no one can relate to, who are eccentric or mysterious just for the heck of it, or whose motives can only be guessed at. Nor is it a reason for writing stories that don't make sense, can't commit themselves or fail to deliver powerful emotions. It is not a manifesto for producing shock or bizarre effects.

Maverick Screenwriting is about getting back to the original magic of the movies and showing us something we've never seen before. It's about finding the form that fits the theme. It's about asking the big questions in life, the ones beyond "What happens next?" and "How's it all going to turn out?", which mainstream movies already have covered.

Instead, *Maverick Screenwriting* asks questions like: "Why are we here?", "What is the meaning of it all?" and "Do we really control our destiny?"

There are no universal, one-size-fits-all answers to these questions, so the answers tend to be personal and unique. This is the opposite of what is usually demanded by the commercial mainstream, who are required to please all four "quadrants" (a marketing term for the key audience groups).

But, you may ask, *Don't you have to write for the market?*

I believe too many writers are being influenced by industry forums and screenwriting teachers who tell them just that. Sure, you have to be aware of what's going on in the market. But not so that you can slavishly follow it, or do what has already been done.

You have to be aware of the market so you know where the gaps are. What nobody else has tried, maybe not for a long time. Then you have to revive it and renew it. Give it a new twist. That's the key.

Maverick Screenwriting is about freeing your imagination. It's about taking a journey to somewhere different. And it's about having the techniques to ensure you take your audience along for the ride.

Why we need Maverick movies

It's a crowded marketplace out there, so film companies rely on every possible hook to gain exposure for their films. It's just so much easier to sell movies that already have a profile as books, TV shows or computer games.

The alternative is to write a **Maverick** film. **Maverick** movies are concept-driven; and original ideas, cleverly executed, are what attract attention and get people talking. Before you know it they're spreading the word by mouth, Facebook and Twitter.

Maverick films do not rely on stars or big budgets, which makes them ideal for first-time filmmakers, even those who aspire to make mainstream films.

But surely the odds are better if you write for the mainstream?

The reality is, if you are a new writer there is little chance of your being hired to write a big-budget movie.

The competition for the main genres is intense. The more high-concept your idea is, the more likely it is to capture something already in the *zeitgeist*, whether it be meteors, terrorism, global warming or swine flu.

When I worked for a major broadcaster, I soon learned that ideas are a dime a dozen. If *you've* thought of it, you can be sure someone else has thought of it first.

In the bars and cafés where writers hang out, they often trade horror stories of their ideas being stolen. That happens much more rarely than people think. More likely they just picked up on something that is out there in the *zeitgeist*. It's amazing how many similar ideas are floating out there at the same time.

This is why I discourage new screenwriters from trying to write high-concept movies. Unless you feel you were born for that reason alone, wait till you've had some experience. Writing a genre movie is tough. You think you can write a better car chase than has been done before? Or tell a cop story with a new twist?

The Wire was a brilliant new twist on the cop show. But it was hardly a new idea to tell a story in the round, connecting characters from every level of society. Dickens used the same storytelling device almost two centuries ago.

It is the *detail* of the world that makes us believe in these connections, and David Simon's knowledge was derived the hard way, like Dickens's. By pounding the streets and knocking on doors.

It takes time to learn the skill of turning research into something living and real – to create the illusion that you've been to distant and wonderful lands, and are merely reporting back. That's best not attempted while you are still learning the basic skills of reading a map.

That doesn't mean you should stick to writing only about what you know. But starting with what you know can be a smart strategy, since what you know best is often unique.

But how do you tell the difference between what is merely new – and what is truly unique?

The search for the New, New Thing

Ever since the early days of film, when movie cameras caught the flight of birds, or frightened petticoated women out of their seats as a train hurtled towards them from the screen, audiences have been looking for the New, New Thing. Hollywood studios try to create the New, New Thing by putting on an ever bigger spectacle. But this obsession is based on a fallacy which I call the **saturation principle**.

To understand what this means, we need to go back to those first experiments in moving film. As soon as audiences became familiar with stunts like the stop-motion tricks used by magician-turned-director Méliès, they wanted more. More than a gimmick or a gag. More than an unbroken reel of time, unraveling a brief moment in history.

They wanted stories that compressed time, that expressed its essence.

This ability to intercut images seamlessly became what is unique about moving pictures. The juxtaposition of one image with another magically lends the two a power which separately they lack.

At first the grammar had to be simple. Early directors had to overcome their producer's insistence that a medium shot of an actor would look like the actor's legs had been cut off. Or that somebody looking, followed by a shot of what they're looking at, couldn't be understood without the addition of a painted eye, a pair of binoculars or a telescope.

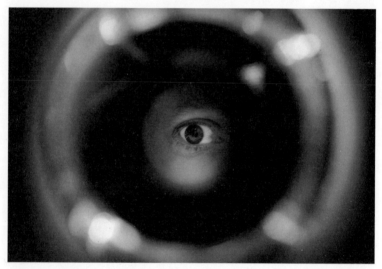

© Getty Images

Nowadays, audiences jump through time and space without batting an eyelid. We no longer need to spell out the whole chain of logic, as film grammar provides us with increasingly radical short cuts. Audiences leap across the gaps quicker, impatient with being led by the nose.

We're running on adrenaline-charged processors, but strangely mainstream movies are not getting more complicated. On the contrary, they read and look more and more like comic books.

Maverick filmmakers, on the other hand, rarely stop to consider whether their obsessions are too elaborate. As Christopher McQuarrie put it:

The Usual Suspects *is what it is because we never stopped to consider the audience as anything but people who loved film as much as we did, who were meticulously anal about detail and ripped films to pieces.*[3]

So what, then, are we using all that processing power for? On digital effects which are ever more detailed, more lifelike. As Charlie Brooker, film critic and novelist, writes about *Die Hard 4*:

Towards the end of the film there's a lengthy sequence in which antediluvian tough guy Bruce Willis hurtles along in an articulated lorry while a fighter jet tries to stop him by machine-gunning the entire world to pieces. The scene grows steadily more outlandish: huge sections of highway buckle and collapse; the truck swerves and tumbles and is literally shredded by bullets; Bruce leaps on to the back of the jet and leaps off just as it explodes in a massive fireball.

And it's boring. Unbelievably boring. At any given moment, only 17 per cent of what you're watching is real, and you know it. You're not immersed in the slightest. At best you're impressed by the rendering of the smoke plumes.[4]

Digital rendering is now so lifelike, that soon it may render movie stars redundant; or able to sit with their feet up, licensing out an image of themselves from when they were younger and better-looking.

The problem is, the more "realistic" special effects become, the less work our imaginations have to do. Our minds absorb, then are saturated by effects at lightning speed. Like a drug addict, we need a bigger hit to get the same high. And every year, trying to outdo themselves, blockbuster movies cost more and more.

All trying to recapture that moment when the Lumière Brothers first projected images on to a wall. No longer a peep show, a private experience, films became instead a shared vision of ecstasy. Finally, the audience knew what it was like to be lost collectively in the action.

In time, actors adjusted to the omniscience of the giant screen, which betrayed every flicker of emotion. They realized they could do more with less. Dialogue was written which allowed actors to say one thing, but suggest another through their eyes.

It was all about being lost in the action. When television brought intimate soaps to the small screen, cinema competed with ever wider, deeper screen formats, from Cinerama to IMAX to 3D.

The immersive nature of 3D is affecting not only the directing but the writing of movies. Shock tactics – the spear flying straight out of the screen – get old real fast (that old train trick again); while piling one effect on top of another can lead to sensory overload.

3D's real strength is in allowing us to feel completely immersed in a scene, to explore it, not from a distance in two dimensions, as we do in the theater, but by actually moving through it in three dimensions. The intrusion of MTV-style cutting yanks us out of this pleasant immersion, becomes distracting.

Screenwriters may write longer, unbroken sequences in the future – like they did at the beginning of moving film. And as they did again in the 1960s, when Nouvelle Vague filmmakers championed the use of long, tracking shots (*mises-en-scène*). Fashions come round again, if you wait long enough.

But the **saturation principle** tells us that the pursuit of spectacle alone is a never-ending, tail-chasing sport.

What audiences really want are stories that replay in their minds long after the images have faded out.

But what if I want to write for the mainstream?

Understanding *Maverick Screenwriting* can help you understand how to write mainstream movies that stand out from the pack. Let's face it: there's nothing harder than writing an action movie that's different. They've raked through all the old comic books, but the superheroes are shrinking, and so are their superpowers.

Genre films have to be constantly reinvented to reflect the shifting preoccupations of their audience: the *zeitgeist* as it is called. The *zeitgeist* is an eclectic mix of everything we absorb from all around us: our culture, music, thought, fashion and politics.

The *Terminator* movies are not just great action movies. They play on that great paranoid theme of science fiction, one which preoccupies us more and more as technology speeds up: the fear that one day human beings will find themselves at war with the machines they have created.

So far, so genre. But what made the *Terminator* movies such a hit was the genius of Cameron's **Maverick**, time-bending concept.

John Connor's return from the future to save his mother's life combines powerful personal motivation with a universal aspiration – that one day our actions may be of benefit to future generations.

Similarly, *The Matrix* didn't just have cool special effects – it echoed the feeling that many of us share in an increasingly virtual, commercialized world: that in another dimension, our real selves are engaged in a more meaningful struggle for what is vital.

These stories connect, because they recognize that much of the time many of us feel disengaged; and for a while they allow us to feel part of something bigger than ourselves, something important.

The **Maverick** approach to storytelling invites us to question whether our habits and routines are blinding us to a deeper reality, one lurking unseen just below the surface.

Maverick films such as *The Sixth Sense* and *The Usual Suspects* go even further, their radical Maverick twists making us reassess everything we thought was true about their world.

Maverick techniques enable you to reflect the reality of a time and place not only by what happens, but by *the way you tell the story.* In *Memento*, we are invited to question whether, in a world where memory is so unreliable, any clues can be trusted.

These films hearken back to the dark, murky world of **film noir**, but instead of Marlowe stumbling through the gloom in search of the criminal, the *audience itself* is invited to disentangle the different strands to reveal the true nature of reality.

While the **Maverick** approach encourages an original way of looking at things, this does not preclude the use of Maverick techniques for adaptations from underlying work.

Recently, films such as *The English Patient, The Motorcycle Diaries, The Constant Gardener, The Last King of Scotland* and *The Diving Bell and the Butterfly* all found uniquely **Maverick** solutions for transforming one medium into another.

Using the **Maverick** approach, period stories can be revived by seeing historic events through the prism of today's *zeitgeist,* as Baz Luhrmann did in his brilliant resetting of *Romeo and Juliet* in gangland Los Angeles.

Bonnie and Clyde retold the myths of the dustbowl bank robbers of the 1930s through the prism of the 1960s. Older critics hated the joyful knowingness of Warren Beatty and Faye Dunaway's characters, their postmodern awareness of their own celebrity. But as a perfect metaphor for the times, it foresaw how the rebellious sixties would turn to hedonistic self-indulgence.

The ability of period movies to transport us into a particular time and place is not just about creating some simplistic "relevance". Nor is it simply about substituting modern language and attitudes. Many costume dramas go wrong by making all the characters talk and act like people do today. If you could truly show how different society was only a couple of centuries ago, people would be amazed.

Didn't everyone tell Mel Gibson no one would ever go see a movie in Ancient Aramaic? What is most *authentic* is always what most amazes us.

As W. H. Auden said, "some writers confuse authenticity, which they ought always to aim at, with originality, which they should never bother about".[5]

Authenticity is the ability to know your world, or to give the illusion of doing so. It is about choosing the right details.

Which brings us to the next question.

Some of the best films have been works of deep realism: aren't these the opposite of Maverick?

You don't have to create an *imagined* world like *Avatar's* Pandora to introduce us to something new. I like nothing better than to be immersed in a detailed, fully conceived world that I've never experienced before, whether it's the *favela* of *City of God* or a subculture of my city that I've never seen before.

Do Maverick films require an element of fantasy?

Not at all. But **Maverick** screenwriting does involve a clear and calculated reframing of the way we look at the world.

On the other hand, not all fantasy is **Maverick**. Movies such as *Shrek*, imaginative though they may be, exist in a consistent reality and deal with familiar emotions and needs.

Of course, ever since *The Wizard of Oz* all the best kids' movies have had a Maverick element: the ability to tell one story for kids, and another – with ironic insight – for the adults.

Is Maverick screenwriting the same as low-budget or "Dogme" filmmaking?

Not necessarily, but it is undoubtedly true that financial constraints as much as stylistic ones encourage imaginative improvisation.

Christopher Nolan knew he was only going to be able to shoot one day a week on his first feature-length film, *Following*, so he wrote the movie in a modular way. Since he never knew what location he'd be in until the day before, he had to rewrite the script as he went along, changing the specifics about each location, which this form gave him the freedom to do.

Cut to the chase: have I got what it takes to be Maverick?

Maybe you bought this book because you fancy you're *already* something of a Maverick. Don't we all like to fantasize that we're rebelling against the norm?

Or maybe we think we're just the opposite: nothing special, even inadequate. Woody Allen and now Charley Kaufman have raised the excruciating examination of personal failure into an art form.

When you realize exactly what makes you different from everyone else, you discover what an interesting point of view you have.

Unfortunately, this artistic truth still vies with the notion that people are born with talent, or touched with genius. They either have what it takes, or they don't. It's the cult of amateurism, nurtured at the altar of privilege. And it's nonsense. Screenwriting is a craft. The dramatic principles can be learned. If you can learn how to apply them, you can also learn how to break them.

And that's exactly what we're going to do.

But first, a cautionary note.

> *There are too many movies that are half-written out there, half-made. They talk about this "independent" movement. It's only independent if the thinking's independent. It's not independent because it was done for a price.*[6]

Oliver Stone, writer/director

The dangers of adopting Maverick as a style

We have a rancher in America's Wild West called Samuel Maverick to thank for lending his name to the high-and-mighty term "Maverick". However, Sam wasn't some kind of well, *maverick*, for refusing to brand his cattle – simply bone idle and preoccupied with the pursuit of his pleasures. He was "The Big Lebowski" of ranchers.

Unfortunately, being different is no excuse for being lazy. Being a truly **Maverick** screenwriter requires work.

Maverick stories are not eccentric for their own sake, nor do they strive to shock or to bore. They do not make a cult out of the bizarre. On the contrary, they celebrate the ordinary: from the small-town habits of *Groundhog Day* to the suburban rituals of *American Beauty*, or the dull, gated community of *The Truman Show*; to the downtown student grunge of Austin's *Slacker*.

These are all **Maverick** films, and the world of each is ordinary in every way. It is the way the stories are told which makes them fresh and original.

The problem is, people are being encouraged to write formulaic screenplays. That leaves those who can't relate to their simplistic messages feeling left out, irrelevant, like whatever they think and feel about the world couldn't be of interest to anyone else.

So they retreat into **Maverick** as a kind of style.

Sometimes people don't want to do the hard work of writing and rewriting a script till it all fits together perfectly; so they call the unfinished mess "Maverick" – when it's simply confused, ambiguous or obscure.

It's a shame, because now that technology enables films to be made more cheaply than ever before, people are rushing into production stories that are thrown together just so they can say that they've made a film.

But there are only so many times you can shake down your friends, family and strangers to fund your solipsisms. Sooner or later you've got to make a story that audiences can relate to, that makes sense of their experience of life.

What if you're not sure that you're truly a Maverick?

Have you ever thought what it would be like to write what you really feel? The things you can never say, because if we all went around expressing exactly what we feel the whole world would be a madhouse.

As Larry David, creator and star of *Curb Your Enthusiasm* says: "Sure, I have a notebook, I write those thoughts down. But I'm not a sociopath. I don't go around saying them."[7]

What if you could get across your own unique way of looking at the world, could give your audience the experience, as Charley Kaufman writes, of "being inside someone else's skin"? What if, just for a moment, you could allow yourself to be unedited and uncensored?

The chances are, if you started doing that, you'd find yourself reaching for the **Maverick** toolbox. And life would start to get a whole lot more exciting.

In this book, you will find tools to make your writing more original and interesting. But this book is not just about tools. It is about learning a creative process that will allow you to go back to the well when your inspiration is flagging; and as you drink from that well, you'll see the world reflected through the shimmering droplets in new and surprising ways.

Splash some on your face, and feel revived, reborn. Undressed, unashamed to be naked at last.

Now dive right in.

Foreword

The Exercises

While this book contains plenty of theory, the proof is in the pudding as far as screenwriting is concerned. If I have not taught you how to apply these principles, what you have learned will have little value.

The exercises at the end of each chapter will help embed these ideas in your subconscious, because they are designed to put you through the mental process, or to allow you to enter the state of mind whereby you can take a **Maverick** slant on things, and see them in another light.

You may want to follow a simple process.

○ Imagine yourself experiencing the point of view or state of mind suggested by the exercise.

○ Now imagine you are floating above yourself, high into the air and coming down into the body of your character.

○ Take a moment to see how they feel – to see the world through their eyes. Now turn up the intensity of the experience, make it brighter, make the colors stronger, the sounds more distinct.

○ Now write down exactly what you experience – and make it real.

It is recommended that you complete each exercise before you proceed to the next chapter. Do not be afraid to let yourself go, or to allow your imagination to run riot. Nobody else is going to see the results (unless you want them to).

On the other hand, you may want to form a small writers' group to give each other feedback on these exercises. These principles are like having a new, expanded palette of colors. Try each one out individually first; soon you will learn to mix and match them, to blend them together spontaneously. Having a creative group around you will give you plenty of ideas that you might not have thought of yourself, for applying these techniques to best fit your theme.

More importantly, you will have learned the habit of thinking flexibly. If you want to write for the mainstream, this will give you the ability to find a new angle, a fresh way into genre material.

It will also give your writing a new shading and depth which can be powerfully felt, without any "technique" being seen.

1 The prequel

Out of the Past, 1947 © RKO/Kobal Collection

> *A film is difficult to explain because it is easy to understand.*[8]

Hold it. Pause right there. First, we have to go back in time. Because if you want to know how to break the rules, you have to know how they got there in the first place.

There has always been a certain tension between art and commerce. Film is an expensive medium, and the costs involved have not always encouraged experiment or improvisation.

The studio system in Hollywood was designed for the production of lavish films on an industrial scale. As such, it succeeded wonderfully. Writers were put on the payroll, and housed in cheaply built huts. Samuel Goldwyn, head of a studio, used to prowl the corridors on the alert for any typewriters that had fallen silent.

In the early days, many screenwriters were distinguished novelists and dramatists. They looked on the fledgling medium of the movies with condescension, if not outright contempt.

They wrote unashamedly popular stories, well-worn variations on plots frequently stolen from their competitors. When they picked up their paychecks, they couldn't believe their luck. Why, in one year they could earn more than they'd earned in a whole lifetime of writing plays or highbrow novels!

Thrown into the "block", junior writers soon learned from the older hacks, who rewrote their pages, what the form was. Very often one writer "shadowed" another: writing the same story in another room, a practice liable to make any writer paranoid. There was little point in pushing a "personal vision". It would only get rewritten. Everyone else's was.

Now Raymond Chandler, whose hard-boiled detective novels written in the 1940s helped inspire the genre of **film noir**, was not a writer who enjoyed being treated like cattle.

Educated as an English gentleman, Chandler had transplanted himself to California, and somehow learned the vernacular – the new slang of the streets and the alleyways – in the way that only strangers can. His books combine wisecracking dialogue with sardonic observation: the outer and inner lives of private detective Marlowe. Over it all, Marlowe's wry first-person narration gives events, told in flashback, a humorous and uniquely slanted point of view.

Chandler accepted a Hollywood paycheck after a number of his books had already been adapted into films. However, the adjustment was not an easy one.

He fumed that having someone in the room while he was writing was an invasion of his creative process, particularly when that person was the younger (but infinitely more experienced) screenwriter and director Billy Wilder, a diminutive German who until recently had barely spoken English. (Wilder went on to write and direct many of the funniest films of the period with some of the snappiest dialogue, like *Some Like It Hot* and *Sunset Boulevard*).

After a couple of weeks' work, Chandler went on strike. He demanded that Wilder stop wearing his hat indoors, and stop making phone calls to his girlfriends during working hours.

Finally, Chandler declared, he couldn't possibly be expected to write unless he was drunk by noon. In spite of this unlikely pairing, Chandler and Wilder managed to create the iconic **film noir**, *Double Indemnity* (1944), in which they finally cracked the puzzle that had challenged all the other screenwriters who had previously adapted his work: how to translate that unique **point of view** to the screen?

Until then, voiceover had been used mostly as a kind of shorthand, particularly in adaptations of literary works. Since novels tend to have more plot than films, all too often the screenwriter will cover up the missing bits – like a decorator painting over the cracks – with narration.

The film adaptations of Chandler's books all tried imaginative but generally unsuccessful techniques to reproduce this point of view. *Murder, My Sweet* (1944) uses highly subjective shots from detective Marlowe's point of view, including a hallucinatory sequence after he gets drugged. The

narration is not always related to what is happening on the screen, but is "syncopated" like a rhythm played off the beat.

The Lady in the Lake went even further, becoming "one of the most extreme experiments with point of view in the history of Hollywood cinema".[9] The camera becomes Marlowe's eyes, while he himself is rarely in shot. Cigarettes are raised to the camera to be smoked, and punches hurled at us. This highly literal approach, unsurprisingly, doesn't really work. **Point of view** has to be more subtle than that – since as soon as we become aware of it, we realize that we're watching something artificial, and the spell is broken.

Chandler's exceptional turn of phrase, allied with Marlowe's unique point of view, made his books hugely successful. It certainly wasn't the plots – which were convoluted and inscrutable, even to the author. When the film adapted from his novel The Big Sleep was being shot, puzzled director Howard Hawks phoned up Chandler to ask who the murderer was. Chandler replied airily (it was past midday, after all) that he didn't have the faintest idea.

In Chandler's work the plots are not as important as Marlowe's **point of view**, which makes everything interesting. Even Double Indemnity, which thanks to Wilder was as tight as could be, still has a massive hole in the plot. Insurance salesman Walter Neff has a plan for the perfect crime. Some accidents are considered so unlikely that they pay out double on life insurance – a "double indemnity". One of these is when someone falls off a train and kills themself. When Phyllis, the femme fatale, walks into his life and he falls for her, they arrange to have her husband bumped off in this way and collect on the insurance.

The idea that Walter would not have seen the obvious flaw in his plan, which he'd been formulating for years, is hard to credit. The very unlikeliness of the accident is its flaw: it immediately causes his wily boss, Barton Keyes, to have a gut instinct (the "little man" in his chest) and investigate further.

Chandler came up with the brilliant idea of having Walter narrate the film on the tape recorder to his mentor Keyes as he's dying. The only reason

Keyes couldn't see that it was Walter who'd set up the whole thing because he was "too close".

Keyes's blindness, and Walter's wounded regret for the pain his actions will cause him, gives the narration an unusual poignancy. Without it, since he can never admit this vulnerability to Phyllis, we would never understand how Walter feels about betraying his boss.

The search for a way of expressing a dislocated **point of view** is at the heart of all **Maverick** films. In Chandler's work, Marlowe's commentary – his point of view – is as important as the events he describes. When he tells us: "I felt pretty good . . . like an amputated leg", the contradiction is both funny and poignant. In his narration, he can make a joke of his feelings, but in life he can never allow them to show. At the same time he lets us know that they are there and that they hurt. This difference between what Marlowe says, and what he is actually feeling, creates **dramatic tension**. In screenwriting terms we say it has **subtext**, the feeling that what lies below the surface carries more weight than what floats above.

When we turn the telescope around and view the world through Marlowe's eyes, his ironic distance and endless wisecracks prevent us from being too affected by the things we witness. Marlowe himself relies on a pint of bourbon, kept within easy reach.

This "cool" and sardonic point of view, along with the whipcrack dia-logue, accounts for the lasting appeal of **film noir**, since it represents not just a style but an attitude to the world: a refusal to accept the outer appearance of things.

At the time, all American films were subject to censorship under the Hays Code (in Britain, the British Board of Film Censors served the same function). Films had to conform to a strict moral code defining not only what could be shown but even what could be implied on the screen. Sex only occurred between married couples; the guilty were punished, and the righteous won out. **Film noir** pushed these rules to the limits. The inability of film noir's heroes to resist temptation was suspected to be subversive, as was the suggestion of dark crimes and sexual perversion hidden just below the surface.

In the following scene from *Double Indemnity,* Walter visits Phyllis for the first time, to renew her husband's life insurance.

                    PHYLLIS
               (*Standing up again*)
          Mr. Neff, why don't you drop by
          tomorrow evening about eight-thirty.
          He'll be in then.

                    NEFF
          Who?

                    PHYLLIS
          My husband. You were anxious to talk to
          him weren't you?

                    NEFF
          Sure, only I'm getting over it a
          little. If you know what I mean.

                    PHYLLIS
          There's a speed limit in this state,
          Mr. Neff. Forty-five miles an hour.

                    NEFF
          How fast was I going, officer?

                    PHYLLIS
          I'd say about ninety.

                    NEFF
          Suppose you get down off your
          motorcycle and give me a ticket.

                    PHYLLIS
          Suppose I let you off with a warning
          this time.

NEFF

Suppose it doesn't take.

PHYLLIS

Suppose I have to whack you over the
knuckles.

NEFF

Suppose I bust out crying and put my
head on your shoulder.

PHYLLIS

Suppose you try putting it on my
husband's shoulder.

NEFF

That tears it.

Neff takes his hat and briefcase.

This scene bats the dialogue backward and forward at ninety miles an hour, keeping the speeding metaphor going, but we know this conversation is about a lot more than car insurance: it's about sex, danger and power. Walter and Phyllis are heading into dangerous territory.

For a long time in Hollywood movies, heroes had been unburdened by guilt or doubt. Given the censor's rules, why should the hero question his purpose? If his resolve did occasionally falter, it was never enough to shake his faith in the righteousness of his cause.

With **film noir**, a new kind of hero started to emerge. In Detective Marlowe, Chandler created a hero who was tough and cynical on the outside, but bruised and vulnerable on the inside.

What motivates Marlowe? Sometimes it's the bills he has to pay. At others, he seems to do things just for the hell of it; or because, beneath that cynical exterior (as Captain Renault says of Rick in *Casablanca*) there lurks an idealist. Sometimes, what Marlowe thinks he is investigating turns out to be not what's important at all. The innocent are often not innocent, or the lines are murky or blurred. He is stumbling along in the dark, toward the light.

Marlowe lives for the present, for whatever walks through the door. He has few illusions or anxieties about his prospects, either for business or romance. Like Rick, last night is so long ago he can't remember, and tonight is too far ahead to think about. Like Willard, the soldier hero of *Apocalypse Now*, he acts for himself; he isn't "even in their . . . army anymore".

For some, this new hero's skepticism about the official line, the desire to get "the real dope", was liberating. **Film noir**'s sharp and cynical take on the dimming of the American Dream chimed with the disillusionment of many soldiers returning from World War II. The films were originally intended to be B-movies, cheap and cheerful knock-offs of pulp fiction. Instead they reinvented the crime genre by suggesting that crime reflected something rotten, not only in human beings, but in the state of Denmark.

Film noir's attitude of cool and cynicism leads rebels of every new generation to rediscover it. But in the anti-communist fervor of 1950s American politics, film noir's cynical take on the American Dream, its obsession with the underbelly of life and the downtrodden, its constant flouting of censorship laws, was seen as a threat to public morals.

In the 1950s, the Cold War between the West and the Soviet Union, with its two competing ideologies of Capitalism and Communism, had a chilling effect on creative freedom. In America, any deviation from social norms was considered socialist-inspired subversion. Under the witch hunts led by Senator McCarthy, many screenwriters with left-leaning sympathies were blacklisted by the studios.

As the new decade brought prosperity, however, many wished to forget the troubles of the past and "fit in". As a result movies became more conformist, and their heroes blander.

This desire not to lift the lid on the American Dream is typified by the delightful series of marriage comedies Doris Day made with Rock Hudson, a gay man forced to play it straight throughout his career in Hollywood.

Across the pond in France, things weren't much better. Between the sheets of the film magazine *Cahiers du Cinéma*, a group of young film critics deplored the predictable, well-mannered studio drama that prevailed in France – the "tradition of quality". Instead, these critics loved the visual storytelling of silent cinema. They loved Italian neo-realism for its sense of spontaneity. They loved Hollywood movies, particularly those made by directors like John Ford and Nicholas Ray who put their own stamp on the major genres (respectively the Western and the melodrama).

What they admired most were those moments when the genre seems to crack apart, and reality breaks through: when their leading men show that at heart they are vulnerable or hurt.

Above all, these critics liked **film noir**, those dark films that expressed a world-weariness and cynicism about the official story and seemed to wink at you as if to say: "This is all I'm allowed to show you. But you and I know the truth is different, eh?"

Jean-Luc Godard was one of those critics, itching to grab a camera and show French cinema how it ought to be done. New documentary-style cameras and fast film meant that film could be more spontaneous, capture more of life on the streets.

For his breakthrough debut *A Bout de Souffle* (*Breathless*), Godard filmed out of the back of a postal van as his characters strolled down the street, leaving passers-by oblivious to the filmmaking going on around them. The film had long, drawn-out scenes that seemed to unfold in real time, interspersed with moments of shocking action and violence that occur almost spontaneously (a technique that Quentin Tarantino was to copy and enhance).

At the time, Godard believed – like the rest of the Nouvelle Vague (or "New Wave") – that the construction of elaborate "montages" was too artificial, too dishonest. Later, he changed his mind, and adopted this and other techniques deliberately to distance his audience, to make them aware that they were watching something artificial. He would read dry economic statistics over the images of two lovers quarreling, or film everything in long shots. His films, increasingly political, became harder to relate to.

However, in the revolutionary *Breathless*, Godard embraced spontaneity. He often didn't write the next day's dialogue until the night before, then read out the lines to the actors on the set. No wonder the actors often sound as though they are trying out the words as they speak them. The radical use of jumpcuts gave the audience the sense of being vaulted in and out of the action, and lent the film an incredible energy. However, as Godard admitted: "I really knew nothing . . . But when [the techniques] are new, there are still no rules, so you can invent."[10]

Always the most political of the Nouvelle Vague filmmakers, Godard shrugged off the "rules": "Who were they to tell us we couldn't do something? . . . We thought of ourselves as commandos attacking film for its complacency."[11]

In Belmondo's small-time gangster Michel, Godard created an entirely new notion of the hero. Pulled over in his stolen car at the beginning of the film, Michel casually guns down a motorcycle cop. Instead of running for it, as any Hollywood hood would do, he is constantly diverted from his plans to skip town – by making love to his American girlfriend Patricia, reciting poetry, or preening in the mirror.

Aware that he is the actor in his own drama, he self-consciously apes the gestures of his hero, Humphrey Bogart. He becomes a character who is all acting, but no action. He talks endlessly of escaping to the Côte d'Azur, if only he can get some money he's owed. The pursuit of this debt keeps him occupied, but we sense it is only for the sake of appearing busy. He would much rather laze about in bed with Patricia, discussing the verities of life. He is as incapable of action as Hamlet.

Belmondo's hero is ineffective; he has no real desire to save himself. At the same time his charm, his disengagement, his ability to remain unflustered, make him the embodiment of cool. He drives the story, but for his own pleasure. Even his last, staggering walk, after he has been shot, seems a self-conscious exaggeration – as if he is still playing a role, rather than paying the ultimate price for his actions.

This approach to character was influenced by the most fashionable philosophy of its time. By the end of the 1950s, existentialism had become the pre-eminent philosophy among artists and intellectuals in France. The existential hero often feels unable to control his destiny, but instead allows himself to be overrun by fate, or by the urge to commit random acts. In such circumstances, the true existentialist must live for the moment.

François Truffaut, who wrote the story for *Breathless* and was Godard's fellow critic at *Cahiers*, had made his debut a year earlier with *The 400 Blows*, a highly autobiographical story based on Truffaut's own neglected and rebellious youth. He followed this up with *Shoot the Pianist*, a story about Charlie, a classical pianist turned bar-room entertainer, forced to take on gangsters to save his brother. Apart from his music, Charlie holds back from fully embracing life, crippled by shyness. He is unable to express his love for his wife, and she ends up committing suicide.

Charlie is an ordinary person reluctantly forced into action, eager to return to the margins of life. While his rebellion is not futile like the boy's in *The 400 Blows*, or Michel's in *Breathless*, it is one in which he has no choice. Caught in a tragic cycle, his new lover is caught in the crossfire and killed. For the existentialist hero, life can be both tragic *and* absurd.

However the new, revolutionary winds of the sixties were blowing, and audiences were soon looking for protagonists who didn't have to apologize for empowering themselves.

By 1962, when Truffaut made *Jules and Jim*, a story about a *ménage-à-trois* (or a threesome – but it sounds more sophisticated in French), the world had changed. The characters had become free to act however they chose, free from guilt or the necessity to act in a way that society approved.

Godard revived Belmondo's gangster in *Pierrot le Fou*, a tale about two lovers on the run, three years later. He was once again a haphazard anti-hero, led by the nose by Anna Karina, a femme fatale who draws him into ever greater trouble, making him question the whole purpose of his existence.

In the end, driven to despair by Anna Karina, Belmondo wraps himself in dynamite and lights the fuse – only to change his mind at the last moment. Too late! He's blown to smithereens. This is **screwball comedy**, which is itself the flip side of film noir. In screwball comedy, women have the upper hand (which seemed so hilarious in the 1950s, they called it "screwball"). In **film noir**, however, this "unhealthy" state of affairs generally leads to violence.

In **classic** screenwriting, strong characters are those who are motivated by the desire to shape the world around them. In **Maverick** screenwriting, characters tend to be less focused on achieving their destiny. They are conflicted, easily sidetracked, prone to periods of apathy interspersed with random, dramatic acts, inclined to change their minds at the drop of a hat.

Ever since the Nouvelle Vague popularized such characters, the best of them have also been passionate and alive, even if their ultimate purpose seems futile. As Anna Karina's character says, "I feel alive, that's all that matters." And Belmondo shrugs after burning their car with a suitcase full of money in the trunk: "Life may be sad, but it's beautiful . . . I suddenly feel free. We can do whatever we want, when we want."

In the United States, the popularity of this Nouvelle Vague or New Wave of films, as it became known, pushed young filmmakers to test – and ultimately overturn – the system of censorship. It was possible now to show criminals as human beings, with the same foibles as the rest of us.

Warren Beatty's production of *Bonnie and Clyde*, the story of two dust-bowl bank robbers from the 1930s, which was highly influenced by the Nouvelle Vague, was initially reviled by critics. But audiences, especially young ones, disagreed. In their style, their attitude, their sexual ambivalence, but mostly in their rebellion, Warren Beatty and Faye Dunaway's characters represented a new generation who rejected the values of their parents: a generation who wanted to change everything.

Above all, they blamed the older generation for sending so many young men to their deaths in Vietnam, for a war that no one could understand.

Easy Rider represented the response of that restless generation, who wanted to opt out of not only the war but society itself. Peter Fonda and Dennis Hopper's hippies take to the road on their motorcycles "in search of America". The soundtrack proclaims, over the sound of a revved engine, "Get your motor running, head out on the highway . . . ",[12] expressing the desire of thousands of young people to hit the road and take life "as it comes".

However, while many copied the new anti-heroes in style, few noticed that the ending of *Easy Rider* predicted that such idealism would soon be out of fashion. "We blew it," Fonda says to Hopper, shortly before the two are blown away by a shotgun-wielding redneck in a pickup truck. Disillusionment was setting in, and turning to self-indulgence. Too much freedom, it was beginning to be possible to see, was not necessarily a good thing.

In **Maverick** screenplays, the characters are often more aware than most of us that they are actors playing in their own drama. They are often self-conscious and, unlike the heroes of mainstream movies, don't simply act but think about acting, and think about the act of thinking. If life is only a movie, then its consequences can't hurt us, so it doesn't matter whether we act, or don't act.

Sometimes life seems to be no more than a dream, an endless mirrored reflection of ourselves, as Belmondo says: "We are made of dreams and dreams are made of us."

He decides to write. "I won't describe people's lives, just life. Everything that takes place between people: space, sounds and colors . . . "

In **Maverick** films, the leading character does not always remain at the center of our universe. Sometimes they step aside, or the world is tilted, and we discover something much more interesting is happening at the edges of the story.

Sometimes, as in Bertolucci's *The Sheltering Sky*, the focus shifts to a different character, and we discover the protagonist is not who we thought it was.

Like Rosencrantz and Guildenstern, supporting characters doomed to wait offstage as Hamlet's drama is played out, **Maverick** characters watch events from the margins.

Like the technicians erasing Jim Carrey's memories in *Eternal Sunshine of the Spotless Mind*, they are trapped in the banality of being watchers, knowing that the true drama is happening elsewhere.

Like the hero of *Being John Malkovich*, they are doomed to watch the world through someone else's eyes. Or like the patient in *The Diving Bell and the Butterfly* with "locked-in syndrome", their only freedom left is the freedom to imagine.

2 The big "what if?"

> *Chain, chain, chain, chain of fools.*
>
> Aretha Franklin

Chain of logic: cause and effect

Classic, three-act structure is great for writing stories that have us asking the questions: what happens next? And how is it all going to end?

In a classically structured script, cause follows effect in an unbroken **chain of logic**, each event setting off the next like a string of Chinese firecrackers.

This chain of logic makes conventional structure great for maintaining suspense and creating anticipation, since it allows us to predict what is coming. The genres carry certain expectations: if it is a comedy, we expect to laugh. If it's horror, we want to scream. We want to be surprised, but we also want our expectations fulfilled.

We expect that in romantic comedy, the lovers will overcome their obstacles. In a detective story, that the investigator will find the truth, and crime be defeated. In a thriller, the threat will be repelled. In horror, evil will be overcome – at least until the sequel.

Classic structure allows you to provide plenty of twists and turns, giving the illusion that the outcome is in doubt, while safely guiding the audience to their destination.

When used in the crassest way, three-act structure can be like driving a mid-range saloon. It gets you where you want to go, but it's not terribly exciting and it's been built by robots.

After all, audiences wouldn't be so consistently satisfied with these genres if they didn't, on some level, desire consistency and predictability from the world. Life is unpredictable enough, so we seek out stories that keep that fundamental uncertainty at bay.

Entertainment is comforting, precisely because it makes us aware that we're not alone in what we feel. We can even laugh at ourselves, as long as we're not laughing alone.

Classic three-act structure is reassuring, precisely because it reflects everything we would like the world to be: consistent, reliable and malleable to our will. Classically structured films are **plot-driven** because they rely on the belief that our actions have necessary consequences. In such a world, "What happens next?", and "How does it all turn out?" become the main drivers.

There follow only two sins in classic screenwriting which an audience cannot forgive. The first is when the **chain of logic** is so obvious that the film becomes boring and predictable.

That's why every good story needs to continually surprise us. Unfortunately, too many movies rely on effects to awe and amaze us rather than the twists and turns of narrative.

The second sin is that the expected and satisfying outcome has been achieved by a cheat. The chain of logic was flawed or incomplete. The beautiful ending was neither hard-won nor deserved. If, for instance, **chance** intervened, the outcome was achieved by an act of fate, rather than the will of the protagonist. Most classically structured films take it as a given that we can all shape our own destiny: that we can learn, and change, and grow. If fate steps in at the last minute, that robs our journey of any meaning. It breaks the chain of cause and effect.

If the world has an underlying logic, then we must be able to learn from it, and put that knowledge to good use. So in **classic** structure the chain of narrative logic allows the protagonist to learn and grow. Ultimately, that knowledge gives the heroine the power to triumph over the forces arrayed against her. In classic structure, this chain of logic has a moral dimension, because it tells us everything is as it should be in the world.

Classic structure works, because it reflects a common aspiration: that if we learn from life we can shape it to our advantage and place destiny in our hands. **Maverick** screenwriting, on the other hand, tends to favor that old adage that if you can't change the world, you may have to change yourself. Taking a different point of view on what we experience can change our feelings about it immensely.

The questions Maverick films ask

Besides wanting to know "What happens next?" and "How will it all turn out?", there are many other questions that we ask of life. Why do we suffer? Is there any sense in it? Why are we lucky sometimes, and sometimes not at all? Do things happen for a reason?

Questions Maverick Films Ask

* Why are we here?

* Do we control our own destiny?

* Does life have a purpose?

* How did things turn out this way?

* What role does fate play in our lives – or synchronicity?

* Are memories real – or distorted and subjective?

* Can we ever really know another person?

These are **Maverick** questions, because they question our very purpose in life. Do we really control our destiny – or is life just one big lottery?

Not only do we question our purpose and whether the universe obeys any laws of justice or morality, we doubt whether our experience of the world is always consistent.

How different the view from the bridge looks when we are in love than when we are mourning a broken relationship!

How quickly time flies at certain times, while at others it just seems to crawl. How different our lives feel when we are young, and experiencing the world for the first time than when we are older and have seen it all before.

Maverick stories are driven by the questions people ask, not the expectations they have. They are driven by a **point of view** that is outside of the ordinary, that stands apart from the norm. Rather than seeing this as a drawback, **Maverick** screenwriters turn this difference into a strength, something which gives them a unique way of looking at the world.

If **classic** screenwriting tends to create heroes who represent an ideal that we aspire to, **Maverick** screenwriting throws up characters who are more like we really are, but who say and do the things we dare not.

Woody Allen and Charley Kaufman have turned neurosis and insecurity into a comic art form. Few people are as tormented as their fictional alter egos, but we all have similar feelings from time to time. We are just more successful at hiding them.

These **Maverick** heroes are not like the heroes of old. They are driven by their insecurity about the world, not their certainty. They are convinced that something is going on beneath the surface, but can't quite put their finger on it. A gap has opened up between perception and reality, and it's not obvious which is which. This gap then becomes a question: a big "what if?"

All stories require a premise, an idea that intrigues us. "What would happen if these two forces collided?" But the **Maverick** premise goes further, requiring us to imagine not only the outcome, but the shift in our way of looking at the world that this would force upon us.

Maverick films are driven by this "what if?", and Maverick characters grab the great "what if?" of life by the horns, leap on its back and gallop off wherever it takes them.

Sometimes this idea is so overpowering it renders these Mavericks incapable of action. They then become **minimalists**. Like The Dude in *The Big Lebowski*, they make an art form out of doing nothing.

From that moment on, they are freed from what Godard called "the tyranny of plot". They can, like Belmondo's character in *Breathless*, act spontaneously, philosophize and make love, rather than obsess about saving their own skin. They can live in the moment, and follow the whim wherever it takes them.

> "You pay a terrific price for a good plot, because the minute everybody is . . . wondering what is going to happpen next, there isn't much room for them to care about how it's going to happen or why.[13]
>
> Stanley Kubrick, Writer/Director

The chain of logic has been replaced by a web of ideas. The story is no longer plot-driven, but **concept-driven**. However, the rules of storytelling still apply.

Mainstream movies are plot-driven

Maverick films are concept-driven

You must still create a desire in the audience "to go on", a need to know. You must still get to the emotional core of your story. If you want to maintain suspense, surprise and excitement without sacrificing credibility, the web of ideas must not get tangled. The **matrix** (you'll learn more about this later) must not have tangled wires or crossed purposes. The story must never become predictable, and the threads that hold it together must be vital and true.

For at the heart of that web lies the **Maverick** premise.

The Maverick premise

In a crowded marketplace, new filmmakers with no marketing money have one thing to fall back on.

A **Maverick** premise.

Maverick stories can be sold on the strength of an idea. Because it is the concept, or hook, that sells the film, they do not need star casting. Because they rely on the cleverness of their ideas, not of their effects, **Maverick** films can often be made on a low budget.

THE CHEAPER IT IS TO MAKE MOVIES

the harder it is to get them noticed

Peter Fonda – producer, co-star and co-writer of the iconic sixties rebel film *Easy Rider* – imagined the image of two Harley-Davidsons blown into the air by rednecks . . . and knew it expressed everything he felt about the war between the generations in America.[14] He raised the money for the movie on the back of that image, and this simple premise: that the more you strive for freedom, the more people will attempt to destroy you.

All films need a strong premise, but **Maverick** films most of all – not only for marketing reasons, but for practical ones too. Without the organizing structure of the **chain of logic**, it's the *idea* that holds a Maverick film together. So it had better be a good one.

A good premise sets up the two great forces which will collide in your story. The story cannot end until these forces have fought each other to the death – literally or through the ideas they represent – or until they have been in some way reconciled.

To maximize the opportunity for conflict, these forces need to reflect the opposite poles of your story. Both should be equally compelling, equally convincing, equally attractive. Each vies constantly for supremacy, and the outcome is always in doubt. If your hero is not torn apart by these forces, she should be.

A **Maverick** premise, however, describes not only the *circumstances* in which these two forces meet, but the leap of imagination required to make it happen.

At the heart of the Maverick premise is a **paradox**. It seems impossible – absurd, even – that these forces could be reconciled. Nevertheless this paradox is intriguing, a puzzle we want solved.

Maverick vs high-concept

The rampant success of *Jaws* and *Star Wars* in the late seventies put an end to the era of eclectic filmmaking which had preceded it. Before the era of the blockbuster, distributors would open a movie slowly, trying to gain word of mouth and positive notices. That way, the reputation of a good product would spread organically.

With the advent of the "tentpole"[15] film, a movie had to open as widely as possible, and how long it ran would depend on how much it made on the first weekend. To do that, so the thinking went, it had to have movie stars and be **high-concept** – something audiences could grasp by seeing the poster. It had to have a **premise** which was striking and which told audiences exactly what to expect.

Let's look at a few examples.

Terminator meets kindergarten kids. In *Kindergarten Cop*, tough city cop Schwarzenegger has to go undercover to teach nursery school. He may be tough, but will he be tough enough to handle the kids? And tough enough to protect them? Will Schwarzenegger discover his softer, childlike side? You bet. And will he also toughen the kids up? Absolutely.

Cynical sports agent rediscovers his soul and becomes a winner. In *Jerry Maguire*, Tom Cruise's sports agent takes a stand against the money-driven ethics of his profession. But if he's going to succeed in building his own business, he's going to have to learn to take personal responsibility, particularly for the single mom who's followed him out of her secretarial job and into his bed, *and* for her son.

He's also going to have to show he can win on terms that the sports business can understand: "Show me the money!" as his one remaining client endlessly refrains.

Hooker teaches corporate shark that he has a heart, and in doing so both are redeemed. In *Pretty Woman*, tough corporate raider Richard Gere hires gauche escort Julia Roberts. These two unlikely opposites nevertheless learn something from each other. He encounters his softer side etc., while she regains her self-respect and self-confidence.

Just to make Richard Gere's transformation believable he is given a couple of "character traits": he plays the piano, which shows he has a soul; and he's afraid of heights, which proves he's vulnerable. In **high-concept** filmmaking, these substitute for internal conflict.

The unlikelihood that in real life a rich, successful man would make an honest woman out of a prostitute is immaterial. The premises for *all* these classic films are ludicrous. Only we don't consider them so, because they reflect our aspirations about how we would like the world to be. In each of these stories, the values of the central character may be challenged, but the underlying assumptions about the world around them never are.

All movies reflect their times, and these films reflect the unashamed materialism that the Reagan era ushered in. Richard Gere's financier will never be short of a few bucks, just because he chooses Julia Roberts. And how much does Tom Cruise sacrifice, really? While Schwarzenegger will prove a man can show his soft side, but still be a tough guy.

The problem with **high-concept** is it can become predictable, and in the eighties movies were becoming more and more formulaic. The screenwriting manuals of the day stressed the importance of the **chain of logic**, in which no scene should fail to move the story forward.

That created an opportunity for a young filmmaker. With his first two films, *Reservoir Dogs* and *Pulp Fiction*, Quentin Tarantino – a big fan of the Nouvelle Vague – did what Truffaut had attempted to do with *Shoot the Pianist*. He blew the **chain of logic** apart, and substituted for it a **web of ideas**.

He showed that you could take a popular genre, like the heist movie in *Reservoir Dogs*, and by jumping in halfway through change its meaning completely. The story becomes no longer, "Will they pull it off?" but "What went wrong, and who's to blame?"

You can *shift focus*. What is important is no longer necessarily what you thought it was: car chases, hold-ups, double crosses. After all, these are just another day at the office for your bad guys.

Tarantino showed killers could be funny and exciting, even when they did nothing more than sit around and bitch. In S*hoot the Pianist*, reluctant hero Charlie, a bar-room pianist, argues at gunpoint with his kidnappers about the merits of a woman wearing stockings rather than socks. In *Pulp Fiction* Tarantino's low-life characters debate the merits of fast food, foot massages and different types of heroin with wit and eloquence, as if these mundanities were important, as if they mattered.

Then every so often somebody's head gets blown off. As in *Breathless*, these moments of **hyper-reality** provide a powerful shock. Tarantino calls this "adding reality to genre",[16] because the more popular a genre, the more likely it is to become formulaic and removed from reality. It has lost the power to be spontaneous and to surprise us. Tarantino's genius was to draw out these violent interludes, and invest them with even greater shock and suspense.

Tarantino showed you could revive and reinvent genre, while giving audiences what they want at the same time.

Maverick concepts are not "high-concept". **Maverick** stories take a notion about the world and pursue it through its unexpected consequences.

Often, when a concept is taken to the end of the line, it will appear to bend in on itself – like the cityscape in *Inception*, or the spoon-bending child in *The Matrix* – and transform into its opposite. Only one thing is certain: nothing will ever be the same again.

Offering your audience this "what if?" is like getting them to choose the blue or red pill which Neo is offered in *The Matrix*. The right pill will change the rules for ever. Take the wrong one and you go back to your ordinary life, and forget that you ever knew otherwise. You sink, like Lester Burnham in *American Beauty*, into a living "coma". You fail to notice what's going on around you. And you never question the whys and wherefores of what you are doing on this planet.

Of course, if we only could become aware of everything that is going on all around us we would be amazed. Turn the microscope on our lawn, and a mesmerizing jungle appears before our eyes (as it does in the **Maverick** documentary *Microcosmos*, as well as the family classic *Honey I Shrunk the Kids* – a great example of using a Maverick premise (i.e. a change in perspective) in an otherwise mainstream film.

A great Maverick premise is one that allows us to shift focus. Take the right pill and you'll be vaulted into the great "what if" of life. You'll see the world in a entirely new way.

Charley Kaufman's screenplays are full of premises which take this leap of imagination, then logically pursue them to the limit.

What if you could control another human being like a puppet? Would you be tempted to use this power for selfish ends? And what would be the consequences?

In *Being John Malkovich* Craig, a puppeteer, fulfils this dream of mastery: to know what it's like "being inside another skin, thinking differently . . . feeling differently", seeing the world "through someone else's eyes". He does so by taking his art to a level beyond even his own imagining: achieving the ability to control not just a puppet, but another human being. This godlike hubris is punished when Craig is trapped inside his former lover's child, forced for eternity to watch her and his ex-wife together in love.

What if you could erase your painful memories? Would you still be the same person? And wouldn't you be in danger of repeating the same mistakes, since you never have a chance to learn from them? What if you did it, and changed your mind halfway through the process? Could you recover those memories? This is a conundrum Leonard struggles with in *Memento*, as he tries to condition his mind through repetition rather than memory; and in *Eternal Sunshine of the Spotless Mind* two lovers face the inevitability of history repeating itself after deciding to rid themselves of each other's memory.

In all Charley Kaufman's scripts the outcome, no matter how absurd, is always a logical extension of the premise.

The ultimate paradox

While many stories have ironic twists, **Maverick** stories take these to the limit in pursuit of the **ultimate paradox**.

In *Memento*, a husband tries to avenge his wife's murder, in spite of his condition of short-term memory loss. How can he put the clues together in a way that will lead him to the murderer if he forgets them as fast as he collects them, if they slip away like sand through an hourglass?

The answer is to tattoo the clues all over his body. But can he really trust what they tell him? Or has the process of pursuing a chain of logic become an end itself? A reason for him to carry on living – and killing?

In *Memento*, the whole **chain of logic** of not just Leonard's story, but the detective genre itself is called into question. Can we ever really trust our memory, or the evidence of our senses?

Lacking memory, Leonard puts his faith in one thing: "You need a system." But without memory Leonard is incapable of learning, and therefore fulfilling the central tenet of **classic** screenwriting: the ability to grow. His "chain of logic" is flawed, because it ignores what is most important in a human being.

In *Festen*, Christian dramatically announces to his extended family that he and his sister used to be sexually abused by their father. Instead of reacting in shock, they do their best to silence him.

Their reaction to this bombshell may be farcical: it may not be realism. However, it does reflect a deeper truth about the way many families behave – which is to avoid uncomfortable topics of discussion whenever possible. In the ordered, conservative world of Sweden, perhaps even more so.

The film's **Maverick** premise takes this common human defence mechanism, and pushes it to its logical conclusion. What if his family don't just disbelieve Christian, but are prepared to go to any lengths to silence him?

Then you have achieved the **ultimate paradox**. You have turned farce into something horrifying, and something horrifying into farce. *Festen* points to the elephant in the room that is hidden in so many families: sexual abuse. *Dr Strangelove* pointed out the absurdity of the threat which the world lived under, but did its best to ignore: nuclear annihilation. Both were able to take a serious subject, and by pushing it to its ultimate, absurd conclusion, make it funny and horrifying at the same time.

In *Adaptation*, Kaufman delivers the ultimate paradox by writing the final act of the movie in a different style from the first two acts. Charlie, a neurotic screenwriter, is commissioned to adapt a book about orchids; but he can't keep himself, and his own angst, out of the story. When Charlie is killed, he is survived by his confident brother Donald, who takes over the screenplay and gives it an action-packed "Mckee" finish. (A comic irony which seemed to elude many outraged Kaufman fans.)

By delivering this ending, Kaufman proved his perfect **Maverick** credentials. **Classic** screenwriting demands unity of tone and intention. Donald's ending is wildly inconsistent with the tone of "Charlie's" section of the screenplay: but as a logical outcome of the story, it is perfect. In Hollywood, you have to adapt to survive.

By handing in a script that dared to mix his fantasy real life with the adapted source material, Kaufman "delivered" what the industry demands, while staying true to his own vision.

Kaufman turned an unlikely subject into a thriller, then subverted the genre by making himself the subject of the story. In doing so, he achieved the **ultimate paradox**.

A paradox is a seemingly sound piece of reasoning
based on seemingly true assumptions that leads to
a contradiction or another obviously false conclusion.

There's something absurd about true stuff that leads
ever so logically to false stuff: and absurd is funny.[17]

A different way of looking at things

In **Maverick** films, the chain of logic has been bent, if not actually broken. Without logic to show the way, **point of view** becomes all-important.

In a **classic** story, the hero and the villain have diametrically opposed points of view. Though we may favour the hero, we see that what the devil has to offer is tempting too. The story pits one against the other, each taking turns on top, seesaw-fashion. We never know whose view of the world will triumph.

However, in **Maverick** screenwriting **point of view** is not just a matter of opinion nor even of the values we hold: it is something which shapes our whole reality. Maverick stories invite the audience not to stand apart but to share that point of view, no matter how uncomfortable or incredible it may seem.

It has been said that every villain is the hero of his own story. In the absence of the **chain of logic**, logic becomes a matter of where we stand. A psychopath is only someone who has pursued their own logic to the limit, unhindered by empathy for others.

A **classic** approach to the serial-killer genre shows us how crazy and twisted the villain is, frightening us while ultimately reassuring us that sanity – and common sense – will prevail.

A **Maverick** film accepts that most of us cannot relate to extreme perspectives. We do not understand what it is like to feel no empathy, because we ourselves are not like that. Rather than judge from the outside, the Maverick screenwriter puts us on the inside, giving us the experience of what it's like to see the world in that way, as Paul Schrader did with *Taxi Driver*. At first we identify with De Niro's "clean up the streets" vigilante. His anger about the decay and decadence around him is understandable, even refreshing in its honesty. Once his character pursues the logic of this point of view and **takes it to the limit**, however, we realize that judging others can lead not only to prejudice but, ultimately, insanity.

In **classically** structured films the point of view, unless overtly announced by the presence of a narrator, is usually invisible. It is not necessary to define this point of view, since it represents values, or a way of looking at the world, with which most of us identify. In **Maverick** films not only our values but our whole reality depends on our point of view.

If a fake world were created around us, accurate in every detail, would we know the difference? And even if we did, would we still prefer the truth?

Both *The Matrix* and *The Truman Show* pose these **Maverick** questions, questions about the very nature of our existence.

We ask these questions because we all have experienced times when reality can become a little distorted. Times when the doors of perception crack open, and the consistency of reality no longer seems so certain.

You may have experienced moments of disembodiment, particularly at times of extreme trauma, when you felt you were floating out of your body and watching yourself from a distance.

You may have experienced hallucination from fever or drugs.

You may have experienced déjà vu, or telepathy, or had your prayers answered. Maybe you feel strangely out of place. These cannot be my parents? Surely I was adopted by aliens!

You may have experienced moments when you felt, like Belmondo mugging in front of the poster of Humphrey Bogart in *Breathless*, that you are an actor playing a role, rather than the person living out your life.

As Jules says to fellow hit man Vincent in *Pulp Fiction*, "Let's get in character."

We all do this, to some degree or other, to rub along with the social order. We wear different masks for our colleagues, our friends, our children or our lovers.

As someone once said, if we all went around expressing our real feelings, the whole world would be a madhouse. But with **Maverick** films we are a little more conscious of who we are and the role we are playing.

We may have fantasized that our true lives are happening elsewhere, that in some parallel universe we are actually doing something noble and heroic, rather than leading our own dull, ordinary lives.

We may believe, like Rosencrantz and Guildenstern, Shakespeare's messengers in *Hamlet* who wait in the wings, that important events only happen elsewhere; ignoring the pageant of life passing before us. As John Lennon so aptly put it: "Life is what happens when you're making other plans." Like the servants in *Gosford Park* who obsess about their masters' lives, we forget that our own lives *matter*.

Once we make this shift, then tossing a coin – or discussing the finer points of hamburgers or foot massages – suddenly matters too.

Maverick screenwriting offers us these shifts in perception, when all at once reality seems to crack open: like the street scene in *The Matrix* in which a seductive woman in a red dress turns out to be a deadly agent, before the screen freezes and the entire sequence is shown to be a training program.

Through this gap comes the blinding realization that we have only been skating over the surface of life. It doesn't usually last long, however. Only until the window slams shut and we're called on stage again, and thrown back into Godard's "tyranny of plot".

Hot tip: shift focus
You can subvert genres simply by focusing on what is normally considered unimportant: by shifting the center of focus.

Many **Maverick** characters lack the motivation or ambition we expect from classic screenplays; consequently, they become drifters and outcasts. Those at the absurdist end of the scale tend to be dreamers who pursue their obsession to the edge and beyond, like Kaufman's alter ego in *Synecdoche*.

Both of these extremes are valued by the **Maverick** screenwriter, because they offer the opportunity for an unusual point of view.

Charlie Chaplin's "Tramp" was the first (and arguably, the greatest) of these **Maverick** outcasts. Always on his uppers, he is bemused and rejected by the world, unsure how to behave. We enjoy it when he pulls a fast one and thumbs his nose at society, usually for the benefit of some poor orphan. Unburdened by responsibilities, he is free, like Belmondo's character in *Breathless*, to be spontaneous, to follow his heart. He is incapable of being a cog in anyone's wheel, especially the relentless wheel of *Modern Times*. He represents the spirit which the assembly-line cannot grind down.

Like Winston, the clerk who rebels against Big Brother in *Nineteen Eighty-Four*, or Truman in *The Truman Show*, the **Maverick** hero never ceases to believe that life and liberty are worth striving for.

The government kept a close eye on Chaplin because of his suspected Communist sympathies. But the Tramp was never really political. Chaplin loved him because he too had once been an outsider, trying to make his way in the New World. And he never wanted to forget what that was like.

Apparently, many of the new immigrants to America felt the same way, as did the millions of others who found themselves left down and out by the Depression.

The persona of the Tramp was so successful that Chaplin was able to start his own movie studio: with the leading director (D. W. Griffith), the leading action man (Douglas Fairbanks), and the leading romantic lady of the day (Mary Pickford). It was a short-lived experiment in giving creative people the power in Hollywood, an experiment that was repeated briefly in the sixties, and again in the nineties with the attempt to bring "niche" arthouse films into the studio system.

It will continue to be repeated as long as **Maverick** filmmakers come along every few years – and overturn the "rules" of screenwriting.

> *It's much better to be non-conformist. Conformism is a limitation on the knowledge of life. It's good not to accept the current reality as eternal and definitive.*
>
> Luis Buñuel, Writer/Director[18]

Maverick stories can be seen from a particular vantage point, a radical or unexpected point of view. Or, they can self-consciously call attention to themselves: "Look at me! I am the Emperor's new clothes!"

They can do this by making the structure itself grab our attention – the endlessly repeating *Groundhog Day*, the backward motion of *Memento*, the fragmented narratives of *Pulp Fiction* and *Before the Devil Knows You're Dead*. All these films use **metastructure**.

Like the Pompidou Centre in Paris, or the Lloyds Building in London, in metastructure the engineering is on the outside, calling attention to itself. But self-awareness (what Brecht called "distancing") can also be created in other ways: such as **transparency**, **breaking the fourth wall** and **voiceover.**

With **transparency**, we see through the crack in reality to what lies beneath, a different reality, equally valid, coexistent.

By **breaking the fourth wall** we tear down the curtain that separates the audience from the action. When a character steps out of role, or addresses the audience directly, the audience become aware that they are watching an illusion. If the audience accept this suspension of disbelief, because they want to know what happens next, then they become *complicit* in the process. Now they are watching the film on two levels: gripped by the story, but aware that it is a fiction (this, *not* having audiences choose the ending of a film, is what interactivity is all about).

Voiceover provides a slant on and different way of *feeling* about the action on the screen. Rather than telling us the story, or worse still, *describing* what is on the screen, voiceover should remind us that everything is open to interpretation, and nothing should be taken at face value.

Since Chandler created Detective Marlowe, voiceover has undermined the reality or truth of appearances. *Alfie's* asides straight to camera reveal a conscience behind the cocky exterior, while Woody Allen's voiceovers undercut his neurotic on-screen persona. In *Fight Club*, Ed Norton's detached voiceover shows how far he has become removed from his own emotions. Instead he leeches off others' suffering by attending endless support groups for conditions he doesn't have.

Self-consciousness or detachment can be created in other ways, by making the characters aware of the unreliability of their own senses. In *Memento* and *Waltz with Bashir* it is memory which is unreliable, while in *Waking Life* it is the slippery relationship between "reality" and the "dream state" which keeps tripping the hero up. Often this shift of perspective has a positive, life-changing effect, by making characters see beyond their illusions, as does Truman in *The Truman Show* or Neo in *The Matrix*.

However, the existential confusion of the characters in *The Discreet Charm of the Bourgeoisie*, who keep waking from each other's dreams, is still not enough to shake their complacency or instinct for self-preservation. So Buñuel leaves them, contemptuously, walking down an endless road to nowhere.

When taken too far, this self-consciousness becomes a complete distortion of reality, an isolating delusion. This afflicts many **Maverick** protagonists, from *Citizen Kane* to *Mephisto*, from *The Aviator* to *Aguirre, Wrath of God*.

Citizen Kane's ruthless pursuit of power for his own selfish ends leaves him surrounded by material wealth, but loveless. "If I hadn't been really rich, I might have been a great man," he cries.

In *The Aviator*, Howard Hughes's obsessive drive to push back the barriers of aviation, his compulsive drive for perfection, leaves him crippled by obsessive-compulsive disorder.

Mephisto's willful blindness to what is going on around him in Nazi Germany and his belief that as an artist he is "non-political" mean that once his friends have all been arrested, he will be defenseless when the Gestapo come for him as well.

Aguirre is convinced by his delusion of an El Dorado to be discovered around the next bend of the river, a golden land which he will make his Empire. In the end he is only Emperor of a few monkeys, all that are left alive aboard his rudderless raft, floating aimlessly downriver.

These characters are so convinced by their delusions that they have allowed a distorted version of reality to overtake them. They have become, as a senior brass describes Colonel Kurtz in *Apocalypse Now*, "unsound".

Sometimes the line between reality and art itself can become confused. In Kaufman's *Synecdoche*, the main character, a theater director, becomes obsessed with re-creating his comically depressive life as a performance piece, true in every detail. This pursuit becomes an illusion which can never be attained, since the story can never be finished. In the end he is replaced, no longer considered capable even of directing his own life.

Ultimately, when the tension between reality and appearance becomes too strained, the distorting glass shatters, revealing a **parallel** or **alternate** reality.

The Matrix offers a parallel version of reality, an illusion that is designed to keep us as obedient slaves. To Truman, his life seems real in every way, but to his audience he is the star of *The Truman Show* – the ultimate in reality TV, an illusion created just for him.

Sometimes the parallel reality is couched in terms of other choices, other roads our characters' lives might have gone down. In *Sliding Doors* we are offered different versions of the way Helen's (Gwyneth Paltrow) life might have turned out, depending on whether she did or didn't catch a tube train. However, this film failed to exploit the potential of the concept by having the two lives intersect in interesting ways: it lacks **transparency.**

In *Run Lola Run*, Lola is given three different attempts to race the clock and make the right choices that will save the life of her lover; in *Source Code*, the fate of an entire city rests on Jake Gyllenhaal's multiple attempts to thwart a terrorist bomber.

Sometimes the parallel realities are different worlds, different lives, that are suddenly brought into relationship with each other. In *Amores Perros*, the lives of the characters in three apparently separate stories are changed for ever by two cars colliding at a crossroads.

In *Eternal Sunshine of the Spotless Mind*, two lovers who erase their memories of each other accidentally meet again, experiencing the same spark of attraction.

In *Inception*, in order to plant an idea within another person's head, we must travel even further – to the dream within a dream within a dream.

Perhaps that's a bit *too* complicated, even for the best of us.

It is a good thing to ask questions, if you want to be a **Maverick** screenwriter. Because if you follow the logic of your own questions, it will inevitably lead you toward a way of telling stories that is unique to you, that's never been done before.

Note I don't say "unique stories" – since all our stories are rooted deep in the myths of our culture, in the patterns of ritual and the different phases of our life span. There really are no new stories.

But it is necessary for each generation to rediscover and reconnect with these myths in a way that is unique to them. To express them in ways we've never seen before. Even if you don't think yours is a **Maverick** story, these techniques allow you to take classic genre and spruce it up with a Maverick twist.

But first, let's remind ourselves of the tools we'll need. The ones every **Maverick screenwriter** should carry in their toolbox.

THE BIG "WHAT IF?"
Recap

* **Maverick** films are driven by the questions they ask.

* In **Maverick** screenwriting, **point of view** shapes our whole reality.

* **Metastructure** draws attention to the structure, adding irony and insight.

* Maverick screenplays substitute a **web of ideas** for the **chain of logic**.

* A great **Maverick Premise** offers not just an intriguing question, but a different way of looking at the world, suggests not only the circumstances in which two forces meet, but the leap of imagination required to make it happen and allow us to shift focus.

* Always respect the chain of logic, but don't make it too predictable.

* Pursue your concept until you achieve the **Ultimate Paradox.**

Exercise

○ Think about an event that happened in your childhood that has influenced you as an adult.

○ Write out the chain of logic that links this to other events in your life.

○ Now, tell the story backward, so that who you are is a mystery that can only be gradually revealed by going back in time.

○ Make the original event a revelation that explains who you are now. Does this change the way you feel about it?

3 The Maverick toolbox

Charlie Chaplin, *Modern Times* © Chaplin/United Artists/Kobal Collection

Writers have to imagine their world

In spite of this obvious truth, ever since the Nouvelle Vague, the auteur theory has held that directors, not writers, are the sole authors of films.

Prior to that, writers had commonly put technical directions into their scripts. In the highly specialized studio system, many directors were trusted with little more than telling the actors what to do.

The Nouvelle Vague was great news for directors, who suddenly became the stars of their own films. Now that directors had become "auteurs", any attempt to direct the film from the page was scorned as trespassing. So how else could the screenwriter make his script cinematic?

The best writers, while avoiding camera directions, simply resorted to subterfuge. From now on pacing, point of view and distance from the action would be read from the rhythm of the sentences, the breaks in the paragraphs, and on how much and with what detail we see what is in the frame. Through the evolution of this new "spec" style,[19] professional screenwriters ensured that they would still be in the driving seat, showing their readers exactly what their movie would look and feel like.

Of course a director adds a whole new dimension to the world the writer has created. But a well-written script should be director-proof. It should be so fully conceived that the experience of reading it is like projecting the movie in your head.

Writers sometimes complain that directors have ruined their great screenplays. But a vividly imagined script is more likely to be enhanced by the director's contribution than misinterpreted.

The tools of a screenwriter

So what are the tools that writers use to conjure up their worlds?

Firstly, there are the ones that screenwriting shares with drama and fiction: **character**, **plot**, **dialogue** and **setting**. You will be familiar with what these mean. All of them can be considered separately, but in a good script they are all connected by the **matrix**, the web of visual and verbal metaphor that links all the themes in your script (more on this in Chapter Twelve).

The Tools of a Screenwriter

Basic tools

o   plot

o   characters

o   dialogue

o   setting

Advanced Tools

o   time

o   point of view

o   reality

In order to understand how they connect, first we have to answer that thorny question: which comes first? **Character** or **plot**? You may have an idea for a story, but no clear sense of what sort of characters should "carry" this story upon their shoulders. You may have an interesting character, but little idea of what you want them to do.

In fact, character and plot are inseparable. You should feel that only this particular character could have taken your story down this particular road. And at the same time that this story is the perfect vehicle for expressing who your character truly is.

Let me give you an example. Let's imagine that on the way home from work, you've had a fender-bender. A minor accident which could have been a lot worse. How do you react?

There are a number of ways that people might respond. Let's imagine you're of a superstitious bent; you take it as a sign that God or the universe is punishing – or warning – you. You'd better put your house in order.

Perhaps you have a cautious personality. Now you can see how dangerous the world is. The best thing you can do is avoid risk. If possible, don't even leave the house.

Perhaps this brush with death is one that you treat with a more spiritual outlook. It has reminded you that our time here is fleeting, and you had best appreciate it. Perhaps now is the time to appreciate what life has to offer. Time to rearrange your priorities.

Then there's the pragmatist. The one who says, this was just an act of fate. It means nothing, unless I allow it to. Like a rider who's been thrown from his horse, he says: "I'm going to get behind the wheel. I'm going to put it behind me. I have to forget about it, get on with my life."

Same situation. Five different reactions, depending on the character. Each character will drive the plot in a different direction, so **character** and **plot** are inseparable. You should be able to cover up the name of the character in your screenplay and identify their dialogue simply from their way of talking. If you cannot, then you have not connected up **dialogue** with **character** – you have not sufficiently individualized it.

If your **character** does not have a relationship with their **setting**, if they do not interact with it, then you need to make that connection.

When all these elements work together, then you have a powerful **matrix**, and you have added a whole new dimension to your film.

Maverick character

A good protagonist needs to be able to think ahead, but also to respond to whatever gets thrown at him in the moment. In other words, he needs a good combination of intelligence and instinct.

The **Maverick** character takes these qualities to the extreme: he is more likely to be driven by **internal conflict** to behave in apparently contradictory, random or spontaneous ways; or to be driven by his own private obsessions, to the exclusion of all others. He is less affected by the outside world, more affected by internal contradictions.

That doesn't mean that **Maverick** characters shouldn't be logical and consistent. Even "The Dude" (in *The Big Lebowski*) has his code: "takin' her easy" (which makes him a **minimalist** – see Chapter Seven). It takes somebody to break into his apartment and pee on his rug, to force him to abandon that code. Only then does The Dude finally lope into action.

A world of values

In **classic** screenwriting the way that a character responds, defines them. In film, the hero's values are judged not by what they say, but by what they *do*. The power of the image is so utterly dominant that we believe the slightest nuance of body language before we'll believe the word of some honey-tongued villain. The flicker of an eyelash, as the silent screen stars learnt, is worth a thousand words.

When movies acquired sound, screenwriters learned how to write dialogue that would allow actors to continue to do that, by giving their scenes **subtext**.

> *If we observe any social gathering, it is clear that the words exchanged between the guests are superficial formalities and quite meaningless, whereas the essential is elsewhere; it is by studying their eyes that we can find out what is truly on their minds.* [20]
>
> François Truffaut, Writer/Director

Of course, the feelings of your character are rarely consistent with their words, because great characters are riven by **internal conflict**. Giving a character internal conflict is not like giving them a character trait — an accessory to be worn around one's neck. Instead, it tells us something fundamental about the two great forces that are at war within your character, as well as in the larger world of your story.

Every person has a **strength** and a **flaw** competing for control within them. Their **strength** is whatever quality gives them the potential to achieve their goals; and their **flaw** is whatever quality has the potential to hold them back, or to sabotage those goals. Being imperfect, we all have these qualities to a greater or lesser extent.

This **strength** may remain hidden till the person has a greater understanding of themselves: which they rarely do at the beginning of their story.

But it must be planted deep in the protagonist early in the story: if we didn't know that Rick in *Casablanca* had a been a freedom fighter before he became a nightclub owner, we would never believe it when he pulls a gun on the Chief of Police at the beginning of the final act of the story. The **flaw** may not be exposed until your hero is put under pressure, but it tends to be revealed earlier.

It is best when these conflicting values can be seen to be flip sides of the same coin. In *The Aviator*, entrepreneur and aviation pioneer Howard Hughes is driven by an obsessive drive for perfection. While this helps him achieve extraordinary success in business, we come to see that these very qualities, when turned inward, are the cause of the crippling obsessive-compulsive disorder that threatens to destroy his private life. Writer John Logan could have used this mental affliction as an accessory, a bizarre character trait. Instead he made it the axis of Hughes's **internal conflict**.

This internal conflict not only provides dimension and interest for your character, it also reflects the larger themes of the story. In *The Shawshank Redemption* Andy, an innocent man sentenced to life imprisonment, is determined to keep his spirit alive, even when this leads him to reckless acts. One day, he uses his privileged access to the Governor's office to relay a Mozart aria over the public address system. This brazen flouting of prison regulations gets him thrown into solitary for so long that we fear he will be a broken man when he finally emerges. The very qualities that allow him to survive his prison ordeal also threaten to break him.

In *Donnie Brasco*, Johnny Depp's undercover cop is sent to infiltrate the Mafia. The better he becomes at playing the role of a mobster, the further he's taken away from his values and identity as a police officer, and the harder it becomes to reconcile the two sides to his life. Soon Pacino's mobster becomes more of a father figure than his own boss.

If your story is a buddy movie, then these values can be shared between characters. In *Lethal Weapon*, Mel Gibson's suicidal nature makes him especially reckless in his police work, and sets him up for conflict with partner Danny Glover, a cautious, stay-at-home, family man. In William Goldman's *Butch Cassidy and the Sundance Kid*, the essential differences in values between the characters, as well as the affection that unites them, are played out right to the end. As the two heroes, both mortally wounded in a shoot-out, dive for cover in a stable, they bicker:

```
                    BUTCH
     Is that what you call giving cover?

                   SUNDANCE
     Is that what you call running? If I
     knew you were gonna stroll...

                    BUTCH
     You never could shoot, not from the
     very beginning.

                   SUNDANCE
     And you were all mouth.
```

It is far more effective to find this central axis within your character than to give your characters lots of meaningless facets. Depth in your story comes not from complexity, but from seeing the themes being played out in every aspect of the story: through the **matrix**.

Once you have defined the hero's values, you can create an antagonist or a force whose values lie at the opposite extreme. Around these poles, you can build your ensemble: a spectrum of characters, each representing different values and responding differently to the dilemmas thrown up by your story. Make sure that you have characters who represent the whole spectrum, or you will reduce the opportunity for conflict – and conflict drives drama.

Your supporting characters also give you an opportunity to reveal different facets of your protagonist and antagonist. It is very difficult to sustain the audience's interest if we only follow the central character's storyline and perspective. You will have to make that story incredibly compelling (and find an equally compelling actor!) for the audience not to get tired of having the same face on the screen all the time.

Of course, rules are there to be broken and some **Maverick** writers just love taking on the challenge. The single perspective storyline can be effective when there are multiple versions of the plot (*Groundhog Day, Run Zola Run*), and the focus is on how the hero deals with each variant. More commonly it is used when your hero's **point of view** is sufficiently surprising and unusual, and can provide us with a *different way of looking at the world.*

Supporting characters and storylines are not there to make your life more complicated, but to open up other aspects of your central characters, and to provide variety of tone and mood. Think of them as relieving the burden on the central story – not just as more balls that you have to keep in the air!

The advanced tools of screenwriting

The elements which give film an advantage over other media, and provide the advanced tools of screenwriting – are **time**, **point of view** and **reality**.

Why do these giving screenwriting the edge? **Time**, because moving images can be played in any order, backward or forward, and at any speed. Only film can achieve such "sculpting in time", as Tarkovsky dubbed it.[21]

Point of view can be changed with the flick of an eye, affecting the appearance and reality of things.

And because film is the most literal of all media, **reality** does not rely on representation, it is a given. In most cases, we accept what we are shown as the way it is.

In **Maverick** screenwriting these ordinary perceptions are challenged. By changing **structure**, we change our perception of **time**; by shifting **point of view**, we alter **logic**; and by manipulating the **matrix**, the interweaving of visual and verbal metaphor, we change our perception of **reality**.

Maverick tools

Like the buildings whose engineering is on the outside, the **Maverick** approach to screenwriting takes techniques which (like all good magic tricks) are meant to be invisible and makes them, if not exactly *visible* – then **transparent**.

With **character**, this can lead to a feeling of self-consciousness or disassociation.

In **setting**, this means that the character does not fit comfortably in their world (like Travis Bickle in *Taxi Driver*), or cannot break out of it

In **dialogue**, this can mean that the **subtext**, or hidden meaning, comes nearer to the surface; or that its meaning is not fixed or definable.

As for **plot**, we've already seen how **Maverick** structure can break the **chain of logic**, and substitute a different organizing logic: the **matrix**, or web of ideas.

So put your seatbelts on, "Warp Factor Ten, Mr Sulu." Let's see how it's done.

Metastructure © Peter Grant Photography

Maverick Screenwriter Tools

Tools	Purpose
	to alter the structure of
o structure	o time
o point of view	o logic
o metaphor (the matrix)	o reality

Section 2
Time

4

Become your own timelord by playing with time and causality

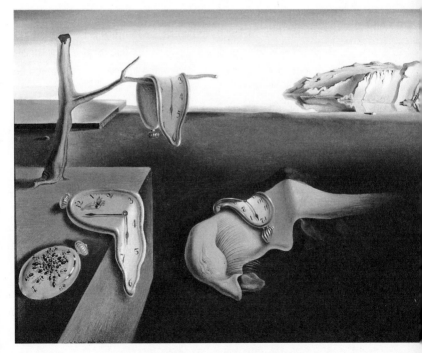

Salvador Dali, "The Persistence of Memory" © Bettmann/CORBIS

> *Don't worry darling*
> *Now don't you fret*
> *We're livin' in the future*
> *And none of this has happened yet*
> Bruce Springsteen[22]

Time is the most important tool in the **Maverick** toolbox. This is moving pictures, after all. In the conventional film, **time** attempts to be invisible, just as the editing strives to be seamless, unless captioned: *Three Months Later.*

Time can be played with in prose, but too many time-jumps can confuse the reader. In film, the visual dimension offers exponentially more inform-ation to anchor us as we jump between time zones.

With *prose*, time runs as fast as the words on the page, according to the amount of detail the writer provides. If you're Proust, you might use an entire paragraph, or indeed entire volumes, to describe the sensations evoked by a single madeleine.

In *film*, not only can we slow or accelerate the pace, we can move deftly back and forth between parallel stories, so that each story informs our think-ing about the other, even though they may have no overt connection.

We can **counterpoint** these stories, or bounce them off each other like electric wires which, when joined, spark and illuminate the theme.

We can **jump forward** in time, or **flashback** to it. We can **fragment** or **unwind** it; we can **run it backward**. We can **overturn** the story so we rush back to the beginning, and view the same events again in a radically dif-ferent light.

Even in a **classically** structured film, there will be variations in the flow of time. In lyrical or meditative moments time moves more slowly, and in action sequences it speeds up until the final moments, when it goes into overdrive and flips the other way: into *slow motion*.

Ever wonder why it does that?

I was once hit by a motorbike as I was crossing the road. I flew about fifteen or twenty feet in the air. As I was flying through the air, I had plenty of time to think about things. I thought about where I would land when I hit the sidewalk, which limbs I would break, and whether it would hurt a great deal. I seemed to have forever to think about all this and more.

When we are in traumatic situations, our brains go into overdrive. Every neural synapse strains to focus on the emergency at hand, and everything which is not relevant is ruthlessly discarded or switched off. As we bring our focus to bear on the situation, our absorption of detail – any of which may be vital to our survival – expands exponentially. The time spent processing all this gives us the illusion that time is slowing down.

In the most famous sequence of *Battleship Potemkin*, made in 1927, Eisenstein experiments with **slowing down** time to capture the confused flight of demonstrators down the Odessa steps as they are pursued by the Tsar's fearsome Cossacks.

How long are those steps, how deep? They seem to go on forever, and as we're pitched from one terrified face in the crowd to another, it's easy to lose our bearings. Shots **overlap** until we're no longer sure of the time sequence. Then time stops for a moment, while a baby carriage teeters, then clatters down, step by step, until it meets its brutal fate at the hands of a sword-wielding Cossack. For a moment, even the face of the filmmaker is featured in the crowd, twisted in horror, all pretense at objectivity abandoned.

In **real time** how long did this event take, as the crowd fled from the Tsar's infantry and the mounted Cossacks? Maybe a minute or two. A crowd can scatter pretty quickly when in fear of its life. But Eisenstein stretches out the sequence to ten minutes or more, to emphasize the suffering and confusion of the demonstrators, and to heighten the suspense.

Ever since then, action sequences segue into **slow motion** as they approach their climax. This mimics the brain's own response to trauma.

Our experience of time is not a constant: it changes according to our state of mind. It can be controlled by the writer both in the ordering of scenes and by the pacing and rhythm of beats within each scene.

These techniques have been used for decades in **classic** screenwriting to modify our experience of time. The last acts of thrillers usually accelerate the pace, spinning out more scenes, played shorter and faster, heightening the feeling that time is running out.

But when given a **Maverick** twist, this effect can also resonate with the frantic feelings of the protagonist. Scorsese does this brilliantly in the last act of *Goodfellas*, mimicking the experience of cocaine paranoia as Henry Hill tries to stay frantically on the move, one step ahead of the game.

At the other end of the scale, **Maverick** films can *stretch* time to an agonizing degree. When time gets elongated it begins to take on the texture of real life, or even **hyper-realism**. In **real time** or slower, our awareness of the ordinary, small things in life is greater. The slightest change in our environment takes on enormous significance.

The brilliant opening of David Lean's *Lawrence of Arabia*, in which a lone figure gradually morphs out of the rippling, burning desert – at first an aberration in the horizon, then gradually revealing itself and coalescing into a bedouin figure – is a great example of this technique. As he approaches we finally register the impossible: this desert wanderer is not an Arab, but a European, and by the end of this sequence we will know that he is a very singular figure indeed.

In Richard Linklater's *Before Sunrise* and *After Sunset*, or Sofia Coppola's *Lost in Translation*, the precious moments eked out between the main characters have the texture of **real time**. Nothing important necessarily happens, but as a result every gesture takes on enormous significance.

In the even more repressed world of *In the Mood for Love*, time becomes a slow-motion waltz, endlessly repeated as the two neighbors pass each other in the street and in the narrow corridors of their boarding house. Nothing ever happens. They never acknowledge each other. They never can do. Then one day they speak.

In the films of Andrei Tarkovsky, time can be stretched out endlessly. In the climactic sequence of *Nostalghia*, a writer struggles to walk the length of an empty Roman bath keeping a candle alight. He dreams that he may be able to save the world if he can get to the other side without the candle blowing out. In spite of its agonizing slowness, the scene builds unbearable tension, not just because of the plot – will he complete the task and save the world? – but also because we know that the effort may well be meaningless and futile.

In Chen Kaige's *Life on a String*, a master musician endures countless hardships in the faith that, as has been foretold, his sight will be restored when he breaks his thousandth string. Needless to say, the tension in this slow but highly poetic Taoist film builds to an excruciating climax through the decades as he approaches his goal. This exquisite film and what it tells us about the dreams that motivate us (regardless of whether they turn out to be true) proves that speed is not necessary to sustain tension.

In fact, the opposite is true. *Slowing down* an anticipated outcome builds tension. *Speeding up* time builds adrenaline, and allows our body to take over without giving us time to think.

> *I had always heard your entire life flashes in front of your eyes the second before you die . . . First of all, that one second isn't a second at all, it stretches on forever, like an ocean of time . . .*
>
> Lester Burnham, *American Beauty*

The shifting sands of time

As I've mentioned, film is the ideal medium for jumping backward and forward in time, because our most powerful anchors are visual. As long as time periods are sufficiently differentiated, the audience need never get lost – unless you want them to!

In *The French Lieutenant's Woman*, we move backward and forward between an eighteenth-century illicit romance and the affair between the two leading actors playing them in a film.

While the two storylines ironically comment on each other, they are distinct and not confusing. Each taken separately is a piece of **classic** story-telling, but the cleverness of Harold Pinter's adaptation is in seeing the novel's commentary on Victorian values through a twentieth-century mirror. The contemporary story, set in the carefree, promiscuous seventies, makes us reflect back on Victorian morality in surprising ways. Sexual freedom has not necessarily made us more free.

In *The English Patient* we move backward and forward between the tragic love affair which brought an Englishman to betray his country and the present day, in which he is a horribly burned patient, gradually remembering his story and realizing the terrible price he has had to pay for his actions.

The fractured intermingling of the two storylines, with the patient's sympathetic nurse offering him a more detached, altruistic alternative to the selfish love of his past, give this otherwise **classic** piece of storytelling a great **Maverick** twist.

Many classic stories are narrated by a character observing events from a different time perspective. The TV show *The Wonder Years*, a series about a boy growing up in the sixties, was built around this premise.

The simple genius of the show was to have the protagonist narrate the story as an older and wiser adult. Events which seem to a growing child to be momentous and earth-shattering can be seen from the perspective of an adult to be a mere ripple on the sea of life.

A story may begin in one time period (usually the preamble, or **set-up**) and then jump to another, which becomes the **present day** of the story. This is **classic** storytelling, as long as the time-jumps are logical, and don't betray the audience's desire to have one storyline to identify with overall.

This desire is perfectly natural. Most of us spend at least part of our day lost either in memories of the past, or in projections about the future. However, we still have a solid anchoring in the present. We like to know where we stand, and consider over-identification with the past or obsession with the future an unhealthy character trait, perhaps requiring years of therapy.

However, the inability to accept the past or face up to the future can be equally problematic. The cynical, world-weary Rick in *Casablanca* suffers from this syndrome. Early in the film his girlfriend rounds on him:

> YVONNE
>
> Where were you last night?
>
> RICK
>
> That's so long ago, I don't remember.
>
> YVONNE
>
> Will I see you tonight?
>
> RICK
>
> I never think that far ahead.

Rick doesn't like to think about the past or make plans for the future. And he won't change till he takes responsibility for his present.

Kubrick's *2001* gave the technique of the Great Leap Forward – a **time-jump** into the future following a short piece of back story that opens the film – a **Maverick** twist, by stretching that time-jump beyond the normal span of human time: from the discovery of tools by apes in the prehistoric era, soon employed with murderous intent against rival tribes, to a future in which space travel is an everyday form of travel, representing everything that is civilized about humankind.

The iconic cut between a bone which has just been used to pummel another ape to death, tossed triumphantly into the air, morphing into a spaceship elegantly spinning through space, pushes the normal convention to its limits: that the opening time frame will in some way motivate, or explain the events that follow.

If we could understand the connection between these events we would understand everything that makes us human, with such a complicated mixture of instinct and intellect. That these two forces can never be reconciled or even fully understood is what makes *2001* such an enduring **Maverick** film.

When jumping backwards and forwards in time becomes too frantic, audiences can have difficulty holding on to the **chain of logic**. However, in Maverick films such disorientation is often deliberately used to give the audience the experience of being inside the protagonist's head.

In *Memento*, the constant slipping back in time reflects Leonard's fragmented mental condition, the short-term memory loss which causes time to roll up like a carpet behind him.

In *Reservoir Dogs* we flash backward and forward between the crisis created by a heist gone badly wrong and the events which brought the gang together; as we, like the characters, frantically try to figure out who's responsible for snitching to the police.

In *Before the Devil Knows You're Dead* a similar scenario plays out between two brothers who have been drawn into an unimaginable crime, shattering not only their lives but the lives of their family. The constant flashing backward and forward reflects our disbelief and frantic desire to know how these two could so completely have lost their moral compass.

In *Eternal Sunshine of the Spotless Mind*, Jim Carrey's character races backward in time to try to retrieve his memories, only to find them dissolving as fast as he tries to pin them down.

In *Being John Malkovich*, the two leading female characters chase each other through Malkovich's subconscious. This takes a convention of classic screenwriting – *flashing back* to traumatic experiences of childhood to explain a character's make-up – and pushes it to a parodic extreme: a montage of Malkovich's Most Embarrassing Childhood Moments ('Malk-o-pee!')

For a comic twist, the writer **shifts focus** by making this the background to the chase, ignored by everyone concerned. When everyone ignores what's clearly most important – that's funny. In this comic situation, the characters become the straight men to the audience's superior position.

In Nicolas Roeg's *Don't Look Now*, we view the frightening visions of a grief-stricken father as projections of the past, when in fact they are psychic portents of the future. It is his future he is haunted by, not the past.

In all these **Maverick** films, the disorientation is an intentional device, intended to reflect the state of mind of the characters, as well as our own curiosity to fit the pieces together and understand how it all came about.

Time can:

* appear to stand still

* jump backward or forward

* decelerate or accelerate

* drift

* unravel or unwind

* fragment

* overturn

* create spiraling or circularity

* switch between parallel stories for counterpoint or resonance

As already discussed, **classic** films tend to ask the question: "What happens next?", while **Maverick** films ask "How did it all come about?"

In the voiceover that opens *American Beauty*, we learn that by the end of the story the narrator will be dead, and that he feels all right about it. The **Maverick** twist of revealing the ending at the outset renders the rest of the film a flashback, a story whose events now seem to have an inevitability. Now we want to know not only how, but why.

Orson Welles's *Citizen Kane* did something similar half a century earlier, opening with a fictionalized newsreel telling the key events in the life of the title character, a newspaper baron who has just died. Why reveal all when the film has only just started?

It turns out that the life of Charles Foster Kane cannot be summed up by its external events. Nor is there one coherent view, as the journalist who tries to track down Kane's acquaintances discovers. No one can even explain Kane's deathbed utterance: "Rosebud", because no one ever really knew Kane (just like no one ever knew Orson Welles).

The clever reframing of the story gives us the illusion of being "ahead" of events, while constantly surprising us that the man behind the public persona is not necessarily whom we would expect. Like the opening of *American*

Beauty, this changes the questions we want answered from the story, and in terms of **time** puts us in the curious position of knowing what's coming, but not knowing how or why.

As well as jumping backward and forward, time can also **unwind** or **overturn**.

In *Memento* the main story is told backward, unwinding toward a starting point which will deliver a shocking emotional climax, while a counter-story runs forward toward the same end.

In Pinter's *Betrayal* the whole story is told in reverse. Beginning with the weary and disenchanted lovers at the end of their affair, we follow events back to the brushing of hands which began it. Who has betrayed whom? Is it the lovers who have betrayed their spouses? Or is it the lovers' own passion that has been betrayed?

In *Jacob's Ladder*, we witness the overturning of a Vietnam veteran's life as he tries to discover the reason for the terrible flashbacks he is suffering. Once a college professor, Jake now works in an ordinary job, haunted by memories of his son, who died in a car accident before Jake was sent over-seas to fight. He discovers that he and his fellow soldiers were the victims of an experiment to see if hallucinogenic drugs would make soldiers more aggressive in combat – an experiment that ended with them attacking each other rather than the imaginary enemy.

As the film approaches its tragic ending, we realize that Jake's quest for the truth, as well as his attachment to his former wife and son, are all that have been keeping him from passing to the other side: in reality, the whole film has taken place as he lies dying in an army forward operating theater. The entire story has been a spiritual journey in the blink of an eye, between death and life, a journey that was necessary in order for him to let go of life.

The Sixth Sense pulls a similar trick. Dr Malcolm Crowe (Bruce Willis), a child psychiatrist, is shot by a former patient who claims that Malcolm failed him. Malcolm recovers and is given a second chance when another boy is sent to him complaining of the same symptoms: that he can see dead people. Will Malcolm believe him? Or will he dismiss this case too with some glib psychological explanation?

As Malcolm becomes obsessed with solving the boy's problem, he suspects his neglect of his wife has led her to start an affair with a younger man. When he finally accepts the boy's story he is able to help him save a little girl's life, but only at the cost of what he should have realized all along. *He too is dead*, and has been since he was shot at the beginning of the film. That is why his wife seems to be ignoring him, why she has another man courting her, and why only the boy can actually see him.

Suddenly we **flashback** to all the clues we might have seen and should have interpreted otherwise: most poignantly, a scene where he is late for a dinner date with his wife to celebrate their anniversary. On first viewing, we take her refusal to respond to his apologies as an angry silence. But as we **overturn** and **rewind** through these scenes, we realize she is celebrating the anniversary alone, in his memory, giving the scene a terrible poignancy.

Films which pull this trick deliver a massive explosive charge at the end of their story. They tell us that everything we have believed to be true up to this point is open to an entirely different interpretation, one more extraordinary yet still entirely plausible. All the clues were there to tell us, had we not been seduced by the emotional pull of the hero's quest.

For this effect to work, you need to lay down markers as you go. These should be almost subliminal: things that stick in your mind without your knowing why. When you travel backward, these markers will light your way, illuminating the new **chain of logic**. This radical realignment of reality has not only to "make sense", but most importantly to provide a profound new understanding of the hero. Otherwise it is only a gimmick.

The Usual Suspects pushed this technique even further by **overturning** at the end a suspect's long confession to the cops, in which he admits to his association with master criminal Keyser Söze. As he leaves the room, the detective realizes the markers are all around the room: scrawled on notes, coffee cups, pens. Has the whole story been one long, brilliant improvisation? Surely only the real Keyser Söze, not the mythical one in the story, could have come up with so brilliant a ruse?

For my money, *The Usual Suspects* overplays its hand. If everything can be made up, then nothing means anything any more. The link between one reality and another becomes too tenuous. In *Jacob's Ladder* and *The Sixth Sense*, the story as we first conceive it still has meaning – if only as a metaphor for the character's journey. It's not completely up for grabs. *The Usual Suspects* is cool and clever, but its revelation at the end is a magic trick – not so much an emotional wrench, more of a pleasurable rush.

Some stories extend this pleasurable sense of déjà vu by using parallel time frames, where events appear to be happening simultaneously. In **classical** storytelling, this provides the opportunity for ironic counterpoint. (Why is it not so ironic if the same events are occurring an hour apart? Because film can offer us the illusion of simultaneity; and coincidence is funny.)

Woody Allen humorously plays off this convention in *Annie Hall* by having Alvy and Annie, in split screen, each seeing their own shrink. "How often do you sleep together?" asks Alvy's shrink. "Hardly ever!" Alvy complains. "Maybe three times a week." Simultaneously, Annie's shrink asks the same question. "Constantly," she wails. "I'd say three times a week!"[23]

However, in **Maverick** films parallel time frames reflect not only parallel actions but different interpretations of reality. In *The Matrix*, the rebels on the ship exist in the same time frame as the action played out in the Matrix, even though they can only view that action as a sequence of data.

In *Inception*, an hour of dreams takes only five minutes in real life, but this is compounded when one goes into a dream within a dream within a dream. So the team have plenty of time to complete their mission in one dream state before their van, careening off a bridge in another, hits the water below.

The appearance of **simultaneity** is often the aim of multi-protagonist stories. Our sense of time is flattened out, giving the forward movement of the plot less importance, since we are constantly moving sideways. When it no longer becomes possible to identify with any one protagonist's time frame, the audience begins to perceive each of the story strands as occurring in a simultaneous present.

When pushed to this extreme, parallel time frames are no longer an obvious construct, as in *The Matrix*. In the hands of Robert Altman (*Mash, Nashville, Gosford Park*), they create a sense of spontaneity, as conversations overlap and the action drifts from one story to another. Like the directors of the Nouvelle Vague, Altman strove to re-create the texture of life with long takes and overlapping dialogue; but to these he added his own brand of multi-protagonist, **interconnecting** stories. The moment we realize we can drop in and out of these stories apparently randomly, while still being able to follow what is going on, we start to lose our anxiety about "What happens next?" and get lost in the spontaneity of "What's happening *now?*"

In his debut, *Slacker*, Richard Linklater took the Altman approach to the limit. The narrative follows a sequence of conversations that hand off to each other like a relay race as people pass each other in the street. The conversations have no direct narrative connection, but reflect the same preoccupations and paranoia about the orthodox view of things. Although we are aware of the day passing, time is flattened out to such a degree that these conversations seem to be occurring simultaneously.

Linklater chose this "modular" form, in which scenes are apparently self-contained and unconnected, because he wanted the audience to experience the same "discomfort and alienation/disorientation" as the characters. But the intricate development of the themes through the different episodes means that the overall experience does not feel unstructured, but deeply woven. As Linklater put it in his production notes, "What seems like a straight line (as narrative) will actually be a circle (emotionally speaking)."[24]

"Dali clock", designed by ChilliChily

Which brings us neatly to **circularity**, the final method for ordering time.

There have always been circular stories, because to our ancestors the cycle of the seasons, the celebrations of the harvests, the rituals of birth, marriage and death, all seemed circular.

It was only after the Industrial Revolution turned **time** into a unit of production that *progress* became a desirable commodity. For Shakespeare, it was enough to know that the heavens were in place, and that order was established on earth. "Progress" would have been a contradiction in terms.

However, **circularity** is still used to reflect lives which follow regular routine or ritual. That may be a life close to nature, or simply one involved with the ritual of family get-togethers at holiday time, as in *Hannah and Her Sisters*.

Generally, in **circular** stories, we have a sense that the end brings us round to the beginning again, but with a new way of looking at things. While outwardly not much has changed, inwardly things are very different.

This convention of **circularity** is taken to the limit in *Groundhog Day*, as we'll see shortly.

We've seen how changing the structure of the story changes our experience of time. Conversely, changing our experience of time forces us to ask different questions of the narrative. This can be summed up in a simple formula.: *Changing structure changes time; and changing time changes structure.*

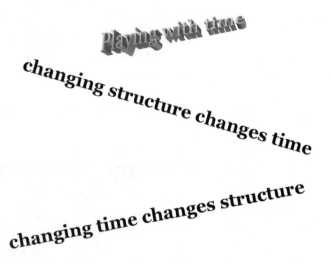

When done arbitrarily, the dislocation of time can become an unwanted jolt, an unnecessary nuisance for those enjoying a smooth ride. But when it reveals a deeper truth about the characters, when it invites us to experience time in a way which reflects the preoccupations of the story, it is a powerful tool.

Of course the very act of manipulating time draws attention to it. But we shouldn't worry unduly about this. As Linklater puts it: "It's okay for the viewer to be aware that they are watching a construct."[25]

As long as we can follow the *emotional line* through the story, we will never lose our way. For like the Yellow Brick Road in *The Wizard of Oz*, this is the thread that will help Dorothy find her way home.

CLOSE UP: GROUNDHOG DAY

Follow the Yellow Brick Road

At the opening of *Groundhog Day*, Phil is as bored as can be with his job as a weatherman at a small-city station. His delivery is as fake as his blue screen. He doesn't have to worry though: he's got a job lined up at a bigger station, in a bigger city.

He hates his job, but there's one assignment he hates most of all. That's when he has to go to Punxsutawney for Groundhog Day. Once again, the emergence of the sleepy groundhog from hibernation will signal whether Spring will be early this year, and trigger celebrations among the townspeople. It's a small-town ritual as hokey as it is pointless, and Phil hates every minute of it. His first sight of his producer for this year's foray reveals immediately how different the two are. Rita delightedly makes finger patterns in front of his blue screen. He pretends to dislike her, while secretly falling in love.

In Punxsutawney Phil delivers his piece to camera with barely concealed sarcasm, impatient to get back to the station. However on the way back the weather turns ugly, as an unexpected blizzard blows in. "I make the weather!" he objects furiously as a policeman tells them to turn round, summing up everything that is self-centered about Phil's world.

Back in Punxsutawney, with the phones cut off and all roads blocked to the outside world, Phil's horror show begins when he wakes up the next morning to discover that he is reliving the same day.

As Phil tries to deal with this confusing new paradigm, he goes through a series of emotions – shock, disbelief, confusion, anger – all the emotions we expect when we experience severe emotional trauma. This is exactly what we expect from the first major plot point in the story – an overturning of the hero's normal way of life. It's not enough just to put a dramatic event at the front of your story – it has to be one that has a powerful emotional impact on your protagonist, challenging them where they are most vulnerable.

Of course, you could put a train wreck at the beginning of every story, but it wouldn't necessarily be meaningful. When James Bond leaves for work in the morning, if an Apache helicopter swoops overhead with frogmen wielding AK-47s leaping from it, that is just another day at the office for 007, and not particularly significant.

The **Maverick** film *Donnie Darko* proved, however, that with a little imagination even random events can be made meaningful. In the opening sequence, a jet engine falls off an airplane and crashes through the roof of teenager Donnie Darko's ordinary suburban home. This completely random event takes on meaning only because Donnie is schizophrenic. For him it's a sign of the impending end of the world, one that requires drastic action.

For Phil, on the other hand, bored and uninspired as he is by life, reliving Groundhog Day is excruciating and torturous. Once he realizes he cannot escape, his only option is to enjoy it.

The turning point comes after Phil has been attempting to overcome his shock by drinking himself into a stupor at a bar in the local bowling alley. He bewails the fact that he is stuck in a place where every day is the same, and nothing he does matters. "That about sums it up for me," says one of his fellow drinkers, reflecting his own resigned attitude toward Punxsutawney. Unlike Phil, he doesn't see this as entirely negative. He guesses correctly that Phil, however, is a "glass half-empty kind of guy".

As Phil drives them home he regrets the fact that all his life he's obeyed the rules. Well, he's not going to live by their rules any more.

With that, he plows their saloon into a mailbox, attracting the attention of a patrol car. One of those rules, Phil announces as he turns off the road and on to a railway line, is "Don't ride on the train tracks." "Phil, that's one I happen to agree with," one of his drinking buddies replies. When they finally career into a billboard, Phil winds down his window to address the police officer who has just caught up with them: "Too early for flapjacks?"

This is a great sequence not only because it shows Phil learning how to take advantage of a life without consequences, but because it gives us a clue as to how he came to be suffering his current malaise. All his life he's done what he's been told, he's lived by their rules, pursuing his career. It's probably a long time since he's done *anything* spontaneous. *Groundhog Day* asks the **Maverick** questions, "How would we respond if there were no tomorrow?" "What would we do if there were no consequences?"

When Phil wakes up the next day, he begins to see the pluses in his predicament. He can turn the endless repetition of his days, the apparent forestalling of his life, to his advantage. He can gain **foreknowledge** and use it to manipulate those around him. He seduces local teacher Nancy by convincing her that he's always held a flame for her, ever since they were in high school together. For better or worse, Phil is learning. In doing so, he is moving forward *emotionally* although **time** has ground to a standstill.

But Nancy is only a substitute for his real object of desire, Rita. Following a casual conversation about what would constitute her ideal man, Phil sets about trying to pretend that he fits the bill. He memorizes her favorite drink, her favorite toast (to "world peace"), her love of French poetry and Häagen-Dazs ice cream. After a romantic date, in which he spellbinds her and convinces her to come back to his place, she smells a rat as he obsesses about getting the details right. She realizes the whole thing has been a set-up. "I could never love a man like you, because you only like yourself," she snarls after slapping him. "I don't even like myself," he replies woefully.

Up to this point, he has been making the most of his situation, but selfishly. Nothing, until his total failure to woo Rita, causes him to question the attitudes which have brought him to such a predicament.

His rejection by Rita convinces him he will never win her over, because she has a natural instinct for a fake. This message is underlined by the volley of repeated slaps which climaxes the sequence as he tries again and again, each time with the same result – as if time has finally been brought to an emphatic halt. Phil, and therefore time itself, has again ceased to move forward. The next morning the clock dial can barely turn over.

Phil sinks into a deep depression, but finds he is as much a failure at killing himself as he is at living. After cycling through the negative emotions of depression, shock, anger and disbelief since his life went into circular motion, he finally reaches blame, and points the finger at the groundhog: "He's gotta be stopped!" But no matter how many times he kills himself or the groundhog, he still wakes up again at the beginning of the same day.

In despair, he reaches out to Rita and accepts her offer to spend the day with him, to see if his preposterous story is true. "I don't know Phil, sometimes I wish I had a thousand lives,' she reacts, for ever looking on the bright, glass-half-full side of things. As she falls asleep in his arms later that night, he has a small epiphany. "No matter what happens tomorrow, or for the rest of my life, I'm happy now." For the first time in his life, this moment is all that matters; *he is content to be in the present*. Even so, when he wakes the next day it's Groundhog Day again. He hasn't learned everything he needs to learn.

Now he determines to be genuinely worthy of her love, and sees his situation as an opportunity to improve himself: to become a jazz piano player, to help little ladies in distress and kids stuck up in trees. He also has to learn, as we all do, that not all our good deeds go rewarded or receive thanks. We have to do things because they're worth doing, not because we expect anything in return.

There is one more lesson Phil has to learn. In spite of his best efforts to save a homeless tramp, the tramp dies anyway. Phil is not a god. Even if we grow up and take responsibility for our lives, that doesn't mean we are always in control.

At the end of the last day, Rita discovers Phil has morphed into the most popular guy in town, and falls asleep once again in his arms. "It's the end of a very long day," Phil admits: measuring not just the length of his predicament, but the distance he has traveled *emotionally*.

Next morning, **time** has finally moved on. Phil looks out of the window at the snowy landscape, and instead of making his escape, declares: "Let's live here!" As in all **circular** stories, he is back in the same place, but with a very different **point of view**.

At the beginning of the film, Phil was in a rut, cynical and bored; the only thing he had to look forward to was the next step on the career ladder. When he becomes trapped in Groundhog Day, he responds at first as most of us would do: with shock and fear. Then he begins to turn the new situation to his advantage, exploiting it for selfish pleasure and kicks.

Up to this point, Phil's changed paradigm has done nothing to change him as a person. It's not until he is rejected by the spontaneous

Rita, who takes childlike pleasure in every new experience, that he begins to change.

The perfect day can be achieved not by meticulous planning, as he imagines, but by living for the moment, and taking life as it comes. When Phil finally comes to appreciate his life, time can move on again, and he can move on too.

> *There are a lot of . . . I guess you'd call them*
> *existential issues, issues dealing with human*
> *existence, that are largely untapped in cinema.*
> *It's just a whole area of thinking about the*
> *world that a lot of people don't do.*
>
> Danny Rubin, Screenwriter, *Groundhog Day*[26]

When you first watch *Groundhog Day*, it's easy to be dazzled by the conceit. The humorous repetition of sequences, never in exactly the same way or with the same outcome, keeps it fresh and surprising. Our concern becomes not with how events will move forward, but how Phil will meet the challenge of making something happen.

We follow the emotional line.

Phil's progression from cynical, egotistic misanthrope to celebrated life and soul of the community is a moral progression as conventional as anything in **classic** three-act structure. What makes this a brilliant movie is the way the **Maverick** conceit suits the theme: Phil becomes stuck in Groundhog Day (a ritual that expresses the rebirth of life every year) because he has ceased to grow.

Maverick conceits are about taking the metaphors we use and making them real. Writing for the screen gives us the unique ability to do this, because we don't have to say to our audience "imagine this", as you would in a novel or a play. Put it on the screen, and that's the way it is.

Though time doesn't progress in a linear sense, Phil's emotional journey toward becoming a generous spirit worthy of Rita's love keeps us gripped and carries us along. We can't wait to see what stunt will become Phil's next opportunity to learn.

When thinking about your character's arc, it's worth remembering that story development is not just about what your character achieves. In **Maverick** films it's also about the **irony** of their predicament. By contrast to the usual genre fare, Maverick stories take us on a journey which often proves to be the opposite of what we expect – like Phil wanting to spend the rest of his life in Punxsutawney.

As a screenwriter, you always want to be asking yourself: what's the worst thing that could happen? And what's the best? How could either of these have unexpected consequences? For Phil, what could be worse than having endlessly to relive the most boring day of his life? And how could he possibly turn it into his best?

If you're going to play with time, point of view or reality, you will only carry the audience with you if they can *follow the emotional line.*

We have to follow the Yellow Brick Road if we ever want to get home to Kansas – or to a better knowledge of ourselves.

Hot tip
*Create empathy by giving your characters qualities,
and putting them in situations that most people can relate to,
no matter how bizarre your story.*

The importance of empathy

In order to have a strong emotional line through your story, you have first to create empathy with your hero. Empathy does not mean feeling sympathy for them, or making the character likeable. It means giving them qualities that we can identify with.

If you have ever known anyone who believed they were perfect, then you know how insufferable they can be. We cannot relate to people who have no flaws. Conversely, it might be imagined that the ideal villain has no flaws, by which we mean human qualities. In fact, the most memorable villains are those whose evil genius is undermined by a human flaw.

How many villains, when they have the hero at their mercy, delay delivering the *coup de grâce* long enough to deliver a triumphant speech about how dastardly their plan has been? This usually gives the hero time to reach up for the gun he's got taped behind his back. The villain's flaw is often pride: they cannot resist boasting about how clever they've been. *Real serial killers* − real psychopaths − lack feeling or empathy, and make boring characters. They reflect only "the banality of evil",[27] as Hannah Arendt described the Nazi leaders.

In *The Silence of the Lambs*, we remember Hannibal Lecter not so much for his crimes as for his wicked sense of humor, which expresses his perfect evil. He delights in cannibalizing his victims, cooked up with "some fava beans and a nice chianti". Yet even Lecter has a human flaw: his pride in his brilliant intellect, which Agent Starling is able to exploit in order to enlist his help in catching another serial killer. We've all experienced the sin of pride, so this vulnerability in his evil armor gives us something with which to **empathize**.

Building empathy is the necessary first step to creating an emotional line. Without it, your audience may admire the twists and turns in your story, but they won't care about its outcome.

Playing with **time** allows the audience to experience the world in a way that mimics the experience of the protagonist, bringing us closer to them. It makes us **empathize**, and hooks us in.

Once the audience is hooked, they'll follow you to Oz and back again.

> *How can I heal if I can't feel time?*
> Leonard Shelby, "Memento"

CLOSE UP: MEMENTO

Time to Burn

> *"All that is straight lies," the dwarf murmured contemptuously. "All truth is crooked; time itself is a circle."*[28]
>
> Friedrich Nietzsche

From the opening image of *Memento*, a bloody polaroid fading to white, Christopher Nolan dramatically signals his intentions: to tell his story **in reverse**. However, as we cut to the black-and-white sequence that runs counter to the backward story, we are thrown very much into the **present**: the killer waking up in a motel room, with no idea where he is and trying to figure out why.

We quickly discover Leonard's "condition" – short-term memory loss – because he finds himself having to explain it "a bunch of times". Ever since his wife's murder, Leonard can't make new memories. He can't remember whether he has a previous relationship with somebody, so he takes polaroid pictures and writes himself notes. And if it's really important, he tattoos it on his body. His biggest tattoo says: JOHN G RAPED AND MURDERED MY WIFE.

In classic **film noir**, the hero is surrounded by characters of uncertain trustworthiness, their stories reflecting the truth like mirages built on quicksand. Nolan gives this convention a **Maverick** twist.

Leonard intends to get revenge for his wife's murder – it's the one thing that gives his life purpose or forward movement. But Leonard's "condition" massively complicates his mission, since it makes the process of accumulating clues, then stringing them together coherently, much more challenging. Why is that good? *Because the greater the challenge, the more exciting it is to see the hero overcome it.*

Leonard knows all about the unreliability of memory from his previous job, and insists this won't hinder him: "Memory can change the shape of a room or the color of a car. It's an interpretation, not a record. Memories can be changed or distorted and they're irrelevant if you have the facts." But can Leonard really be sure of his facts? His scraps of paper, notes with crossings-out and files with pages missing don't fill us with confidence.

Nolan tells the main strand *in reverse,* thus mimicking Leonard's own experience of the world. Leonard can't remember what he's just done, and neither can we, because we haven't seen it yet. By having each sequence begin where the next one ends, we move gradually backward down the upward escalator of time.

Leonard's experience is like having the carpet of memory rolled up behind him. He can keep the thread of understanding going by sheer willpower, by "acting on instinct" rather than memory. He can condition himself to respond in certain ways, even if his mind can't remember why.

Even so, we see him lose that thread repeatedly. Once, hilariously, in the middle of a chase where he can't remember whether he's the one doing the chasing or the one being chased. And once, poignantly, when he "wakes up" on a toilet seat with a bottle of whiskey in his hand. He tries to figure out whether he feels drunk, having forgotten that he grabbed the bottle to use as a weapon against his pursuer, whose bathroom he's hiding in and who's likely to burst in at any moment.

Leonard's constant experience of "waking up" means that he has to think on his feet, which is a great quality for a protagonist. He has to assess the situation a hundred times faster than most of us. Like Ray Liotta's character in the final act of *Goodfellas,* Leonard lives in a state of mental hyperactivity, as his situation can spring surprises on him at any time. The endless calligraphy on his body is an attempt to imprint something that will stick.

Leonard doesn't like to talk on the phone, or to people when they're wearing sunglasses, because he needs to see their eyes.

He needs to be able to judge, in the moment, whether he can trust them. He's pretty good at that, because he used to be an insurance investigator who could "see through people's bullshit".

Except for the Sammy Jankis case. We learn about Sammy through a series of flashbacks told chronologically in the black-and-white sequences: the **forward** storyline. Shot in a gritty documentary style, they provide a more objective truth. In them, Leonard talks about the Sammy Jankis case because it helps him understand his own. Sammy also had short-term memory loss. It was Leonard's job to decide whether the cause was physical or mental, in which case the policy didn't pay off. If it was physical, Sammy should have still been able to learn through repetition, but he didn't. He should have been able to condition himself.

Leonard rejected the claim and got himself a promotion. But now he realizes he was wrong: "Conditioning didn't work for Sammy, so he became helpless. But it works for me. I live the way Sammy couldn't. Habit and conditioning. Acting on instinct." Ultimately, willpower can take the place of almost anything, even memory.

As for the look of recognition which he thought he saw in Sammy's eyes, he knows what that is now, because he does it himself every day: "You're supposed to recognize someone . . . You bluff it to seem less of a freak." In Leonard's case, this kind of bluffing is a matter of survival. But the film invites us over and over again to empathize with Leonard's condition, in the chilly recognition that it's perhaps not so different from our own. Haven't we all, at some time or other, pretended to recognize someone in order not to hurt their feelings?

The film plays this trick with us time and time again. In some senses his condition has made Leonard the "freak" that Natalie, the woman he gets involved with, accuses him of being: someone whose situation is almost beyond our understanding. Yet we're constantly invited to experience through the backward movement of time situations which seem familiar – but topsy-turvy.

When Leonard wakes up next to Natalie, we instantly know he can't remember either who she is, nor how long he's known her. It's the familiar scenario of someone waking from a one-night stand unable to remember what happened the night before, but taken to the extreme – because Leonard *really can't* remember what happened. This is funny because it plays off a situation we recognize, yet gives it a completely different meaning.

Actual memory loss is probably quite rare. Most people just prefer not to remember what makes them uncomfortable. As Teddy, the unreliable cop who befriends Leonard, puts it: "So you lie to yourself to be happy. Nothing wrong with that – we all do. Who cares if there's a few little things you'd rather not remember?"

But Leonard's condition gives an ironic twist to the post-coital embarrassment of the one-night stand. He can't swear that he's had a night to remember, or promise that he'll give her a call. On the contrary, he promises he *won't* remember her. She replies, "I think you will." Why? Because she is manipulating him into killing someone for her own reasons? No. This is an insight we can only enjoy when we **overturn** at the end of the film, when we understand her deeper motives. In the **eternal present** of the story, the beat-by-beat experience of watching the film, it feels more poignant. Even though she knows about his condition, the woman in her, the lover in her, wants to believe that the intimate experience which they have shared will be remembered.

Leonard's condition gives him an easy "out". Because Leonard is surprised to find Natalie's enemy Dodds bloody, beaten and gagged inside a closet (something he did earlier – but can no longer remember), he can present himself as the victim of circumstance. Had the story played in forward motion, we might have seen him as someone all too willing to carry out a beating on his girlfriend's behalf. Nevertheless, the structure makes us *empathize* with Leonard's point of view, no matter how skewed; since he doesn't remember seeing Dodds before, and neither do we.

Leonard is freed from suffering the consequences because he can no longer follow the **chain of logic** that leads back to his own actions.

In *Groundhog Day*, Phil is freed from consequences because **time** has ceased moving forward. Leonard is freed from consequences because time is being erased behind him. He can no longer be sure of his motives, apart from the one tattooed on his chest.

Sometimes the audience is fooled into making the wrong assumptions, because they don't know the back story either. A great example of this is when we see Leonard wake up to find a hooker snorting cocaine in his bathroom. Sure, the guy may be lonely, but somehow this doesn't sit well with someone who claims to be obsessed about his wife's death. For a moment, we lose empathy for Leonard. Only later, when we see the earlier part of the scene, do we realize the hooker is part of an elaborate ritual designed to make him remember his wife's presence, to ensure that he never forgets. Because if he forgets he loses his motivation – and so does the story.

Knowing Sammy Jankis's helplessness in the face of *his* "condition" makes us admire Leonard's refusal to give up his goal or become a victim. But, as the story goes on, we begin to wonder how much of Leonard's goal is misguided or illusory.

Even if he achieves it, as Natalie reminds him, he won't remember it. He won't even know it's happened. "The world doesn't disappear when you close your eyes," he responds. "My actions still have meaning, even if I can't remember them." Unlike Rick in *Casablanca*, who lives for the moment by choice, Leonard has no choice in the matter. Leonard has to keep the memories alive, in order to keep his motivation strong.

This is a Maverick **twist** on the convention of revenge plots: which is that the longer vengeance is delayed, the more it becomes a self-serving action to justify the time that has been wasted, and the pain that has been endured. As Hamlet's prevarication proves, revenge is a dish best served hot.

The pain of his wife's murder is all that Leonard has to hold on to, since the satisfaction of revenge, short-lived though it may be in the **classic** tale of vengeance, will be even shorter for him.

Is the act of pursuit more meaningful for him than the outcome, which can never be satisfactorily achieved, because he can never be sure he has got the right man? The **Maverick** approach to **time** in *Memento* forces us to ask different questions: not just will he achieve his goal – but will it be worth it?

At the end of the film, when Leonard realizes that Teddy may have tricked him into killing the wrong "John G", he doesn't pause to reconsider his commitment to vengeance, though he's already got it wrong once (nor does the hero in the **classic** vengeance tale – usually because he's got the taste for killing, not because he's forgotten he's done it). Instead, he says "You'll be my John G," as he triggers the events that start the backward story of the film. As Leonard puts it: "Do I lie to myself to be happy? In your case, Teddy, yes, I will."

The circular shape of this story breaks the principles of **circularity** mentioned earlier. Leonard may never find the right John G, and killing the wrong one may just get to be a habit. He appears to be in an endless loop, and unlike the heroes of most circular stories, who return to Kansas with a fresh view on life ("Toto! We're home!"), Leonard may never learn from his mistakes. As Nolan puts it: "Sometimes forgetting can be a freedom, as well as a handicap."[29]

Because the climax of the Sammy Jankis story dovetails into the climax of the main story, we find ourselves wondering what Leonard has really learnt from Sammy's story, which also ends tragically. When Sammy's wife comes to Leonard to find out the truth about her husband's condition, he tells her the problem is mental. Later he admits: "I thought she just needed some kind of answer. I didn't think it was important to her what the answer was, just that she had one to believe." Sammy's wife goes on to test him, by asking him repeatedly to administer her insulin shot. He does, and she dies.

Was Leonard's attitude to her any different from Teddy's or Natalie's, both of whom are manipulating Lenny for their own ends, telling him what they think he wants to hear? Is Sammy Jankis's story, as Teddy suggests, just a cover for his own? Was it really Leonard's wife who had diabetes, not Sammy's, as Teddy alleges? Did Leonard accidentally kill his wife? All these possibilities exist because of the unreliability of our narrator, each intriguing but impossible to affirm.

Leonard is in the opposite position to Phil in *Groundhog Day*. Phil enjoys the possibilities of a life lived without consequences, whereas Leonard constantly has the sense that something is wrong, but doesn't remember what. He is searching for a back story that he cannot remember. He feels guilty but doesn't know why. Maybe this cycle of killing the wrong person, *any* person, in revenge for his wife's death has been going on for a long time. If he can't remember, can't hold on to the moment, how does he know who *he* is? As Teddy points out: "You don't know who you are, who you've become since the incident."

In the most moving scene of the film, Leonard lies awake in bed with Natalie asleep on his chest, thinking about his wife. "I don't want to wake up every morning thinking she's still here then realizing that she's not. I want time to pass, but it won't. How can I heal if I can't feel time?"

Living in the moment is an ideal that we would all like to attain. But on its own it's meaningless. Without the ties of memory, without the benefit of learning from the past, we can't hope to develop and progress as human beings. Leonard's situation is a **Maverick** one, but his dilemma is universal. All of us need to be able to overcome the hurt of the past, and move forward with our lives.

How does the backward momentum of *Memento* change our experience of the story? It allows us to experience the world as Leonard does; it brings us closer to his point of view, which allows us to empathize with him, even when he's wrong.

While **time** may move backward in *Memento*, the emotional charge of Leonard's journey grows greater as the film progresses, as we realize the degree to which he has been manipulated, to which he has manipulated himself. Nor does the film fail to deliver the classic last-minute confession by Teddy, which promises to pay off the suspense and end the mystery, and provide Leonard with all the answers. But can Teddy's story be trusted when he is pleading for his life? Can it be trusted any more than Keyser Söze's in *The Usual Suspects*?

The backward movement of time in *Memento* gives us the sense that everything ought to be familiar, but isn't. We share the sense of loss, of something missing. "It's like I've woken up in bed and she's not there because she's gone to the bathroom or something."

Memories are like that. People leave impressions in our lives, even after they have moved on. We have all felt a sense of loss at some point in our lives, so we find ourselves empathizing with Leonard's predicament, which at first we saw as so different from our own.

Most **voiceovers** offer us the benefit of hindsight by placing the events in the past. But Leonard narrates in the present tense, opening up the emotions of a character to whom we might otherwise find it difficult to relate: "So where are you? You're in some motel room . . . you don't know how long you've been there, or how you got there . . . " By using second-person narration, it's as though he is standing outside himself watching, inviting us to feel the same way.

As Leonard puts it: "We all need mirrors to remind ourselves who we are. I'm no different." Don't we all wake up sometimes wondering who we are and why we're here?

The radical restructuring of **time** in *Memento*, along with its strong **genre** elements, make these existential questions suddenly seem vital, intriguing and important.

CLOSE UP: PULP FICTION

When Quentin Tarantino made his second feature *Pulp Fiction*, he revolutionized not only independent films (Harvey Weinstein, co-founder of the hugely successful independent producer and distributor Miramax, called his company "the house that Quentin built"),[30] but genre film as well.

With *Pulp Fiction*'s enjoyable, oddball characters and super-cool gangsters, offhand, over-the-top technicolor violence, and sassy and funny dialogue, few people stopped to worry that the story itself was far-fetched, improbable and took bizarre turns.

In addition, the film jumps between several story strands without regard for chronological order. That this did not bother audiences or dampen the runaway success of the film proves that complexity of form does not necessarily make a film less accessible.

By contrast, Hollywood movies in the late eighties had become formulaic and plot-driven. Tarantino, in his many hours working at a video store, had gained an almost encyclopedic knowledge of film: the good, the bad, the popular and the obscure – from Far Eastern chop-socky to fifties crime pot-boilers.

Tarantino's genius was to take all these elements and forge them into something new. While liberally referencing other films and turning genre convention on its head, Tarantino seems to bring little that is autobiographical to his films. (Harvey Keitel, impressed by Tarantino's knowledge of the gang world, was amazed to discover that he had gained most of this knowledge from films.)[31]

However, that doesn't mean that Tarantino's style and preoccupations are anything less than uniquely personal. The clever challenge behind *Pulp Fiction* is to take a film which celebrates – even fetishizes – popular culture, seriously.

Pulp Fiction opens in a diner as two lovers, Honey Bunch and Pumpkin, debate taking their crime spree to the next level. Why risk it holding up liquor stores, when they could hold up a diner full of customers? With their baby talk, pet names, and live-wire affection for each other, these two seem like kids who are playing at being gangsters, like Bonnie and Clyde or Belmondo in *Breathless*. They leap up and pull guns from their waistbands, launching into a dramatic and well-rehearsed routine.

Vincent and Jules, whom we cut to in the next scene, are made out of different metal. Cool, laid-back, they shoot the breeze about Vincent's recent trip to Amsterdam, where he reveals the locals eat mayonnaise with their fries, and call a quarter-pounder a royale. If they weren't wearing their film-noirish black suits, they might be heading to a ball game, a sales call, or a plumbing job.

Indeed, as soon as they stop and pop the trunk, the two start kibitzing about the tools they've been given. "We should have shotguns for this kind of deal," says Vincent.

Inside the apartment building, they stop outside a door. "It ain't quite time, let's hang back," says Jules, as though they had an appointment. As they take a stroll up the hall, they continue their debate about whether Marcellus, their boss, overreacted by throwing out of a window a Samoan whom he found giving his wife Mia a massage.

Jules thinks he did, but Vincent isn't so sure. Jules claims a foot massage doesn't mean anything, and that even he's pretty good at them. "Would you give a guy a foot massage?" Vincent asks, amused. When Vincent mentions that Marcellus asked him to take Mia out while he's away, Jules is concerned. "It ain't a date," Vincent insists. Suddenly, all the casual talk about foot massages is not just a way of passing time, but of *raising the stakes*. Marcellus is a violent, jealous man. If Vincent puts one foot wrong with Marcellus's wife, it's curtains for him.

Jules hushes him. "Let's get in character," he says, before they knock on the door. Their approach is very different from Pumpkin and Honey Bunch's, however.

Inside, Jules confronts the college kids who owe his boss the proceeds of a drug deal. Instead of "acting the heavy" as he might in a more conventional film (as Honey Bunch and Pumpkin do), Jules takes a friendly interest in the burgers the kids are eating, where they bought them, and what they're drinking. However, Jules's violation of Brett's space by munching on his burger reveals the scary **subtext** behind the casual chit-chat: he intends to consume them, utterly destroy them. His confession that: "I can't usually eat 'em 'cause my girlfriend's a vegetarian. Which more or less makes me a vegetarian too," only makes his carnivorous pleasure that much more flagrant.

Tarantino's dialogue scenes (like Kaufman's) break all the rules taught to new screenwriters about the extent of dialogue and length of scenes you should write. Before *Pulp Fiction*, the idea that killers would be discussing burgers on the way to a hit rather than the details of the job would have been considered absurd in a mainstream film. "How does all this dialogue move the story forward?" the producers would have asked.

A warning, though, before you rush to copy their example: you had better have a natural ear for dialogue, as both these writers have, and an instinct for using it as a dramatic tool. Otherwise it will just be talk, talk, talk.

Though it may be inconsequential, Tarantino's dialogue is never just "talk". The genius of his approach is in repeatedly laying down themes that seem accidental, then picking them up later charged with new meaning. These threads running through the story help to hold it together, even as we're jumping backward and forward in time, testing the chain of logic.

Let's cut back to the apartment room, with Jules picking up on the theme of the "royale with cheese" which seemed so incidental in the previous scene. He asks Brett why he thinks it's called that in France, and Brett takes a stab at "the metric system?" "Check out the big brain on Brett. You'a smart motherfucker," Jules says admiringly, but also somehow threateningly. Jules asks where the suitcase is, and Marvin starts to tell him, but Jules interrupts: "I don't remember askin' you a goddamn thing." Brett tries to apologize about the situation with Marcellus, but Jules punctuates this by plugging three bullets into his room-mate Roger's chest. "Oh, I'm sorry. Did that break your concentration? I didn't mean to do that. Please, continue. I believe you were saying something about 'best intentions'." Jules dictates the pace, and no one gets to talk without his say-so. He uses dialogue as a means of control, as a weapon.

In the next few moments he reduces the college-educated Brett to incoherence:

> JULES
>
> What country you from!
>
> BRETT
> (*petrified*)
>
> What?
>
> JULES
>
> "What" ain't no country I know! Do
> they speak English in "What"?
>
> BRETT
> (*near heart attack*)
>
> What?
>
> JULES
>
> English-motherfucker-can-you-speak-it?
>
> *When Brett says "What" one more time, Jules*
> *presses a .45 to his cheek.*
>
> JULES
>
> Say "What" again! C'mon, say "What"
> again! I dare ya, I double dare ya
> motherfucker, say "What" one more
> goddamn time!

Jules, the autodidact gangster who quotes from Ezekiel, enjoys nothing more than reducing this smart white college kid to speechlessness.

The longer he can **stretch it out** the greater the suspense, since we know that he hasn't come here to shoot the breeze.

By contrast, Jules's recitation from the Bible before he shoots Brett dead is pure rhetoric. It starts with a justification: "The path of the righteous man is beset on all sides by the inequities of the selfish and the tyranny of evil men." Then builds to a murderous rage: "I will strike down upon thee with great vengeance and furious anger those who attempt to poison and destroy my brothers."

Why does Jules need to go through this ritual before he shoots somebody? Perhaps because the artificiality of the language keeps him at one remove from the emotions which he might otherwise feel. Perhaps to call upon some spurious authority for his actions, because he does not believe the justifications he makes to himself. Perhaps to foreshadow what will happen in the end, when these words will come to have a transformative meaning, a message of forgiveness.

Dialogue can be used to **pace** time, to draw it out or punctuate it. It can lull us into a particular mood, which can then be powerfully broken by action, since on screen what characters do always carries more weight than what they say.

When a character delivers a long **monologue**, as Jules does here, it has the effect of halting the action. In most situations, this is a good reason not to write excessive dialogue. But when used effectively, it shifts the emotional weight of the scene from the speaker to the listener. We feel Brett's terror more because he is powerless, and all he can do is listen.

A moment after Brett is killed a friend of theirs comes crashing out of the kitchen, shooting and yelling: "Die! Die! Die! Die! Die! Die!" with each bullet that empties the chamber. We don't see what happens, only his expression of amazement before he's shot to pieces.

Instead of showing us the other side of the shot, the miracle which turns out to be not only the inciting incident, but one of the most important moments in the film, we **jump** to much later in Vincent's story. On his way to meet Marcellus, Vincent runs into Butch, whose story is going to dominate the second act. Butch, an aging fighter, agrees to throw a fight for Marcellus. We then continue with Vincent's story as he scores some heroin.

At his dealer Lance's, Vincent gets a rundown on the brands available, particularly the one that's a "fuckin' madman". When Vincent, fresh from his visit to Amsterdam, expresses some skepticism, Lance replies: "White people who know the difference between good shit and bad shit, this is the house they come to." They may as well be discussing fine wine. We are invited to value these distinctions equally, whether between burgers, soap stars, foot massages or drugs. In doing so, Tarantino challenges us to believe that these things are as important as anything else.

As if to drive home the point, we cut to a slow-motion, highly stylized sequence as Vincent prepares and shoots up the drug. It's hardly glamorized: the syringe looks filthy, while the extreme close-ups of needle, skin and blood are not for the queasy. But in **heightened reality** the blood swirls like an abstract painting. It is the elevation of drug-taking to an almost mystical ritual, a fetishization of the mundane. By the end of the evening, it will seem almost grotesquely different.

Hot tip: get closer

When you slow down and enlarge what is happening on the screen, you increase its importance.

You also increase our ability to absorb everything about it, and what it means.

Vincent calls to pick up Mia. She leaves a note for him on the door to come in, then speaks to him through an intercom while getting ready.

Over dinner, Vincent rolls Mia a cigarette, and she offers him a sip of her five-dollar milk shake, so he can judge whether it's worth it (another fine distinction). They both agree to ignore each other's germs. After this disassociated start, the conversation between them is soon in danger of running dry.

                    MIA
          Don't you hate that?

                    VINCENT
          What?

                    MIA
          Uncomfortable silences. Why do we
          feel it's necessary to yak about
          bullshit in order to be comfortable?

                    VINCENT
          I don't know.

                    MIA
          That's when you know you found
          somebody special. When you can just
          shut the fuck up for a minute, and
          comfortably share silence.

                    VINCENT
          I don't think we're there yet. But
          don't feel bad, we just met each other.

                    MIA
          Well I'll tell you what, I'll go to
          the bathroom and powder my nose,
          while you sit here and think of
          something to say.

Until now Tarantino's dialogue, with its high rhetorical flourishes, has called attention to itself through sheer bravado and ballsiness. So when the conversation does finally run out, we feel the unspoken physical **subtext** that much more strongly. The less these two have to say to each other, the more their sexual attraction *screams* at us.

This shift from verbal to physical reaches its climax on the dance floor, where the two show how much their bodies are in sync. Back at Mia's place, Vincent wrestles with his reflection in the mirror, telling himself to leave. Before anything can happen, Mia mistakes Vincent's heroin stash for coke, and snorts enough to knock her out.

This is the second of several bizarre accidents (the first – the "miracle" – has happened but we haven't seen it yet) that occur in the film. Vincent throws Mia into his car and tears over to the last person you would look to for help in an emergency: the slovenly Lance. He calls Lance on his cell phone, and as Lance tries to cut him off, Vincent punctuates their call by driving into their front porch. (Now that everyone has cell phones there is no excuse for stopping the action during a phone call – and it's even better if you can literally drive the action from one caller to the other.)

It turns out Lance does have some adrenalin, and after flailing through the piles of mess in his room in a failed search for a medical textbook, he advises plunging the needle straight into her heart. "Then what happens?" asks Vincent desperately. "I'm curious about that myself," responds Lance.

The contrast between their hysterical, offbeat conversation and the serious task at hand makes for a hilarious scene.

The dialogue is punctuated by Mia's bloodcurdling scream as the needle plunges through her breastbone. Her recovery is unbelievable, absurd, ridiculous; but we don't mind because we're laughing at the miracle of these messed-up characters bringing her back to life.

The shaggy dog story

The story now jumps to the boxer Butch's back story, and another monologue – or one-sided scene, as I prefer to call it.

This is the long shaggy dog story of how Butch inherited the watch that is going to become key to his story. His father's war buddy Captain Koons tells him how three generations of warriors kept this watch through as many wars, till he and his father were taken prisoner in Vietnam. After his dad died of dysentery, Koons made the ultimate sacrifice and hid "this chunk of metal" up his backside for four long years. With that image fresh in our minds, he continues: "And now my boy, I'm giving it to you."

This hilarious story delivers a punchline that plays two different ways. For most of us, this is a gift we could do without. For Butch, it's a rock-solid motivation, not only to be a survivor, but to make sure the watch survives with him.

One-sided scenes place the emotional weight on the character reacting, rather than the one doing the talking. The strength of the reaction is magnified because the one who's talking usually has the power. Butch's reaction to being offered the watch is cleverly held back till we **flashforward** and find him, on the night of the fight, waking with a start and ready to go into action.

By any measure, this story is a tall tale; a roll-call of hoary old war movies all rolled into one **back story** of a watch. Why does Tarantino throw us such a line? He does it because, in a little while, he's going to ask us to believe something even more unbelievable: that Butch would risk almost certain death, after having ripped off Marcellus, by returning to his apartment to retrieve this watch.

Tarantino knows that if you want the audience to believe something unbelievable, you'd better come up with a strong back story, or a powerful motivation for it. So he places the most absurdly compelling obligation on Butch: to repay the sacrifice and heroism of his forefathers by never losing that watch. We know it's contrived, but because it's funny and has a great payoff, we accept the underlying premise. Butch will do anything to get it back.

After Butch, incredibly, not only beats the other fighter in the ring but kills him, he makes his escape. At a motel room, his girlfriend Fabian is waiting. The two engage in some baby talk, before making love. The scene seems to stretch out forever, as if they had all the time in the world, just like Michel and Patricia, the lovers on the run in *Breathless*.

Tarantino loves these extended *mises-en-scène* (as did his heroes in the Nouvelle Vague) so much that they're given their own chapter headings in the film. Like Kubrick's six "non-submersible" sequences around which he claimed to structure his films,[32] the **"real time"** feeling of these episodes gives cohesion to what might otherwise be a confusing structure.

By slowing everything down to "real-time" (which seems slower in films than in real life, and less natural since film is **compressed time**), we are beguiled into lowering our guard until the moment when Butch realizes that Fabian has forgotten his watch, and the tension builds to a fury.

Now we are ready to believe that Butch will go and do something that even he admits is stupid.

Butch manages to sneak into his apartment without being seen ("they keep underestimatin' ya"). He slots some Pop-Tarts into the toaster, then notices a compact submachine gun on the counter. The toilet flushes. As Vincent emerges, clutching a pulpy novel, he gets knocked backward by a hail of bullets. We know what a vicious killer Vincent is, so the fact that Butch avoids being killed by him is almost a miracle.

An even greater miracle follows when Butch spots Marcellus crossing an intersection and attempts to mow him down. Just as he thinks he's got away, he's hit side-on by a car coming from the other direction. Butch, banged-up, hobbles away pursued by an equally limping Marcellus, and ducks into a pawn shop. Butch knocks Marcellus out but is in turn knocked out by the hillbilly proprietor, who takes the two of them down to the basement dungeon for some sadistic fun with his even weirder brother.

While Marcellus is being sodomized, Butch magically manages to get his hands free. After a moment's hesitation, Butch realizes that he – the inheritor of the watch! – can't leave even his most dangerous enemy in that predicament. He finds a handy samurai sword and slices open one of the brothers before Marcellus gets himself free and shoots the other. On condition he keeps silent about the whole episode, Butch finds himself forgiven.

When Butch returns to Fabian, he confesses this has been "without a doubt the single weirdest day in my entire life". And yet we are only two-thirds of the way through the film.

We then cut back to the miracle which was withheld from us when the fourth college kid rushed out of the kitchen shooting. Despite shooting from point-blank range, his bullets all miss, and he is mown down by Jules and Vincent, who then take his roommate Marvin hostage. In the car, Jules insists Vincent acknowledge it was a miracle and not a "freak occurrence". While they're arguing about it, Vincent's gun accidentally goes off, splattering Marvin's brains all over the back seat. They pull into Jules's friend Jimmie's suburban house, and wait for Mr Wolf, Marcellus's fixer, to get them out of their predicament.

Under Mr Wolf's strict guidance the car is cleaned up, and Vincent and Jules hosed down, before Jimmie's wife gets home. Dressed in Jimmie's white bread T-shirts and shorts, not looking remotely tough, they end up at the diner, where Jules insists he is retiring. As we swing right round to the beginning again, Honey Bunch and Pumpkin begin their hold-up, looking every inch their parts.

But we now know that they are no match for Jules, who already has his gun out under the table. He is not impressed when Pumpkin sticks his gun in his face. Incredibly, instead of blowing them away,

Jules decides to use this as the first step toward his new life, and lets them get away with his money; but without his boss's suitcase. (Can't let go of the McGuffin! See below.)

Why does Tarantino hold back the conclusion of Jules's story to the end, when Butch's story chronologically succeeds it? Why bookend it with Honey Bunch and Pumpkin?

> *Of course a film should have a beginning, a middle and an end. But not necessarily in that order.*
>
> Jean-Luc Godard, Writer/Director[33]

As Godard understood, when thinking about how to structure your story, the actual chronology of events may be your least concern. What's more important is the *emotional arc*. But whatever the order, your story still has to deliver the same things as any **classic** screenplay. It has to build to an emotional climax that surprises us, yet seems entirely plausible. This is exactly what Tarantino does.

In Jules, Tarantino created one of the most memorable, larger-than-life, bad-ass gangsters ever. On a practical level, if Jules and Vincent's story had been told in chronological order, it would have been over about a third of the way through the film, which would have been disappointing. And he would be asking us to believe that such a terrifying hard-ass has a religious conversion and is reformed in the blink of an eye. Which would be melodrama (or pulp fiction).

So instead of telling the story in chronological order, Tarantino opts to tell it in order of increasing improbability. Like the frog which fails to notice the water heating up in time to jump out of the pan, the audience are sucked in, bit by bit. The story makes us swallow the least implausible things first, until step by step we accept stranger things might just happen.

In a world where a young couple who call each other baby-talk names hold up a diner, there are also hitmen who shoot people while thinking about lunch. So far, so good. Now the water heats up a little more. Vincent is spared from doing anything foolish with Mia, only to have her do something far worse. On the verge of dying, she is brought miraculously back to life by the most unlikely of saviors. With the help of a very shaggy dog story, we are asked to believe that Butch would go back to his apartment just to collect a watch, and that a professional killer like Vincent would be caught on the toilet by an amateur like Butch. Butch then accidentally runs into Marcellus, and accidentally finds himself the prisoner of sex perverts. Miraculously Butch escapes, and most miraculously of all, he is moved by human decency to go back and save Marcellus.

After the miracle of the bullets, Vincent, an experienced gunman, accidentally lets his gun go off in Marvin's face. And a seemingly impossible situation is saved by the mysterious Mr Wolf, who symbolically hoses them down and makes them reborn. Jules, who accepts the miracle, is saved – while Vincent, who does not, will shortly be killed. That Jules would allow some young punk to wave a gun in his face, take his money and forgive him is a miracle indeed.

But why does Tarantino want us to believe all this? Because the movie is a *pulp fiction*, an homage to those episodic, lurid crime and horror thrillers printed on cheap paper with cheap plot twists and paper-thin characterizations to match. He wants us to "get" all this, to enjoy the movie and pop references, and to value them as much as he does.

At the same time he wants us not only to believe, but to *care* about Jules's epiphany. He wants us to *empathize*. He does this by resolving Butch's story first, even though in real time it comes later. If Butch can become a hero by saving the man he's just double-crossed, then surely even Jules is capable of conversion? *Make us believe something unlikely first. Then we'll be prepared to believe something extraordinary.*

Beneath all the blood and guts, the double crossing, the drug-taking and sodomy, this is a very moral film. This is signaled early on, in the continual debate about ethics and values – not just of burger chains, but foot massages and heroin too. The story is full of characters "saving" each other, and the film offers us not only one powerful moral dilemma (Butch going back for Marcellus), but two (Jules deciding not to shoot Pumpkin and Honey Bunch).

But what does it all mean? Is life a miracle, or just a series of bizarre accidents? As in many **Maverick** films, there is more than one way of interpreting the hail of bullets which fails to hit Jules and Vincent. If you choose to believe it doesn't mean anything, you may wind up like Vincent, and die unredeemed. Or you could see it as divine intervention, like Jules, and decide to start anew.

Or you could take the view, like Tarantino, that everything in *Pulp Fiction*, like everything in pop culture, is of value, if we choose to see it so. And everyone, even the lowest of low-lifes like Jules, is capable of redemption – and therefore worth taking seriously.

The radical approach to **time** in *Pulp Fiction*, with its extended scenes intercut out of sequence, highlights the melodrama. The miraculous twists and turns of the plot – the **metastructure** – hold our attention. However, it is the things which seem offhand and incidental, even throwaway, that turn out to be the most important. That is what makes this a great **Maverick** film. While delivering on the genre elements, violent action and suspense, Tarantino has shifted focus. He has turned Rosencrantz and Guildenstern, the dice-playing messengers in *Hamlet* (as reimagined by Tom Stoppard), into the main players. He has made us empathize.

The McGuffin

I know what many of you are going to say. "You haven't mentioned the briefcase!" What does that mean? There is no need to mention the briefcase,

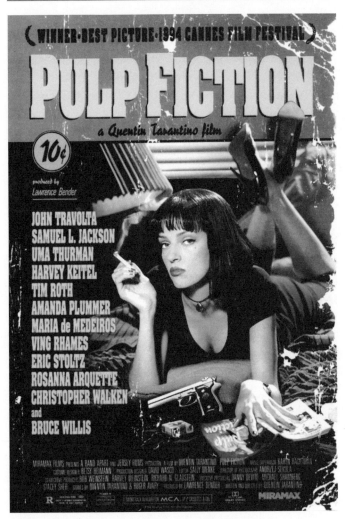

Pulp Fiction, 1994 © Miramax/Buena Vista/Kobal Collection

because the briefcase is just a McGuffin, something which seems terribly important, but isn't.

The **McGuffin**, a device popularized by Hitchcock, is something which everybody wants to get hold of. It is the motor of the film, but in the end is just a pretext for moving things along. Like Ugarte's "exit visas" in *Casablanca*, people may kill each other for them, but they are meaningless in themselves. They are often there to distract us from something that is illogical in the story, and which the writer is hoping we won't notice. In this case, it is the idea that Rick, a guy who "sticks his neck out for no one", would agree to look after the papers for Ugarte, a cut-rate thief.

In *Pulp Fiction,* the briefcase has a different purpose. It is there as a nod to the reader: there's your motor, the piece of plot that drives the story forward. But don't take it too seriously (see, it glows!), because you're going to find that everything which seems banal or incidental is actually what is most important. The briefcase's hold on the plot is so strong that even after Jules's conversion, he is still prepared to kill or die for it.

In this film, what seems most important is an illusion, while mundane things are treated as though they matter hugely.

Maverick screenwriting is about *shifting focus.*

The **McGuffin** keeps the forward momentum of the story going when the radical reordering of the chronology might leave us feeling adrift. In *The Big Lebowski*, the bowling sequences are one big McGuffin intended to give spine to a story which, with The Dude at the helm, would otherwise meander from place to place.

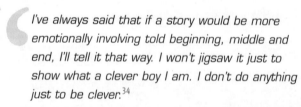

> I've always said that if a story would be more emotionally involving told beginning, middle and end, I'll tell it that way. I won't jigsaw it just to show what a clever boy I am. I don't do anything just to be clever.[34]

Quentin Tarantino

Time: coda

Reordering **time** in your script opens up a world of possibilities in the way you tell your story. As with all **Maverick** techniques, it should only be done for a purpose. That purpose is to reveal a deeper truth.

Changing chronology not only shifts the burden of the story from the "what?" to the "why?", but also alters our sense of what is important in a story. In *Groundhog Day* Phil is bored with life. The passing of time is immaterial as long as he is spiritually and emotionally stuck in a rut. Once you've defined the central value of your character in this way, then you can start to think outside the box. You can play with **time** to give the audience the feeling of that experience.

Even when the passage of time is something we can no longer keep track of, as in *Memento*, we still have to have a purpose in life, and we can renew that sense of purpose, day by day. The backward structure of *Memento* gives us that experience.

In *Pulp Fiction*, the reordering of time allows us to believe that miracles can come true, even to characters whom we don't normally think of as being worthy of them. **Maverick** screenwriting reminds us that no character is incapable of being taken on an incredible journey.

In each of these films, our focus is shifted from the plot to the themes because **Maverick** films are **concept-driven**, not plot-driven. As the forward movement of **time** becomes less important, in *Groundhog Day* and *Memento* the importance for their characters of living in the moment is greatly heightened. In *Pulp Fiction* the extended, ultra-real time episodes elevate the ordinary to the **mythical**.

In all these films, the things we don't normally notice suddenly become very important. We have *shifted focus*. Like all great **Maverick** stories, these films play with time to allow us to appreciate the world in a new way.

> *Good movies are unpredictable but logical.*
> *Mediocre movies are predictable and logical.*
> *Bad movies are predictable but illogical.*[35]
>
> Andrei Konchalovsky, Writer/Director

TIME

Recap

* Our experience of **time** changes according to our state of mind. It's not a constant.

* Changing structure changes **time**; changing time changes structure.

* Classic films ask the question: "What happens next?" **Maverick** films ask "How did it come about?"

* Any radical realignment of reality has to not only "make sense", but provide a profound new understanding of our hero.

* In **Maverick** films parallel time frames reflect not only parallel actions, but different interpretations of reality.

* Slowing down an anticipated outcome builds tension. Speeding up **time** builds adrenaline.

* **Maverick** conceits are about taking the metaphors we use and making them real.

* You will only carry the audience with you if they can *follow the emotional line*.

* In order to have a strong emotional line through your story, you have to first create **empathy** with your hero.

* Create **empathy** by giving your characters qualities and putting them in situations that most people can relate to, no matter how bizarre your story.

* **Maverick** stories are not just about what your character can achieve, but the irony of their predicament.

* If you want the audience to believe something incredible, come up with a strong back story or a powerful motivation for it.

* **Playing with time** allows the audience to experience the world in a way that mimics the experience of the protagonist, bringing us closer to them and making us empathize.

* Actual chronology is less important than your emotional arc.

Exercises

○ Write a scene in which time seems to slow down for your heroine. What does she notice that she wouldn't notice otherwise? Now *shift focus* and make this the element that "turns" the scene (changes its outcome). Bring your scene back up to **real time** by the end. Pay attention to the transitions.

○ Write a sequence in which "time flies by" for your hero. Avoid the obvious ways of measuring time. Pay attention to the pacing in your scenes. Create momentum by "coming in late and getting out early".

○ Write a sequence intercutting between two **parallel** stories. Make sure that each sequence *plays off* the other, but also that each represents a *different view of reality*. Again, pay close attention to the transitions. Are you cutting on an image, a sound or an action; one that echoes, or contrasts with it?

Section 3
Reality

5 The different levels of reality

Star Trek, three-dimensional chess © Paramount Television

In the hands of a **Maverick** screenwriter, reality is a malleable tool. The Maverick screenwriter does not seek to reflect reality as it is. He considers that, like Lester in *American Beauty*, most of us are sleep-walking most of the time anyway. We are floating through the world, our lips are moving, but we are really not seeing or hearing or saying anything.

We need to be reminded that we are alive, and this requires us to be shaken out of our usual point of view, to become conscious of the significance of our smallest actions. Like the writer in Tarkovsky's *Nostalghia*, we need to carry that candle across the swimming pool, to keep the flame of life alive.

Most of us forget that we experience many different types of reality in a day. We wake out of our dreams, and then daydream our lives away. In the car or the subway on our daily commute, we zone out the other passengers. We enter the virtual reality of our computer screens and communicate with people continents away, who seem more real to us than the people who live next door. Sometimes we feel disconnected, and sometimes we are lost in the moment. Sometimes our reality becomes hypercharged with adrenaline, distorted by powerful emotions like anger, fear or jealousy.

Many of these different levels of reality can be suggested in film, which is at heart an illusion – the illusion that when still images are passed before our eyes at the rate of 24 frames per second they will appear to be in motion.

We willingly suspend our disbelief so long as that smooth forward motion is maintained; so long as we're not snagged by anything that seems forced, unnatural, illogical or out of character. The slightest whiff of any of these false moves will cause us to snap right out of it. Any shift in reality needs to match the mood.

So what are the different levels of reality you can work with?

All art is, in a sense, **compressed experience**. We expect art to reflect the important things in life, or at least the significant ones. We do not expect a day of movie time to be like a day of our own. Drama is life without the boring bits, seen from the perspective of hindsight. We rarely see the patterns in life when we are experiencing them, unless it's to complain, "Why does this always happen to me?" or to proclaim, "Everything's going my way!"

Life is mostly routine, with a little random chaos thrown in. Sometimes more chaos than routine – the times drama tends to be interested in.

Ordinary reality is represented dramatically by what we call **naturalism**. Naturalism is the illusion that while life experience may be compressed, it represents a consistent reality, told from a consistent point of view. Stories have a shape and a meaning which can be discerned by the hero and manipulated to her advantage. Naturalism reflects a world in which we can in some way influence, or shape, our own destiny.

In **ordinary reality**, though a story may have dramatic events, and take strange and unexpected turns, these are still seen as extraordinary, not everyday occurrences. The world has meaning, and is knowable. Generally, **point of view** is invisible, or clearly identified. It doesn't shift.

(Occasionally, this principle of consistency – like all rules – can be broken in a **classic** screenplay, but if so, it is done invisibly. In *Platoon*, the voiceover of Charlie Sheen's infantryman is at first the naive one of a new recruit, writing to his grandmother. But gradually, imperceptibly, it shifts to the point of view of an older, wiser man looking back on his experiences. Yet nobody noticed because, as Stone has remarked, it "wasn't logical, but it just made sense".[36] The voiceover mirrors the audience's own changing feelings about the war, while the more reflective tone suits the build to an almost mythical finale.)

Naturalism often incorporates **realism**, but they are not the same thing. Many fantasies are told in a naturalistic style, i.e. when animals are given human characteristics. Once the rules of a world are established, stories such as *Jungle Book*, *Shrek*, *The Lion King* or *Bambi* proceed naturalistically.

The **social realism** of a filmmaker like Ken Loach, on the other hand, excludes all improbabilities. The filmmaker has to be able to say this could have happened, or it did. While such stories may strive for realism, they are in fact artfully designed to deliver a moral message. In social realism, causes rigidly lead to effects, which in turn imply necessary remedies. In the worst forms of social realism, characters can become types rather than individuals, since individuals are more likely to be unpredictable and therefore to challenge the all-important **chain of logic**.

Even realism can be given a **Maverick** twist, when it allows us to detail certain experiences that are unknowable, or which no single point of view can adequately describe. Greengrass's *United 93*, about the 9/11 hijackings and that flight in particular, takes a story whose details we can only piece together from the outside, and tells it from the inside. This works, not in spite of, but because most of the audience already know the external facts. As with *Citizen Kane*, which begins with an extensive newsreel telling the life story of its protagonist, that is not the point.

Movies like *United 93* or Greengrass's *Bloody Sunday* attempt to give us the feeling of being there, no more and no less. We are not asked to interpret or to explain, only to experience what is unimaginable or what, till now, could only be seen in a thousand contradictory fragments. *JFK*, though in a more mainstream genre style, does the same thing. It takes the "truth" and pokes a thousand holes in it, weaving together a series of fragmentary alternatives, seen from multiple viewpoints. The conspiracy, if it exists, is too big for anyone to see at once.

The open-endedness of these films, the sense that truth is not finite or black and white but problematic, is what makes these films **Maverick**.

The opening sequence of *Saving Private Ryan*, on the other hand, is **hyper-realism**, a distorted, subjective time-bending sensory overload that mimics brilliantly the experience of being in battle. Sadly, after that the film becomes more conventional.

Hyper-realism demands that we look at the detail of the world in a way we have never noticed before. In *The Thin Red Line* we can stop in the middle of a firefight to notice how beautifully the long grass sways in the wind, emphasizing the ephemeral nature of the soldiers and their conflicts, which will soon be buried in the dust of history.

In hyper- or **ultra-realism**, ordinary objects become metaphors simply by the intensity of our looking at them: for Ricky in *American Beauty* even a plastic bag blowing about in the wind can take on a life and meaning of its own, become like "God looking right at you".

Naturalistic stories also use metaphor, but more subliminally. In Loach's *Kes* we know that, for the put-upon boy who has raised a wild kestrel, the hawk represents freedom of the spirit; but nobody ever comes out and says it (unlike in *The Matrix*, where the meaning of the "The Matrix" is endlessly explained). By contrast, Tarantino wisely deleted some dialogue from the shooting script of *Pulp Fiction* which explained in detail the meaning of Butch's watch. Nor, in *Kes*, would the boy himself be able to put such a concept into words.

In **minimalism**, metaphors are even more submerged, or non-existent. The whole idea of giving symbolic weight to anything gives the world more meaning than most **minimalists** would want. If everything is meaningless, why give one thing more value than another? This refusal to recognize the value of things which other people consider important is what makes **minimalist** films funny.

In **heightened reality**, however, we are in a world where objects and situations are temporarily distorted and given extra weight in order to add to their emotional or symbolic value. It's like adjusting the controls on your TV set.

Heightened Reality

can be realized through

- comic exaggeration
- dreams
- idealized or traumatized memories
- distortion through illness or exhaustion
- intoxication
- fantasies
- mental illness
- supernatural or spiritual events

Heightened reality can be created visually by sharpening or blurring an image, by magnifying it, or by turning up the brightness or color. It can be suggested by camera moves or lenses. However, it is most effective when it relies solely on the emotional resonance of the image, vibrating in tune with the overall **matrix** of the film (see Chapter Twelve).

These distortions of reality can be brought about by exhaustion, intoxication, or ecstatic or depressive emotional states. It could be the snow-capped mountains that Clint Eastwood's character in *Unforgiven* enjoys after recovering from a fever; or the candles the boy has burning in the church in *The Sixth Sense*, with which he tries to keep the darkness and the fear at bay.

Comedies of manners often use **heightened reality** to satirize the social niceties which we unthinkingly obey, barely aware that we are acting like robots. However heightened reality, through whose distorted glass we can still see the world as we know it, is only the first level of altered reality.

Exaggerated reality is like drawing a face on a balloon and then blowing it up as far as it will go. It's still recognizable, but distorted. Once it goes beyond what we would expect to encounter in ordinary circumstances (unless we happen to work in a mental institution), once the characters become obsessively blinded or driven, or the plot takes impossibly melodramatic turns (as in *Pulp Fiction*), we enter the realms of **black** or **broad comedy**, **farce** and **altered reality.**

Of course, the lines between these different levels are somewhat fluid, and depend on the treatment.

Horror films work mostly on the level of exaggerated reality. Unless the evil seems sufficiently real, we will not be frightened by it; and we enter the realm of fantasy instead. (Which is why one of the few genuinely frightening moments in *The Lord of the Rings* is when Frodo and Sam crouch in the hollow of a tree, as the horses of the Black Riders snort and paw the ground above. The threat is no longer one of supernatural evil, it is the visceral one of an animal trying to pick up a scent.) **Horror** is about the crossover between forbidden territory and ordinary life. *The Blair Witch Project* is a film whose brilliant **Maverick** twist is to keep the evil firmly rooted in the imagination, at the level of heightened reality. The exaggerated, horrifying "truth" of the film is played out entirely in our minds, rather than on the screen, contrary to genre convention.

In film, memories can be accepted as literal truth – our internal record of our own history. More often, however, they are taken to be subjective, and so are part of **heightened reality**. However, as we've learned from *Memento,* memories are often unreliable. Things we find painful are conveniently forgotten; and things we want to hold on to are seen through rose-tinted lenses.

In extreme cases, memories can be entirely rewritten, and those who do so will swear that the airbrushed fantasy is the truth. The truth can be locked up by the subconscious, so that we are none the wiser. Sometimes, we keep secrets even from ourselves.

Dreams are like puzzles where some of the pieces are always missing. We think that if we can only put them all together they'll make a picture that we can understand; but the meaning is always slipping from our grasp. Dreams, like memories, can often be of a fragmentary nature. They are part of an **altered reality** that nevertheless seems to have an oblique relationship to the truth.

At the same level are **fantasies** or **daydreams**, projections into a future we would like to bring about, or a past that we would like to rewrite.

Other states of mind can also move from level to level.

Exhaustion, illness, hunger or thirst can **heighten** our perception of reality – the beads of moisture on an ice-cold beer bottle, or the creaking of a floorboard. Sometimes, intoxicants offer a state of reality that is at one remove, a refuge from the intensity of the present.

Taken to an extreme, these states lead to **hallucination**, the substituting of one established reality for another, equally convincing one. Then there is **mental illness**: a journey to another land from which we cannot always return. For sufferers, reality is not to be trusted or relied on.

These altered states of mind can be enlightening, illusory or a curse. There are some who say reality is beyond, and behind, the surface of things; while others say reality is all we've got.

What's important is not what you yourself think about the world, but *how your characters think about it,* and how you can represent that state of mind by expanding the borders of your fictional reality.

Just an awareness of these possibilities will begin to move your writing away from *naturalism* – the illusion that a story accurately reflects our normal perceptions of time and space.

Then finally, there is **alternate** or **parallel** reality, the creation of other worlds that operate independently of our own and according to their own rules. Plenty of **classic** films provide a parallel supernatural reality, but it is the shifting line between these worlds that denotes a **Maverick** approach.

Toy Story 3 cleverly takes us through four **levels of reality** in as many minutes. The opening sequence is a Western-style actioner in which Woody and all the other toys play absurdly heroic versions of themselves. Have the writers changed the rules of this highly successful franchise? Not at all. We are just seeing the adventure Andy – as a kid – is playing inside his head, as he gives his imagination free rein (**parallel** reality).

Then we cut into "Andy's reality" (**altered** reality). One again, Woody and the others are pretending to be inert toys, careening this way and that as the kid hurls them about. ("Great improv," they congratulate each other later.)

Then what we are watching becomes part of Andy's mom's home video, an idealized flashback montage of Andy's happiest moments growing up, always in the company of his toys (**heightened** reality).

Then we are into the "true" and present reality (**ordinary** reality) of the film – one in which toys are alive and have feelings. At the moment they are feeling abandoned, since Andy, who is now a teenager, no longer plays with them. The existential dilemma faced by the toys is beautifully summed up by our passage through these different levels of reality.

Classic screenwriting uses altered states of reality, but the boundary between them and ordinary life is usually clear.

In *It's a Wonderful Life* George gets a chance to see what the world would be like if he'd never been born. The genius of the **Maverick** twist in this **classic** film is to take his despairing cry: "I wish I'd never been born!" literally.

In this **alternate** reality, we see everything that is good in the town transformed into something harsh, selfish and greedy. Meeting the same characters in the alternate reality lends a **transparency** (see Chapter Eight) to both levels of reality, while George's positive feelings about his **ordinary** reality are colored by his experience of the alternate one – two levels of reality, both distinct, and each influencing the way we see the other.

Different Levels of Reality

- ○ hyper or ultra-realism
- ○ ordinary reality
- ○ heightened reality (altered states of consciousness)
- ○ exaggerated reality (comedy, horror)
- ○ altered reality
- ○ parallel or alternate reality

Exercises

- ○ Write a scene with **perfect reality.** Boring, isn't it? Now, make it interesting by cutting it down to half the length and keeping what is *emotionally* important.

- ○ Write a scene in which your heroine transitions from one **level of reality** to another and back again. This could be a daydream, a memory, a fantasy or an emotional or physical trauma. Pay particular attention to the transitions! Use the final transition to "turn" the scene.

DIFFERENT LEVELS OF REALITY
Recap

* All art is **compressed experience**.

* **Naturalism**
  – is the illusion that life represents a consistent reality, told from a consistent point of view
  – reflects a world in which we can in some way influence, or shape, our own destiny

* In naturalism, **point of view** is invisible, or clearly identified. It doesn't shift.

* **Social realism** excludes all improbabilities, and therefore requires a rigid **chain of logic**.

* **Maverick realism** allows us to detail certain experiences that are unknowable, or which no single point of view can adequately describe.

* **Hyper-realism** demands that we look at the detail in a new way.

* In **hyper-realism**, objects become metaphors simply by the intensity of our looking at them.

* **Naturalistic** stories also use metaphor, but more subliminally.

* In **minimalism** metaphors are more submerged, or non-existent.

* In **heightened reality**, objects and situations are temporarily distorted and given extra weight in order to give them added emotional or symbolic value.

* **Exaggerated reality** is recognizable, but distorted.

* In **Maverick** films, we have the sense that truth is not finite or black and white, but problematic.

6 Absurdism

"Every existing thing is born without reason, prolongs itself out of weakness, and dies by chance."[37]

Jean-Paul Sartre, Existentialist

The only sane response to an insane world

If you ever feel that your efforts are futile, or that the deck is stacked against you, if you feel that you are powerless against the forces arrayed against you, if you feel that the rules, or beliefs, by which others live their lives make no sense –

Then you might start thinking like an **absurdist**.

The recognition of the absurd and chaotic state of the world is a liberating force. To accept it is to accept that we will always look for meaning in the world, and rarely find it.

It is also to see the world as a giant cosmic joke, which delights in irony, pulling the plug on our sense of order and security. No matter how much we try to take control over our lives, life delights in playing tricks.

Once we start accepting this aspect of the world, and stop expecting life to give us what we "deserve", we start living in the moment, since we have no idea what tomorrow will bring. We start taking a more playful attitude to the world, and embrace its contradictions.

Absurdism is about taking an absurd notion about the world and pushing it to the limit. Absurdism may test an idea that we all share – but how far are we prepared to take it?

Absurdism is about saying the unsayable, imagining the unimaginable, and still making sense.

How can we be sure it makes sense? By creating a strong emotional line, of course, and weaving it into the thread of logic. In absurdism, character and plot are as irrevocably linked as in **classical** screenwriting.

Stories can be **absurdist** by dint of the way the universe acts upon a character. Or they can be absurdist simply because the character perceives things as so. Such characters are so self-obsessed, they see the world as revolving around their own particular angst.

In *Annie Hall*, Woody Allen took the genre of romantic comedy, with its usually reassuring reconcilement of lovers, and gave it a **Maverick** twist.

The Graduate may have signaled the dawn of the "New Wave" by rejecting middle-class notions of fulfillment through marriage, but *Annie Hall* rejected

135

the idea that the war between the sexes can ever be won. It showed that relationships were messy and confusing, and didn't always end well. But in typical **absurdist** fashion, it also accepted that, to paraphrase Alvy Singer (Woody Allen's alter ego), we're like sharks that have to keep moving forward. We are programmed by instinct and need to keep trying.

The problems between Alvy and Annie are not substantial ones, as is usually the case in romantic comedies. There are no parents standing in the way, no rivals or previous entanglements. The only thing preventing the couple from enjoying happiness together is Alvy's neurosis, his depressive view of the world (he'll only buy Annie books that have "death" in the title), and the fact that Alvy won't embrace new experience or anything outside his comfort zone. As his mother puts it, he was always "outta step with the world".

Alvy's neurotic pessimism is shown as being entrenched from an early age, when he stops doing his homework because he's learned the universe is expanding. Many of us have unstable childhoods, but Alvy's is so in a literal sense – since he lives under the Coney Island roller coaster.

Alvy has a "hyperactive imagination" and has difficulty distinguishing between "fantasy and reality". This facet of Alvy's character allows Allen to introduce numerous **Maverick** techniques. In his memory, pretty girls step out of the action and mug for the camera. He imagines anti-Semitism to be everywhere. When someone says "d'you" in a record store he believes they're saying "Jew", and that they're playing Wagner just to annoy him.

Neurosis is a form of obsession with one's problems and anxieties. It places the character at the centre of their own universe and colors everything they look at. Rather than being open to new experience or new influences, Alvy tries to shape the world around him in his own image. He wants Annie to be as obsessed with death as he is; and when he hears an academic pontificating in line at a movie theater about the writings of sociologist Marshall McLuhan, he imagines pulling McLuhan out from behind a hoarding to puncture the pretensions of his tormentor (thus **breaking the fourth wall**).

Absurdism is about taking what is hidden and thrusting it into the light. In architecture this could be compared to the famous Lloyds Building in

London, in which all the plumbing and wiring is on the *outside* of the structure. So when Alvy and Annie enjoy their first drink together, Allen *shows* us the subtext in the form of subtitles: "God, I sound like a jerk." The normal insecurities and awkwardness which we all feel around someone we're attracted to are magnified by being written on the screen, the neuroses forming an almost impenetrable barrier to their ever enjoying an easy and natural relationship.

The contrast between the characters trying to act cool and sophisticated, while underneath feeling uncomfortable and self-critical ("Christ, I sound like FM radio. Relax") makes for a funny scene.

When Alvy visits Annie's WASP-ish family, he imagines that, to the Jew-hating grandmother his Jewishness is not just evident, but visible on the surface – that he has been transformed into an Orthodox Jew, in full Old World regalia.

When Woody complains that Annie "feels distant" when they are making love, she denies it, but her soul actually climbs out of bed in search of something to keep herself occupied. "You've got my body, why do you need my mind?" she asks, confirming his worst fears.

All of these "tricks", these momentary lapses from naturalism, are funny because they give substance and weight to what's in Alvy's head. They're funny because none of these anxieties is as serious as he imagines it to be. And because most of us will have experienced similar feelings from time to time, we can laugh at ourselves as well, relieved that we haven't been exposed in the same way.

Great comedians say the unsayable, they puncture the balloon of social convention and reveal the maelstrom of human emotion inside. Because most of us cannot live with this constant intensity of emotion, we observe these conventions. If we all went around saying exactly what we feel all the time the whole world would be a madhouse.

And because most of us are at heart romantics, we create art – as Alvy does in his play based on his and Annie's relationship – in which, unlike in classic **film noir**, everything comes right in the end.

> *Life is so much luck. And people are so frightened
> to admit that. They want to think that they control
> their life. They think "I make my luck." And you want
> to keep telling yourself that you're in control, but
> you're not in control. Ninety-nine percent of it is
> luck, the luck of the genes, the luck of the draw,
> what happens during the day, the bomb that goes
> off on the other guy's bus.*[38]
>
> Woody Allen

Chaplin's Tramp may have been the first notable film character to stand on the outside looking in, but the outsider's point of view has often been a launching pad for **absurdist** stories.

While the Tramp was an outsider for economic reasons (*Modern Times* suggests he might have had a hard time holding down a job, even if there hadn't been a Depression!), and Alvy Singer distances himself by his own neurosis, others find themselves outside the mainstream of family, community or society by choice, attitude or philosophy.

In *The Big Lebowski* The Dude, a laid-back hippy with a "takin' her easy" attitude, is someone with few needs, apart from his reefer and his bowling team. He is shaken out of this minimalist idyll, however, when some heavies piss on his living-room rug, mistaking him for someone else. His quest to get compensation soon throws him into an absurd ransom plot straight out of **film noir**, complete with fake kidnappings, double crossings, gold-diggers and *femmes fatales*.

The challenge facing the average detective in film noir is hard enough, but *The Big Lebowski* is funny because The Dude is probably the character least likely to be handed this role (just as in *Pulp Fiction* Lance is the character least likely to be performing emergency medical procedure). As he puts it himself: "It's a complicated case, Maude. Lotta ins. Lotta outs. And a lotta strands to keep in my head, man."

The **classic** convention is to create characters who have, at the very least, the hidden potential to achieve their goals, qualities they can draw on to help them in their task. But **Maverick** stories often call on characters who are ill-fitted for their roles – or, like Craig in *Being John Malkovich*, all too well suited for their improbable tasks. It's absurd to think The Dude can go head to head with gangsters – but that's what makes it funny. It also challenges the writer to find unexpected ways in which The Dude's qualities can turn out to be useful.

To counterbalance The Dude's laid-back style we're given his sidekick Walter. A Vietnam veteran and a smoking powder keg of repressed rage, Walter is a perfect example of a character who sees everything through his own highly subjective filter. For him, everything is a metaphor for Vietnam ("I did not watch my buddies lie face down in the muck for that . . . "). Walter's short fuse gets The Dude in all kinds of trouble – and by comparison The Dude seems diplomatic and rational, which is the whole point.

Hot tip
Make your flawed hero more sympathetic by giving supporting characters similar but more extreme values.

For Walter the world is lawless and chaotic, and you need to be a no-holds-barred warrior to deal with it. For The Dude, rules and laws are mostly to be circumvented, and those who impose them are not to be trusted.

Since both men are in thrall to a golden past, these **absurdist** characters are not primarily motivated by shaping their future. The **film noir** plot may carry them along for a while, like a tide pulling refuse in its wake, but ultimately the machinations of rich men and their trophy wives are not what matters to them.

More important are the things you can count on – like bowling. This provides the anchor in their lives, and also the spine of the story, rather than the convoluted kidnapping plot, which turns out not to be a kidnapping at all.

As in many **Maverick** *films, the trick is in* **shifting focus** *away from the things the genre normally considers important.*

Unlike in **film noir**, where the hero is trying to find his way in a morally corrupt universe, the heroes of the Coen brothers' films are "trying to find a code of conduct in a world of madness".[39] "This is not Nam. This is bowling. There are rules," as Walter puts it. "All I wanted was my rug," The Dude insists. In such a world, the characters need something they can hold on to: so they go bowling.

Curiously, it is not until the final scene that we see either The Dude or Walter bowl. The script records that they are "pretty good". Here, they are no longer outsiders; they are in their groove. As The Dude puts it, life is "strikes and gutters", but "The Dude abides".

"I guess that's the way the whole the whole durned human comedy keeps perpetuatin' itself, down through the generations," as The Stranger, the film's narrator, puts it. Which is as good a definition of **absurdism** as any.

While *The Big Lebowski* works on the level of comic exaggeration, *Festen* works on the level of **altered reality** – but an altered reality in which everything has the appearance of truth.

Festen delivers one of the great inciting incidents when a grown son addresses the large, extended family who have gathered to celebrate his father's sixtieth birthday at the hotel they run. When Christian accuses his father of sexually abusing him and his twin sister over a period of years, the initial shocked silence is soon replaced by social embarrassment and an eagerness not to let anything so preposterous – which the father denies, accusing his son of being "over-tired" – interrupt their pleasant lunch.

Festen takes a giant stick of gelignite and drops it into their lobster soup bowls. Instead of watching the bomb go off, as we would expect in a "social issue" drama, the family do their best to disarm it. But Christian will not be silenced, even after he is thrown out, beaten and tied to a tree.

This satire on bourgeois complacency, and its fear of confronting an ugly and painful truth takes a big "What if?" and logically follows the consequences. What if you told someone the terrible truth about your family, and everybody just ignored you? Unfortunately, this happens – all too often.

This scenario – even down to the "pressure-cooker" device of having the staff steal the guests' car keys – is not *realistic*, but its hilarious consequences are played out naturalistically. It enters the realm of fairy tale, but a fairy tale in which everyone involved pretends nothing out of the ordinary is happening.

In one of the most disturbing scenes, Christian's father confronts his son in a deep, dark wine cellar that resembles a dungeon. With creepy sincerity, he tells Christian he should contact the police if he really believes his story is true: because he personally has no memory of it. Almost before our eyes, we see Christian reverting to a confused, terrified child. He apologizes and insists he must have made a mistake, blaming it on the pressure of work.

Before our eyes, we see Christian deny the reality which he knows to be true. In **altered reality** *things which are false can become true, simply because the characters believe them to be so.*

If Alvy is alienated by his own neurosis, and The Dude by society in general, in *Dr Strangelove*, an absurdist political satire about nuclear war, it is humanity itself which is rendered absurd by the possibility of nuclear annihilation.

When a renegade General in charge of a US airbase orders his B-52 bombers to attack the Soviet Union, the American president is forced to give his Soviet counterpart the coordinates to destroy the aircraft in order to prevent a nuclear war.

When one of the planes manages to get away, we learn that their bombing raid will automatically trigger an all-out nuclear strike thanks to the Soviets' new secret "Doomsday Machine".

This dark material, however, evaded serious treatment. According to Kubrick:

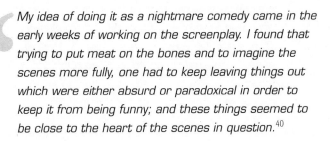

> *My idea of doing it as a nightmare comedy came in the early weeks of working on the screenplay. I found that trying to put meat on the bones and to imagine the scenes more fully, one had to keep leaving things out which were either absurd or paradoxical in order to keep it from being funny; and these things seemed to be close to the heart of the scenes in question.*[40]

The screenplay soon coalesced to include a host of larger-than-life characters: the cigar-chomping base commander, paranoiacally convinced that his drinking water has been poisoned by Soviet agents to rob him of his manhood; the mustachioed English air force officer seconded to the base, who with polite restraint and contained hysteria tries to deal with the insanity around him; the drawling Texan air force pilot who dons his cowboy hat and jumps astride his nuclear payload to guide it home; and the thwarted and crippled Dr Strangelove himself, the Nazi-loving German scientist who plans to retreat to his underground bunker and sit out the nuclear conflict while repopulating the human race with eager females.

In spite of this comic exaggeration, Kubrick strove for realism, particularly in the flying sequences. The set for the fictional "War Room" was so impressive that, on first visiting the Pentagon, Ronald Reagan is said to have asked to be given a tour of the (non-existent) room.

However, it wasn't only the design, but the performances that Kubrick wanted to be truthful. As he wrote in the preamble to the shooting script: "The story will be played for realistic comedy – which means the essentially truthful moods and attitudes will be portrayed accurately, with an occasional bizarre or super realistic crescendo."[41] And in handwritten notes found with an early draft, Kubrick reflected:

> *The serious writers of the twentieth century have taken themselves too seriously. Cynicism, loss of spiritual values, two world wars, the communist disillusionment, psychoanalysis has forced the twentieth-century writer to keep his hero uninvolved, detached, burdened with problems of relating to life. Coolness or at least madness seemed the only path open. If the modern world could be summed up in a single word it would be absurd. The only truly creative response to this is the comic vision of life.*[42]

When the world is going mad all around us, sometimes **absurdism** is the only sane response.

Festen alters reality to create a funny "What if?", but then logically follows the consequences. Once we have suspended our disbelief, everything else follows in a naturalistic if heightened fashion.

Maverick films such as *Being John Malkovich* take this a step further by beginning with a "What if" and then taking us through a series of increasingly unlikely consequences.

When something is as absurd as that, how do you keep the audience along for the ride?

CLOSE UP: BEING JOHN MALKOVICH

The world of *Being John Malkovich* is quickly established. From the opening, a technically accomplished but self-indulgent puppet show, "Craig's Dance of Disillusionment and Despair", we realize that Craig is the kind of artist whose feelings are turned inward on himself. Unemployed, he's jealous of the success of his famous rival Derek Mantini, a cheesy commercial entertainer. "Consciousness is a curse," he tells the chimpanzee, one of the menagerie of animals that his wife Lottie keeps in their cramped apartment.

Craig is so out of touch with his audience that, when he puts on a sidewalk puppet show, he doesn't realize that his erotic version of *Abelard and Heloise* is unsuitable for children, and gets smacked in the face by an angry parent.

Soon Lottie is pressuring him to get a job, and Craig reluctantly begins scanning the classifieds. Fortunately, an ad in the paper says Lestercorp is looking for someone with "unusually nimble and dexterous fingers", and Craig fits the bill.

Hot tip
*When you want your audience to believe a very big "what if?"
always get them to believe something easier first.*

It is *unusual* that Craig should find a job so completely suited to his unusual abilities, but it is not impossible. In a **classic** screenplay, this coincidence would have been disguised. But here it draws attention to itself, because if the writer can make you believe this, he can make you believe the implausible things that follow.

Craig and Lottie's world is deliberately portrayed as drab and humdrum – not the sort of place where unusual things happen. After all, how odd is it really – maybe a little eccentric – that she keeps a miniature zoo in their apartment?

So when Lestercorp turns out to be on the 7½ th floor of a very ordinary-looking office building, which can only be accessed by jamming the lift with a crowbar, everybody treats this as perfectly normal, and it feels like nothing strange has occurred.

However, from the moment we enter the 7½ th floor we enter seamlessly into another level of reality, where the ceilings are half the normal height to keep down the "overheads".

Just as we are wondering whether to suspend our disbelief, we are deliberately distracted by a series of hilarious misunderstandings. (In hypnosis this is known as an "interrupt", a momentary confusion designed to jolt the subject from one state to another.)

The receptionist mishears everything he says, and dismisses him as a "mumbling job applicant". When called in for his interview, Craig discovers that the secretary has convinced her clear-speaking boss, Lester, that he has a speech impediment.

Because Craig can see through the injustice done to Lester (despite the credence to which he gives her "Masters in Speech Impedimentology"), his exposure of this lesser truth allows us to forget about the bigger "what if?" – whether we believe in the world of Lestercorp in the first place.

And because we see Lester as the "victim" of this fraud, we don't challenge his eccentricities. Instead, we sympathize – which is important, since his character will have to "deliver" the most outlandish aspect of the plot: the hijacking of John Malkovich as a "vessel" to prolong Lester's life.

Craig's nimble fingers do their magic, and he is duly hired. His first task is to sit through a corporate video, explaining how the 7½th floor came about. We are invited to laugh at this hokey story about how the "Captain" created a special floor for his vertically challenged lover. Why not? Isn't that the way we feel about all corporate videos?

As we flatter ourselves with our superiority to such propaganda, we forget to question any longer whether there could *really* be 7½ floors. This, in magic, is what we call sl*eight-of-hand* – the making of a big, false movement in order to disguise a smaller, more covert one.

This dubious back story about the Captain is as important as the back story about Butch's watch in *Pulp Fiction* – not because we necessarily believe it, but because it entertains us, *which gets us to buy what happens next.*

And because Maxine, his fellow new employee, calls it "bullshit", we recognize her as someone who tells it like it is, and she doesn't seem to notice how odd it is that Lestercorp is on the 7½th floor. We like her just the way we like Craig for telling Lester that he doesn't have a speech impediment. If Craig has been shown to be such a truth-teller, why should we doubt anything he says from here on in?

So when Craig drops a file behind a filing cabinet, and discovers a portal into the brain of John Malkovich, is that really such a big leap of faith? After all, Malkovich isn't even doing anything very interesting – just reading the paper and having his coffee. What could be more normal?

This is just one example of how the **Maverick** structure of *Being John Malkovich* takes us through multiple levels of reality.

The process works by creating *susceptibility* – a willingness to suspend disbelief because certain things are shown to be demonstrably true, so that others, treated in exactly the same way (but far more unlikely), will seem convincing as well.

Hot tip
*When you want the audience to accept a big lie,
tell a small one first.*

We tend to accept the view of reality of whichever character we most empathize with, particularly if they are pointing out what is self-evidently false. We say, how clever of them to have noticed! Which means we're more likely to accept reality as they see it next time round.

We can use this character's belief in the new reality to vault us over the gap – the gap between expectation and a new reality.

For instance, when a character for whom we already have empathy, like Maxine, believes that Craig has "magically" guessed her name (when he has obviously used a trick), we are far more likely to believe it when Craig does something truly magical, like becoming John Malkovich.

From the outset, Craig is aware of the moral implications of his discovery. He tells Maxine that it raises "all sorts of philosophical-type questions", and it's a real "metaphysical can of worms". He can no longer go on, he declares, living life as he has lived it till now.

This is the purpose of all inciting incidents – to **overturn** the world of the hero so that life can never be the same again. In a conventional screenplay, this "meaning" would have been left in the subtext, and taken on board subliminally.

Instead, when Maxine is so openly unimpressed – she hasn't a clue who John Malkovich is – we laugh with her at Craig's pretensions. *But we no longer question the event itself.*

However, Maxine soon sees its commercial potential, and convinces Craig to start selling tickets. Unlike Craig, she has no moral qualms about exploiting the situation.

Remember, giving supporting characters more extreme qualities than your protagonist makes your hero more sympathetic. And because Maxine is so overtly out for herself (for her the world is divided between "those who go after what they want and those who don't"), Craig's artistic ambitions, though self-serving, seem more forgivable.

Complications follow immediately. Lottie takes a trip inside John Malkovich, declares it to be "sexy", and decides she wants to be a man. Instead of expressing amazement at this turn of events, Craig is more concerned to know why she chose an *allergist* to consult with. And so, once more, we are dealt a *sleight-of-hand*.

Being John Malkovich obeys many of the conventions of **classic** storytelling – the inciting incident, for instance, sets off all kinds of moral and practical complications for the characters – but the twists and turns of **absurdism** are sharper and more radical than **naturalistic** storytelling.

Nevertheless, despite its series of unfolding realities, *Being John Malkovich* never loses its audience, because we *follow the emotional line*. The story snatches Craig's subconscious desires and hurls them into reality, then pursues them to the end of the line.

Intermission
(something we thought you ought to know)

Triangles

Most good stories are based on **triangular** relationships. This is because two-sided relationships can get very predictable, like Craig and Lottie's. Without any outside force to relieve the pressure (which is why Lottie so desperately needs animals as child substitutes), life can get boring.

Ever had an argument with a loved one that just seems to go round and round? Two-sided relationships are like that.

As soon as you introduce a third corner of the **triangle**, however, life gets a lot more unstable, and therefore dramatically a lot more interesting.

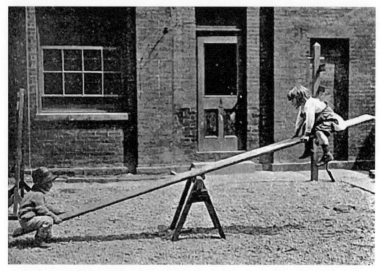

Jean Lee Hunt, *A Catalogue of Play Equipment* (1918), digitized by Project Gutenberg

We all know two's company and three's a crowd. That's because as soon as you have three people, two always take sides and the third feels left out. *This creates tension, and tension demands action to resolve it . . .*

So when Lottie decides she can only "actualize" herself as a man, this sets up a romantic triangle of such overwhelming complexity that it parodies conventional romantic complications. Lottie only feels comfortable as a man, and as a man she feels attracted to Maxine. Maxine only feels attracted to Lottie when she is inside John Malkovich, and Craig can only trick Maxine into loving him if he pretends to be Lottie.

This is a fantastic set-up for a triangular relationship, as it provides no hope for resolution, but endless comic permutations!

When creating an improbable situation, you always need a character who can voice the audience's own scepticism. If the character is someone we enjoy disproving, all the better. In *Being John Malkovich* that role is ably filled by John Malkovich. Like many actors, the character Malkovich appears somewhat prissy and vain, and overly concerned with the exact hue of his towels. Hilariously, although Craig speaks of him as "one of the great American actors of the twentieth century", he is constantly remembered for a role he never played – a nightmare for someone whose identity is bound up with their image.

In a film that is inextricably about identity ("Am I me? Is Malkovich Malkovich?" asks Craig after discovering the portal), nobody in this film is happy in their own skin (apart from Maxine, who's just naturally sexy). Craig wants the "thrill of seeing through someone else's eyes", Lottie wants to be a man, and Lester wants to do the ultimate and assume another body, so he can live forever. Malkovich is portrayed as one of those actors who is only comfortable when playing a role, perhaps because he doesn't feel entirely comfortable with himself.

When Malkovich shares his paranoid suspicions with his friend Charlie Sheen, Charlie is excited about the idea of meeting the girl who is "channeling her dead lesbian lover". Charlie doesn't question the premise; on the contrary, he drools over it. We know the "truth" is even stranger, and so enjoy seeing through Sheen's lurid fantasies.

The audience always enjoy knowing more than the characters. When this dramatic irony goes beyond knowing more of the plot, to being able to see through to another level of reality, then we experience the joy of **transparency** (see Chapter Eight).

Hot tip

The audience's ability to disprove the illusions of the characters reinforces the "truth" that you want to sell them.

When Malkovich barges into the queue for the Malkovich experience ("Ever want to be someone else?") and dives through the portal, he is confronted by the nightmare scenario for an actor – one in which every character is a mirror image of himself.

Good screenwriting is about making the internal external, but **Maverick** screenwriting goes one step further: it takes the metaphors we use to describe our dreams and nightmares, and makes them real.

The film moves into the next level of reality when Craig, now with Maxine, fully assumes John Malkovich's identity. In another brilliant *sleight of hand* she and Craig (in the guise of Malkovich) visit Malkovich's agent to inform him of his new career direction: to become a puppeteer.

The agent is so obsequious to his star client's whims he doesn't even bat an eyelid, while Craig and Maxine sit there like two giggling love-birds who can't believe their luck. And because we enjoy the sycophantic agent's willingness to be fooled, we don't question any longer whether Craig can pull off the deception of Being John Malkovich.

And so the film pulls its ultimate dummy (or body swerve, if you prefer). Because we have been taken step by step from Craig's first awkward discovery of the portal to his complete assumption of John Malkovich's identity, we can accept this as the next logical step (highly important, since the actor Malkovich must now convince us that he is inhabited by Craig, and later Lester as well – an amazing feat, some-what overlooked by the critics).

Just in case we don't buy it, we are treated to a pseudo-documentary about Malkovich's rise to famous puppeteer, almost a parody of Craig's wildest dreams – and another "reality marker" – like the TV show about Mantini, and the corporate video about the "Captain". But this second-act triumph, as in any classically structured screenplay, is not the end of the story. Craig begins to suffer the consequences of ignoring his reservations about the moral implications of what he has done.

Maxine's love for Craig begins to wane as she becomes pregnant and yearns for Lottie. And now Craig starts to suffer the unexpected consequences of being "inside someone else's skin". We all dream of being someone else: someone richer, more famous, more good-looking. If we could be all those things, everyone would love us, wouldn't they?

But would they love us for ourselves?

Everything that Craig has achieved is an illusion, because he is loved for being John Malkovich, not for himself. So sick is he of his new identity that, in a parody of the famous scene from *Spartacus*, he rounds on an over-friendly barfly: "I AM NOT MALKOVICH!"

Finally, Craig takes moral responsibility and gives up Malkovich so that Lottie, whom Lester has pretended to have kidnapped, can be freed. And at that moment Lester enters the "vessel" of Malkovich, and Craig discovers he has become trapped in the body of Maxine's child, condemned to see Maxine and her lover forever through someone else's eyes.

Be careful what you dream of, in case your dreams become a reality.

If you are a screenwriter, take your wildest fantasy and pursue it to the end of the line, to see where it takes you. Now make it brighter, more glittering. Now make it so shiny it's almost painful. Does it still look so alluring?

when you pursue your greatest fantasies
TO THE LIMIT

WORST NIGHTMARES

ABSURDISM

Recap

* Recognising the **absurd** and chaotic state of the world can be liberating (and funny too).

* **Absurdism** is about
  - saying the unsayable, imagining the unimaginable, and still making sense
  - taking an absurd notion about the world, and pursuing it to the limit

* **Absurdism** favors the **outsider**'s point of view.

* In **absurdism** things become absurd just because a character perceives them to be so.

* Great comedy punctures the balloon of social convention and reveals the maelstrom of human emotion inside.

* The trick is in **shifting focus** away from the things the genre normally considers important.

* Make your flawed hero more sympathetic by giving supporting characters similar but more extreme values.

* **Techniques of persuasion:**
  - the **interrupt**, a momentary confusion designed to jolt the subject from one state to another
  - the **sleight-of-hand**: the making of a big, false movement in order to disguise a smaller, more covert one
  - **susceptibility**: a willingness to suspend disbelief because certain things are shown to be demonstrably true; so that others, treated in exactly the same way (but far more unlikely), will seem convincing as well

* When you want your audience to believe a very big "what if?", always get them to believe something easier first.

* We will accept the **view of reality** of whichever character we most empathize with, particularly if they are pointing out what is self-evidently false.

Exercises

○ Write a scene in which the world is shown to be ironic or absurd. Show how this insight completely changes the point of view of your character, and the way they respond to the world.

○ Use one of the **techniques of persuasion** to convince your audience that something absurd is logically true.

○ **Triangles**. Ever heard the saying: two's company, but three's a crowd? Write a scene in which this becomes painfully obvious. Make sure the scene has some "business" to drive it and to camouflage the subtext; but this subtext must explode out on to the surface at some point to "turn" the scene.

7 Minimalism

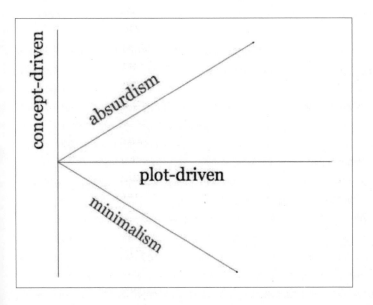

When nothing else works, do nothing

In **metastructure**, the plumbing is on the outside. The structure calls attention to itself because the normally submerged organizing principles of **classical** structure have been broken: causality, linear structure, consistency of reality or point of view.

Classical structure works because so many of these unspoken rules mirror our ordinary experience of reality. For instance, most of us see the world through a single point of view (unless we happen to be very indecisive, or schizophrenic). Without the usual organizing principles, the audience can get lost, and so sometimes an artificial structure – the bowling tournament in *The Big Lebowski*, for instance – can help keep us on track.

In **metastructure**, the writer wants you to see the architecture because, when the logic is exposed, you're more likely to accept whatever goes along with it. Unlike with **naturalism**, the **absurdist** writer is not afraid of the audience being aware that they are watching a construct. Absurdism is, by definition, self-conscious.

In **minimalism**, the structure is submerged or invisible. The landscape is flattened out, with fewer obvious features to orient yourself by, fewer milestones or turning points along the way.

This does not mean that minimalism does not create tension – or offer surprises – quite the opposite. But it tends to do so through quiet revelation or cumulative feeling, like a great tidal wave rather than a roller coaster.

In **absurdism**, characters are often carried away by the momentum of their obsessions or fantasies. In **minimalism**, characters are more likely to be wandering the landscape without any sense of direction or clear motivation.

Minimalism takes the typical dramatic set-up – a pressure-cooker situation where characters who have been thrown together have to work through their problems – and intensifies it.

Absurdist drama often involves outsiders – the joker characters from fairy tales who enter a community and turn it upside down (*Groundhog Day, Festen*). **Minimalist** characters often feel confined by their circumstances or overwhelmed by the forces surrounding them, environmental, social or personal. Minimalist characters can be so overwhelmed by their internal conflict that they become paralyzed. The forces struggling within them cancel each other out, until they are incapable of acting (or they implode, like Vera Drake, a woman who seems to shrink in size the more pressure is applied to her).

Their predicament can be summed up by the final words from his novel *The Unnameable* by master minimalist Samuel Beckett: "You must go on; I can't go on; I'll go on."

While **absurdist** characters often feel unable to conform to society, **minimalist** characters often feel disempowered. Like Rosencrantz and Guildenstern, Hamlet's messengers who were put centre stage in Tom Stoppard's play and subsequent film, they believe great events are what happen elsewhere, while they are held, in a kind of limbo, and rolling dice is as good an indicator as any about where life is headed.

Sometimes that powerlessness can be created by restricting **point of view**. In Hitchcock's *Rear Window* Jimmy Stewart's character Jeff, confined to a wheelchair after breaking a leg, becomes intensely curious and frustrated when he believes he is witnessing the aftermath of a murder from his window, but feels powerless to do anything about it. Although the film suggests all kinds of off-screen drama, this **mainstream thriller** leans toward **minimalism** because the main character feels unable to affect the dramatic events going on all around him.

In Polanski's *The Pianist*, Wladyslaw Szpilman, a concert pianist, escapes from the ghetto where the Nazis have imprisoned Warsaw's Jews, and hides on his own in a series of increasingly desperate bolt-holes. He is forced to watch from his window the Warsaw Uprising being bravely fought by his fellow Poles and ultimately defeated. He is powerless to help, or even to exist, since he has become a non-person, a kind of living ghost.

When his hiding place is discovered by a German officer who has been billeted in the rooms below him, he is asked to prove his story by playing the piano. It has been years since Wladyslaw has touched a piano, but his fingers have never ceased to move in imaginary recitations of the classical repertoire. His shaky but achingly beautiful performance, to save his life, illustrates how we can be stripped of everything that makes us human but still retain our human spirit. And with that one act, he is brought back to life.

Minimalism can be brought about by the inaction or powerlessness of the characters. There may be plenty of action in a minimalist film, but – bending the rules of this visual medium – that action is usually off-screen. *The Blair Witch Project* combines both aspects, stranding a documentary film crew in the woods where they have gone to investigate a local legend about a murderous witch. They soon find themselves lost and surrounded by frightening signs and sounds of something evil.

The brilliant **Maverick** conception, however, is that all this is left to the imagination: we never see anything horrifying actually happen, only hear it or see its consequences. And yet, with all the rest of our senses heightened, this film is highly frightening; and a brilliant solution for filmmakers working on a microbudget.

Minimalism can also be created by restricting the free will of the protagonist. In *Leaving Las Vegas* the protagonist is a lowly development executive in Hollywood, who gets fired because of his drinking problem. He resolves to drink himself to death in Las Vegas, where alcohol can be obtained round the clock. Even when he meets a hooker with a heart of gold who takes him in, he cannot change the course he has set himself. All he can give himself is a brief epiphany, the knowledge that he has been loved for himself, and for himself alone.

In *Vera Drake*, a story set in post-war, still food-rationed London in 1950, a middle-aged woman proves herself to be a good wife, a loving mother, and a caring neighbor. One of her caring acts is to help "girls who have got into trouble", by giving them back-street abortions. While she herself has never taken any money for this service, she is unaware that the friend who refers girls to her is charging for the service. The premise cleverly turns on its head the stereotype most of us would have of an illegal abortionist. The story builds up her world in small scenes of everyday life and service, with cups of tea for family and friends to keep up the spirits, while the men swap war tales.

When a girl she "helps out" ends up being rushed to hospital and almost dies, Vera is arrested. From this point on, we watch her slow destruction by the system, as justice follows its course. Running counter to it we are offered the storyline of a young girl from one of the well-to-do families Vera cleans for, who is able to pretend mental instability, and pay a private doctor to get round the law on abortion.

In spite of the good intentions of those who enforce it, the law is shown to be a blunt instrument, inexorably and indiscriminately grinding down those who are caught in its net. While most of the characters are looking forward to getting on with their lives in the post-war world, the system is shown to be backward and cruelly dated, and Vera, as a poor, working-class woman, is powerless in the face of it.

Vera Drake has strong elements of **realism**, but like *Leaving Las Vegas* leans toward **minimalism** in the slow inevitability of the working out of its plot. As one of Vera's fellow prisoners, in for the third time, puts it: "We just do our best, love."

In *Breathless* Belmondo's character has the illusion of spontaneity and free will. When a motorcycle cop pulls him over in his stolen car, Belmondo unhesitatingly shoots him. He makes various efforts to call in a loan so he can split town, and to change his car for a "clean" one. But these are just ways of "making" busy. In fact, he is more interested in flirting with Jean Seberg, and discussing every topic under the sun, than in making a getaway.

Hovering around the peripheries of the gangster genre, *Breathless* is the story of someone who plays at the idea of being a gangster, even to the point of his final melodramatic death stagger. Belmondo is imprisoned by his own image of himself, and so his downfall is inevitable. Belmondo is a **minimalist** character trapped within his own **metastructure**.

In *Slacker*, the forward progression of plot has been annihilated altogether, apart from our vague sense that time is passing and the day growing longer. The story works as a relay race of obsessional conversations, each couple handing off the baton to the next as they pass like ships in the night.

As Linklater has put it: "The scenes and characters change . . . but the preoccupations . . . remain the same."[43] There is a succession of scenes, but the landscape of plot has been flattened out into a pancake-shaped plateau, giving us the sense that these conversations are going on simultaneously, on any given day of the week, among the disenchanted of Austin, Texas.

Without the usual narrative progression, the film is, writes Linklater, "much more interested in who you are than what you're doing". The slowing of the narrative wheel allows us to notice more, in more detail, about the characters.

But the act of talking so obsessively seems to neutralize their ability to take any action. In true **minimalist** fashion, the tension comes from "characters' desire to act contrasting with their inability to do so".[44] For this to change, the characters would have to step off the merry-go-round and let the plot gallop back into life.

CLOSE UP: LOST IN TRANSLATION

Sofia Coppola's *Lost in Translation* is a delightful reinvention of **minimalism** which avoids the earnest, downbeat tone which plagues many minimalist films.

Minimalism, with its tendency to pared-down stories, can be a bolt-hole for writers unwilling to write emotion or to create dimensionality. But working in a minimalist style should not mean that characters are superficial or lacking in interesting qualities.

However, it can mean that those emotions are often buried deep in the **subtext**.

When minimalist characters are not paralyzed by inaction, they can have an almost autistic singularity of purpose, as in *Leaving Las Vegas* or *Paris, Texas*. It's as though all this repressed emotion has been translated into brute, unthinking *purpose*.

On the surface in *Lost in Translation* very little seems to happen between the two main characters, stranded together in their high-rise hotel in Tokyo. Bob is an American movie star, flown in for a high-paying commercial which bores and humiliates him, while Charlotte is a newly married Ivy Leaguer, still looking for direction in life.

The tension of not-happening between them is electric; in spite of this, the roller coaster of emotions takes us on a journey that seems epic in scope.

Bob feels distant from his wife in every sense of the word, he feels that his children don't need him, and he feels lousy about himself for doing this commercial when he should be making a film.

Charlotte has come with her photographer husband, whom she has recently wed, but who spends most of his time away doing photo shoots. But she feels alienated from the world he mixes in, particularly the young starlet Kelly, who is also staying at the hotel. Charlotte knows she is privileged and should be enjoying herself, but wonders why, when she visits an ancient temple, she is unable to feel any emotion.

These two alienated characters are trapped between the artificial surroundings of the hotel and the strangeness of the world outside.

In such a situation, something is often "lost in translation", meaning that characters find it difficult to communicate across the barriers that they have, in their own minds, erected around them.

This makes **minimalism** the opposite of **realism**, in which those barriers are regarded as real rather than a product of the imagination; but both thwart the will of the protagonist equally. This miscommunication is hilariously dramatized during the shooting of the commercial, when Bob's brief queries receive long tirades from the director in response, yet are translated by the translator only as: "Slower. And with more intensity." In **minimalism** everything is reduced to the banal; lofty ambitions are undercut, and great ideas are punctured, letting the air out.

Cut off from the world, the protagonists are thrown into intense intimacy. As Bob and Charlotte hang out they find it natural to share their confusion, as well as to laugh at the absurdity of it all. When Charlotte wanders off, bored, from her husband's friends, she runs into Bob. He whispers conspiratorially: "I'm trying to organize a prison break. Are you in or are you out?"

Excitement can best be dramatized by showing characters embracing spontaneity. As Bob and Charlotte run through the streets of Tokyo, their actions embrace the spirit of Belmondo in *Pierrot le Fou*: "We can do whatever we want, when we want." What they do and in what order isn't important.

When I put my hand on your knee, that's wonderful. That's what life is about: space, feeling.

Ferdinand, *Pierrot le Fou*

Before meeting Charlotte, Bob couldn't wait to get back home. Now he agrees to a TV interview that will delay his departure. But though he and Charlotte lie side by side, chatting through the insomniac night, their relationship remains determinedly platonic. This time, when Charlotte travels to Kyoto and witnesses a traditional wedding, she is moved to tears. She is able to feel at last. Following tradition, she writes a note (we'll never know what she wishes for) and ties it to a holy tree.

These are not big events, but they express major shifts for these characters. When Charlotte hurts her toe, Bob rushes her to a hospital; the scene is not about how serious her accident is, but about the quality of his attention.

So when Charlotte discovers that Bob has broken the unspoken pact between them by having a one-night stand with a klutzy jazz singer, she taunts him that maybe he's more comfortable with someone "nearer his age". The betrayal seems the greater because, in spite of their connection, they themselves have chosen not to cross that line.

Though they soon make up, their parting is awkward, neither of them willing to express their true feelings. In the limo to the airport, Bob happens to catch sight of Charlotte in the street. He rushes out to her and they hug. He whispers in her ear. We never hear what he says, whether it's a consolation or a confession of love.

Like the prayer Charlotte leaves hanging on a tree (and which in *In the Mood for Love*, Chow leaves nestled in a hollow), **minimalism** fades out with a whisper, not a bang. It requires the audience to lean forward to make that connection. Never mind heroics. Minimalism asks simply, do the acts of man live on after we die? Do we leave a trace, is there still an echo?

Whatever it is Bob says, it's a crossing of the line between them into a state of intimacy which can never be enjoyed, only savored in the memory. It's an action of the smallest, most minute sort; but it matters more than anything.

That is the beauty of **minimalism**.

If Bob and Charlotte had decided to have an affair, the sexual tension would have been broken, and the value of their relationship cheapened (which is why Bob broke the rules by sleeping with someone else).

If Charlotte's husband John *were* having an affair with Kelly, the story might have taken a more dramatic turn, and vaulted out of **minimalism**. But he probably wasn't. Because if he had, Charlotte would have had a motive to act, which would have turned *Lost in Translation* into a more conventional story.

Sometimes a little uncertainty is not a bad idea.

> *Just say two plus two.*
> *Let them say four.*[45]

Billy Wilder, Writer/Director

CLOSE UP: IN THE MOOD FOR LOVE

In the Mood for Love is set in the claustrophobic world of Chinese exiles in Hong Kong after the Communist takeover in China. We know nothing of these "larger world" issues, however, because this is an exercise in **minimalism**.

Sofia Coppola uses a similar approach in *Marie Antoinette*, her ornamental successor to *Lost in Translation*. *Marie Antoinette* focuses on the fantasy world of the French aristocracy, which they continue to revel in until the revolutionaries are at the gates. The **matrix** of the film is unashamedly one of confectionery – that superfluous culinary art which reached its zenith in the eighteenth century. Like the characters, it impresses and fizzes for a moment, but is soon consumed and forgotten. We have no idea that the peasants are revolting, that there is turmoil in the streets, because neither does she.

Ignoring the political context of its own period, *In the Mood for Love* turns it all into subtext. We don't know the back story of these immigrants;

all we know is that they are part of an endangered white-collar community, who live in poor, cramped quarters while trying to maintain their former social pretensions. They share an intense sense of yearning and nostalgia – a sense of the fragility of life kept at bay by the playing of endless mah-jong games. Indeed, the Chinese title means "age of blossoms", a reference to the fleeting pleasures of youth; and the film is full of subtle references to the passing of the seasons.

The mah-jong marathons, like all gambling, are a way of confronting the chaos of the world and attempting to impose order upon it, a pattern that we can profit from. Some days we win, and some we lose; but we find it reassuring to believe that there is an underlying logic to justify the massive displacements of our lives. And so the landlady Mrs Suen hosts the games in the knowledge that they provide comfort for the displaced.

Chow and So are two tenants in this boarding house, who find themselves passing, like ships in the night, on their nightly journey to the noodle bar. Their walk, shot in slow motion as an aching waltz, stretches their short journey into an epic dance of solitary feeling, emphasized by the swaying of hips, the cupping of a cigarette while ducking from the rain, because neither can break the barrier to speak.

Until finally they find themselves in their corridor, and each remarks on how they have not seen their spouses for some time, since they have been traveling on business. Their tentative friendship is solidified at a diner when Chow asks So where she bought her bag. He is sure his wife would like something like that. Well, perhaps not something exactly like that, she sensibly suggests. After all, they are neighbors.

So asks about the tie Chow is wearing – she would like to get one just like that for her husband. That's tricky, he replies, because his wife bought him this one when she was away on a business trip.

The subtext of this conversation is that Chow has also acquired such a handbag, and So's husband such a tie, at the same time.

Following Billy Wilder's dictum, the audience are left to make the vault of understanding: the spouses of these two have been having an affair.

In **classic** drama, this would have led to gnashing of teeth and a melodramatic outburst. In **minimalism**, the characters must contain themselves. So and Chow are in a foreign environment, where community cohesion is everything.

Instead, the two meet again over lunch. So accuses Chow of having an affair, and bursts into tears when he admits it. He then accuses her of being weak in confronting her husband. This, we realize with a double-take, is only a rehearsal – for the moment when she must confront her husband for real.

Even though they are only acting out roles, she bursts into tears: "I didn't know it would hurt so much." Like Belmondo, these two are playing at confronting life; for So will probably never work up the courage to confront her husband. Even though we are aware that they are playing roles, that this is a self-conscious act, the emotions this "play" summons up are real.

As all actors have found since the beginning of time, acting creates unusual intimacy between the actors. It creates a safe space, a place to "play" at one remove from the person herself. It allows emotions to be expressed that otherwise would remain buried, with the option to disown them as not being truly yours. And so Chow and So play with each other's emotions without truly owning them.

In this sense, **minimalism** is the opposite of **absurdism**. In *Being John Malkovich*, Craig's problem is that he goes the whole hog. He doesn't just own his own emotions, he wants to own someone else's.

When Chow, frustrated that their relationship can never lead anywhere, announces he is leaving to take a job in Singapore, So at first coldly responds that she never thought he would fall in love with her. But as she speaks her fingers dig into the flesh of her arm, revealing her internal conflict.

When she breaks down, he reminds her again that this is only a rehearsal. These characters feel so constrained by their situation that they can only "try out" their emotions. Real action is impossible; Chow can only lamely advise: "keep a closer eye on your husband".

Like Bob and Charlotte, neither can act because action is impossible. And yet, the nightly trek to the noodle stall reveals something they have in common. In the stifling intimacy of the boarding house, they are lonely.

The drama the two are acting out is soon extended to the martial arts serials which Chow begins to write, increasingly relying on her advice. In one of the finest sequences in the film, she is surprised late in his room by the arrival of a number of guests at the flat for a mah-jong session. For her to leave a married man's room at night might create unwanted attention. So Chow shares his noodles with her, and waits for the moment when So can make her escape.

However, the mah-jong turns into another marathon session. She stays not only all night (chastely in his spare single bed), but the day after, when he phones in sick to her work, pretending to be her husband. When she can finally slip out, she must do so in the too-small shoes of his wife; she leaves behind a slipper which will become important in the finale.

Their restraint makes them superior to the gossip of the other boarders, but if they're willing to explore their relationship in such intimacy as an "act", why not go the whole hog? Why not have an affair, since everyone thinks they are doing so anyway?

Not-acting proves to these characters their superiority to their spouses, and makes the emotional betrayal acceptable. But it also means they are shutting themselves off from something important in life. When Chow invites So to accompany him to Singapore, she hesitates too long, and misses him.

Next year she travels to Singapore and visits his apartment while he is out. A few years later, he visits Hong Kong, and hears that a woman and her son have taken over the boarding house next door never realizing that it might be her. And so, once again, they miss each other, like ships passing in the night.

In **minimalism**, the pain of unrequited love is a powerful theme (that is why the film adaptation of *Captain Corelli's Mandolin* was less successful than the novel – they gave it a happy ending!) Never underestimate the power of **restraint** in writing, of holding back or implying more than you are showing.

Minimalism is often a tragic form, with its opportunities missed and love unrequited. But it can also show the transient beauty of life, and the moments of brief epiphany. (David Lynch abandoned his usual penchant for dark absurdism with *The Straight Story*, a perfect minimalist film about an old guy traveling cross-country by lawnmower – a movie whose message could only be described as *do it slower*.) Remember also that **not-acting** is not necessarily a cop-out. Sometimes, as in *Lost in Translation*, it can be a tender gesture; or as *In the Mood for Love*, a heroic one.

In Herman Melville's short story, "Bartleby the Scrivener", a copy clerk responds to his boss's requests to work by politely replying: "I prefer not to." Even after he has been fired, he keeps showing up for work and when asked to go home will only continue to reply: "I prefer not to." Sometimes, even quiet gestures can be heroic.

> VLADIMIR: Well? Shall we go?
> ESTRAGON: Yes, let's go.
> *They do not move.*
>
> Samuel Beckett, *Waiting for Godot*

Exercises

○ Write a scene in which as little as possible happens, but make it as exciting as possible (and don't forget to "turn" the scene). Remember to **shift focus** so the emphasis in the scene is on the things we don't usually notice.

○ Write a montage in which your heroine singlemindedly struggles to learn something practical, feels the pleasure of achieving it, then experiences it becoming second nature. Make sure your heroine experiences temporary setbacks

MINIMALISM
Recap

* The **absurdist** writer is not afraid of the audience being aware that they are watching a construct. Absurdism is, by definition, self-conscious.

* In **minimalism**, by contrast, the structure is often submerged or invisible.

* **Minimalism** creates tension, and offers surprises, through quiet revelation or cumulative feeling.

* **Minimalist** characters feel confined by their circumstances, or overwhelmed by the forces surrounding them, be they environmental, social or personal.

* **Absurdist** characters often feel unable to conform to society. **Minimalist** characters, on the other hand, feel disempowered; this feeling can be heightened by restricting **point of view**.

* **Minimalism** can be created by restricting the free will of the protagonist. Make their desire to act contrast with their inability to do so.

* When **minimalist** characters are not paralyzed by inaction, they can have an almost autistic singularity of purpose.

* In **minimalism**, unlike in **realism**, the barriers between people are imaginary.

* In **minimalism** everything is reduced to the banal: lofty ambitions are undercut and great ideas are punctured, letting the air out.

* Social and political contexts are kept in the **subtext**; so is emotion.

* Never underestimate the power of **restraint**, of holding back or implying more than you are showing.

8 You left my umbrella where?

Tenniel, The Caterpillar, *Alice's Adventures in Wonderland*
© Bettmann/CORBIS

Alternate and parallel realities

Parallel and **alternate** realities offer the greatest scope for your imagination, but they also require the greatest discipline and organization.

After all, you are going to have to be your own architect, biologist and engineer. You are going to have to lay down the rules and stick to them; because any hint of randomness is going to pop the bubble of your world.

Unlike in **absurdism**, where each "what if?" leads to another, creating narrative momentum, **alternate** or **parallel** realities require the creation of a consistent world.

In *Inception*, a team who enter the dream world in order to plant a belief, hatch up the idea of creating a dream within a dream. As they enter one level of reality after another, we are left feeling that this is an unending hall of mirrors in which the ultimate truth can never be relied upon.

In *The Matrix*, on the other hand, the world is so consistent that most human beings mistake it for reality. Neo first has to learn that what he thinks is reality is an illusion. His world was long ago taken over by machines, who turned human beings into gigantic battery farms, creating the Matrix to give them the illusion that they were still free. Neo is finally able to overcome the machines by learning, not just how to travel between the two worlds, but to actually see through the illusion of the Matrix: to see its **transparency**.

Whenever you create a **parallel** world, you create the expectation in the audience that the **alternate** world in some way comments upon our own. Part of the fun may be in getting the audience to tease out that relationship.

In the seventies, the Cold War and its threat of global nuclear annihilation led to an anxiety about our possible future need to escape this planet. The space race to the Moon stimulated imaginations with the possibility that somewhere out in space there might *really* be **alternate** worlds.

However, in the hands of science fiction writers, those **alternate** worlds were always likely to be a reflection of our own. In *Planet of the Apes*, a crashed astronaut finds himself on a planet where apes enslave human beings. At the end of the film, he discovers the half-buried Statue of Liberty reaching out of the dirt, and realizes in despair that this planet is his own.

Journey to the Far Side of the Sun pulled a similar trick. When a new planet is discovered on the far side of the Sun, a space ship is launched to explore it. After a crash landing, the astronaut is convinced he has landed back on Earth, not realizing that he has landed on the other planet, which is a mirror image of our own. However, in this case critics agreed that a mirror image was not really interesting enough – a **parallel** world needs to be skewed to reflect some interesting revelation about the Earth.

In *2001*, the parallel world that an astronaut finds on the far side of a black hole is so tilted that **time** has flattened out altogether: allowing him to experience his birth and death simultaneously.

No matter how distorted the representation, or how warped the mirror, we always expect this **alternate** reality to be in some way a reflection of our own, not just a projection of a fantasy.

I debated long and hard with a writer who had written a clever script about a world very like our own except in one fundamental detail. But why had the world come to be this way? What had caused these people to lack something so essential? The writer was reluctant to explain; and so this imaginative script remains unmade.

Usually we expect an explanation for how an **alternate** world came into being. It may be like Pandora in *Avatar*, a distant world we have yet to discover, or as in *The Matrix*, an artificial construct created in a future ruled by machines.

It may be that, like the angels who walk invisibly among us in *Wings of Desire*, their presence is a **parallel** reality whose existence we have felt but never seen. Or it may be, as Morpheus says in *The Matrix*, something "you can't explain but you feel it".

The more exotic the **alternate** world, and the more different it is from our own, the more clearly its rules need to be articulated. Establishing the credibility of this world is more important than plot complexity, which can get in the way of our appreciating what makes this world different.

James Cameron, whose scripts are often underrated, appreciated this when he created a world of dazzling detail and originality in *Avatar*. Those who criticized the story as being simplistic failed to understand that the film could not have borne a more complicated plot. Nor does it need it. Because *Avatar* has a brilliant **Maverick** premise – that a human being, plugged into an alien body, might come to not only understand this alien race, but to find his loyalties conflicted.

When Jake, a disabled army veteran, replaces his dead brother, a scientist who had been trained for the Avatar mission, he has a massive chip on his shoulder. He also has a secret agenda: the promise of brand-new legs if he spies for the military, who see the Avatar mission as being "soft" on the enemy, who are resisting their attempts to mine the planet. The act of being a Pandoran, of feeling not only physically restored but powerfully enhanced and in harmony with the world, makes Jake think like an alien and change his loyalties.

We have to explore this world in detail, to appreciate it in the same way Jake does, otherwise we will never understand why he would risk his life to defend it – against his own species, if need be. Jake's dramatic arc from em-bittered, wounded warrior to empowered Pandoran, using these powers to defend the weak, both to heal and to fight for peace, is a **classic** one. At the same time, it requires a great leap of imagination – the **Maverick** premise conceived by Cameron.

Of course the plot, a variation on the Western stories of US cavalry scouts "going native", from *Broken Arrow* to *Dances with Wolves,* is far from new. The brilliance of Cameron's conception is not simply in creating a world that represents a beautiful, more spiritual vision of life; but a character who can provide a bridge into that alien mentality.

(Cameron has a knack for reframing well-worn stories. By framing *Titanic* with the story of a young woman's liberation, he turned a tragedy into a redemptive epic.)

Whereas in the Western the scout might have been of mixed race, or brought up by natives, giving him an instinctive feeling for both cultures, Cameron imagines the next logical step: a future in which it may be possible to be part-human, part-alien, and to choose the alien vision, a vision of the world we have lost, over our own. The hope being that we may take a look at what is still precious and beautiful on our own planet, and preserve it before it is too late.

If **minimalism** is ultra-reality, **alternate** reality suggests that the truth (unlike in **realism**) is not immediately apparent. It has to be searched for, and that search changes the protagonist profoundly.

This drawing aside of the veil connects with a deep human need: to believe that we can pierce through the lies and misconceptions all around us, and see what lies beneath. It connects with a profound hope as well: that in doing so, we can find a way to live without the restrictions that we rail against, just like Jake and Neo.

When you create an **alternate** reality, you need to find a way for the audience to connect that reality with their own needs and aspirations. You also need to give them a "way out" – a return to normality at the end, or its replacement with a new normality.

In *Synecdoche*, a depressive director wins a "genius" grant to create a performance piece. His attempt to find something "real" by re-creating his own life in endless detail, is not only self-defeating but ultimately unfulfilling for the audience, since Kaufman's character can never learn anything or find redemption, because, like Phil in *Groundhog Day*, he can never move on.

The more alien your parallel reality, the more important it is to give your characters an emotional arc. If **absurdism** is taken to the point where the characters can find no meaning or way to make sense of things, then your story as a whole becomes meaningless.

On the other hand, beware of explaining everything. *The Matrix* is remembered for the cleverness of its action and ideas, not for the endless pseudo-profound explanations of "the meaning of the Matrix".

As Kubrick said of the follow-up to *2001* (which he was not involved in): "Know what they did? They explained everything. They told you what everything meant. Killed it. You tell people what things mean, they don't mean anything any more."[46]

In *Source Code* Colter Stevens, an army helicopter pilot hovering between life and death, is given a mission to return to the past to prevent a terrorist attack. Using a new time-loop program, his mind is inserted into an alternate reality where he is a teacher on a train which is about to be the first target of the bomber. He can't change the past, but he can get enough "intel" on the bomber to stop his next move. Since Colter has only eight minutes of brain time before the train is blown up he is inserted repeatedly, each time learning a little bit more, not only about the bomber but about the teacher's beautiful companion Christina. Unlike Phil in *Groundhog Day*, Colter learns at lightning speed. He seizes the moment.

Source Code cleverly combines a mainstream thriller plot with this **Maverick** conceit. It sets Colter the challenge not only of thwarting the terrorist plot, but also the rules of the program – of reality itself. Colter not only saves Christina but slips into her reality, thus cheating death. How exactly does he do it? We'll never know. For some, this will be a cop-out. Others will go with their emotions, and admire Colter's ability to turn this reality to his advantage (as Craig, Leonard and Phil strive, but fail to do): to shape the world around him, as heroes do.

Colter, mortally wounded, is himself hovering between one reality and another, creating a bridge between the alternate or **parallel** reality and the **ordinary** reality of the story. That bridge should never be completely transparent because, without some distortion, there is no mystery.

> To me a film that answers all your questions is pointless . . . If you don't give them something to take with them, you are a thief, a lousy storyteller. To that end, you also have to take something away from them, rob them of some fulfillment. Without mystery there is no love affair.[47]
>
> Christopher McQuarrie, Screenwriter, *The Usual Suspects*

Transparency

Ice Hotel © Peter Grant Photography

My words fly up; my thoughts remain below.

Shakespeare, *Hamlet*, Act III, Scene 3

The process of **transparency** is key to **alternate** and **parallel** realities, and to many other **Maverick** techniques.

Bad films have no transparency, or too much; but **transparency** is at the heart of what makes films exciting.

Film is a highly literal medium. We tend to take what we see on the surface as reality, or truth. Unlike in novels, we cannot reveal the feelings of the characters, unless we use that creakiest of devices, the voiceover (we'll discuss how to use it better later). Having characters describe their feelings through the dialogue is known as writing "on the nose" and except in rare instances it feels unnatural. Instead, we have to work from the outside in. We have to find some way to pierce through the shiny surface of illusion.

The usual way to do this is by creating **subtext**. **Subtext** is the awareness that what the characters are saying is at odds with what they are thinking or feeling. This makes the audience want to explore further and uncover the truth.

In film, actions and body language speak louder than words. As Hitchcock put it, dialogue should be "something that comes out of the mouths of people whose eyes tell the story in visual terms".[48]

If someone is saying they feel fine but their body language and actions tell you otherwise, then the audience feels a tension between the two. If a character is spinning a beautiful tale but their body language is shifty; if they swear they're telling you the truth, but they can't look you in the eye – then you have **dramatic tension**, or **subtext**.

Subtext is like an iceberg: 80 per cent of it is submerged underwater. This is where the emotional weight of the scene lies, not in the "business" on the surface.

The **business** of the scene is the activity that drives it. This is not necessarily "plot" stuff in the larger sense; it can be quite trivial. But it needs to keep us interested or amused, and be the motor of the scene. The more static and intimate the scene, the more important this **business** is. Even if

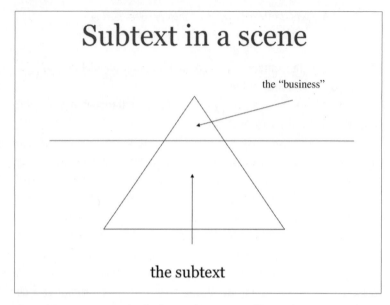

your characters are only sharing a chat over coffee, make sure you have some **business** for the scene.

This is not just to create visual interest, but to ensure that you create **subtext**. Action, not words, reveals the true feelings of your character; and so if you have not created actions for your character all the way through the scene, it will be hard to discern how they truly feel.

I have seen this problem so many times in students' screenplays – long dialogue scenes in which it is impossible to tell whether the characters are being honest or lying, ironic or understated – *because we only have their words to judge them by.* In a film it is action, not words, that we put our faith in.

Of course, bear in mind that the more static your scene, the more the smallest gestures will be magnified and take on greater significance.

In *Kramer Vs. Kramer*, Kramer is woken up by his young son the night after his wife has walked out on them. The boy is late for school, and Kramer has to scramble around the unfamiliar kitchen to rustle up some French toast, while reassuring his son that everything is going to be just fine. In spite of his jibes about "All the best chefs in the world are men – I bet you didn't know that," and "Daddy not only has to bring home the bacon, he has to cook it too," we sense that Kramer is floundering, as he makes a mess of everything. Finally he picks up a red-hot pan and drops it with a clang, shouting "Damn her!"

His true feelings have finally burst out of the subtext, as they must. The **subtext** carries the emotional weight of the scene. We feel it lurking beneath the surface like an unexploded bomb. We long for the moment when, like Neo bursting out of Agent Smith's body in *The Matrix*, it will smash through the surface, relieve the tension – and change everything.

In **Maverick** screenwriting, the subtext is taken further.

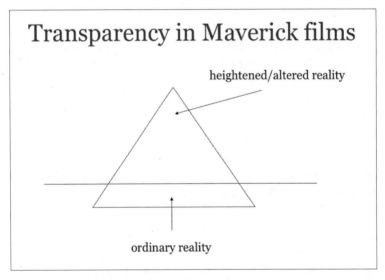

Transparency in Maverick films

heightened/altered reality

ordinary reality

Heightened or **altered** reality is like a neon sign grabbing our attention, swallowing up the darkness. In a cleverly written film, we can still see reality shining through; we have a reality check.

Annie Hall uses **transparency** as a gag played out in a variety of ways: when Alvy and Annie are flirting, the subtext of their seething awkwardness and embarrassment is printed as a subtitle on the screen ("Christ, I sound like FM radio. Relax!"). When Alvy complains Annie is distant during their love-making, her spirit floats free from her body and steps out of bed.

One of the greatest pleasures of *Being John Malkovich* is seeing the character of Craig, or Lottie, or Lester *coming through* John Malkovich. That is **transparency**, but so is Craig pretending to guess Maxine's name just by the cues on her face. We can see through the trick, but admire how clever it is anyway.

In *The Wizard of Oz*, Professor Marvel guesses at once that Dorothy is trying to run away from home. While she has her eyes closed, he sneaks a family photograph from her bag and uses it to create a "vision" of her family home in his crystal ball. "It's just like you were reading my mind!" she responds, amazed. Although we see through his trick, we see also the deeper, kindly motive – to convince her to return home.

When Dorothy travels to Oz, Marvel will be transformed into the Wizard, a character just as phony as his counterpart in Kansas. The use of the same actor gives us an ironic insight into the Wizard's character, because we have already met him in **ordinary reality**, where he is essentially the same character: a shyster with a good heart.

The conceit of having all of Dorothy's neighbors transformed into characters in Oz made *The Wizard of Oz* the first children's movie which worked on different levels for children and adults, since kids usually don't spot that the same actors are being used. However, this **transparency** gives adults an ironic insight which adds an extra dimension to the story.

> *I think that a film should have a clear story and it should have, if possible, something which is probably the most difficult thing in filmmaking . . . a little bit of magic.*[49]
>
> Emeric Pressburger, Writer/Director

The two main characters in *In the Mood for Love* role-play imaginary conversations with their spouses. Is the way they imagine them colored by their feelings for each other? Undoubtedly. Through the role-play – the **business** of the scene – we see the shadows and shimmering reflections of their hidden feelings like goldfish darting beneath the surface of a pond.

In *Rear Window*, Jimmy Stewart sees what he believes is the aftermath of a murder through his neighbor's windows, which his confinement with a broken leg forces him to gaze through all day. Do the events he witnesses add up to the conspiracy which he imagines? We can only see what he sees, and let our imagination do the rest. That is **transparency**.

Transparency creates ambiguity, the feeling that something may have more than one meaning (not, as some people seem to believe, a meaning which is confused or obscure). Ambiguity is tantalizing, since it suggests that more than one version of reality may make sense.

> *To declare that existence is absurd is to deny that it can ever be given a meaning; to say that it is ambiguous is to assert that its meaning is never fixed, that it must be constantly won.*[50]
>
> Simone de Beauvoir

At the end of *Jacob's Ladder*, we realize that the story we have been watching is not reality, but a metaphor for Jake's spiritual journey from life to death. All the time we thought he was living he has been dying on a surgeon's table. This **overturn** – an ending that makes us rush back back to the beginning – creates a flash of **transparency**, like a powerful beam piercing through the darkness. Now we see everything in a new light.

However, it's a **transparency** that we can only enjoy retroactively, as we review in our minds (or through a flashback) everything we've seen before, and the clues we've missed.

The **overturn** mimics the experience of our lives flashing before us; or, as in *2001*, **time** itself stretching out into an endless corridor. The **overturn** gives us a last chance to figure out how we got here, and the meaning of it all, before we move on to the next level of reality.

A decade later *The Sixth Sense* pulled a similar trick. Dr Malcolm Crowe, a celebrated child psychiatrist, is confronted by a former patient who breaks into his home, accuses Malcolm of letting him down, and shoots him. Malcolm recovers and is given a second chance with a new child, Cole, who comes to see him with the same symptoms: the belief that he can see ghosts.

Will Malcolm fall back on rationalist medical explanations for what is affecting the boy? Or will he show some humility this time and accept the possibility that what Cole is telling him is the truth?

In the brilliant **overturn** at the end, Shyamalan pulls the rug on Malcolm, as he realizes that Cole *really can* see dead people. And the proof . . . ? Malcolm realizes, with a shock of awakening, that he himself has been dead since being shot at the beginning of the film.

A flashback sequence sends us rushing back through all the clues we failed to see. Most poignantly, in the scene when we thought his wife was angry at him for turning up late for their anniversary dinner, we now realize it was *her* anniversary dinner – in silent memory of him.

As in *Jacob's Ladder*, the rush of insight solves the "problem" of the film, its mysterious non-sequiturs, everything that doesn't quite make sense; it also resolves the internal, emotional problem of the character.

In *Jacob's Ladder*, Jake finally understands how his own army conspired against him, a metaphor for the war that divided America itself. The turmoil he feels is the grief of leaving his loved ones behind – the process we all must go through before we can let go and face whatever lies beyond.

In *The Sixth Sense*, Dr Crowe is able both to put right the mistake he made before, by saving another child's life, and to "let go" by realizing how, far from being disloyal, his wife loved him and still grieves for him.

Similarly, *The Usual Suspects* **overturns** the whole of Verbal's evidence, as we pan across the Post-It notes and papers spread around the walls of the detective's office and realize they contain the entire story woven out of random names and places. In the blink of an eye Verbal is shown to be a master of improvisation; a character whom we thought peripheral and now see to be the mastermind behind it all.

We love characters who think on their feet, and think spontaneously (not *randomly* – spontaneous decisions make sense, even if they're the wrong ones!) Still, for me *The Usual Suspects* makes that link between the truth and the lie too tenuous; because if nothing we have been watching has been true, why should we care? We do not have enough of a stake in the heist story, because the most important character is missing. We can admire the brilliant **sleight-of-hand** as a clever con, but we are not moved by it.

All these films give us **retroactive** transparency, the ability to see through the veil of unreality only when we reach the end of the film, when we **reverse**, **rewind** and **reassess**.

But these are magic tricks, mere sleights of hand compared to the next level of **transparency**.

In Hollywood today, **voice** is too often suppressed; or else ironed out by numerous rewrites. And nothing is discouraged more than that old theatrical fillip: **breaking the fourth wall**.

Breaking the fourth wall doesn't simply mean having the character address the audience, as Woody Allen does in *Annie Hall*. Sometimes it can be about the audience becoming aware of the authorial voice that is guiding the narrative or commenting upon it. Or it can be turned into a **Maverick** conceit, as in *Adaptation*, by inserting the author into the drama.

In *Adaptation*, Charley Kaufman the sensitive screenwriter is struggling to do an adaptation of a factual book about rare orchids. Kaufman creates a doppelganger in the form of his coarse twin brother Donald, who eventually gives the story the "Mckee" finish that it needs to become a successful film.[51] By splitting himself into two characters, Kaufman externalizes his own inner conflict between writing art and entertainment, and creates a **transparency** whereby we can clearly see that the way a story is told is a projection of the character of the writer.

In **parallel** or **alternate** reality, **transparency** is between one conception of reality and another.

In one of the most interesting conceits of *Inception*, the team must carry out a mission in dream time before their van, which has careened off a bridge, hits the water and jolts them out of their dream. Since dream time is so much longer than real time, we are able to watch long action sequences while cutting back frequently to the van moving fractionally toward the water.

While the concept is fascinating, the lack of an obvious relationship between the snow-clad armies fighting each other in dream time and the van falling through the air makes this **transparency** less effective than it might be.

By contrast, in *Synecdoche*, the lack of differentiation between the director's real life and his fictional re-creation of it makes the real-life element of the story less compelling than it could be.

Complete transparency makes the **ordinary reality** of the story less compelling, because our attention is drawn straight to the **subtext**. We need a stake in ordinary reality, so that we want to return to it in the end, as we must. **Transparency** shouldn't just be a mirror image, nor can the mirror be so muddied that the reflection is impossible to see.

However, when used to the right degree, **transparency** lends great emotional depth and poignancy to **Maverick** stories.

Breaking Through the Fourth Wall

Transparency

- creates irony
- gives an audience the "thrill of recognition"
- informs both levels of reality
- adds emotional depth
- draws attention to the structure

CLOSE UP: THE TRUMAN SHOW

Since birth, every action of Truman's has been on *The Truman Show* – from youth, through teenage years, to the present. Truman is the longest running, most popular soap opera in the world. Everyone loves *The Truman Show*.

Only Truman doesn't know he is in it. He has no idea he is part of a reality show in which everyone else is an actor. Even his wife subliminally sells products while serving up breakfast.

Yet from an early age something in Truman has yearned for escape, and he has fantasized about exotic travel to far-off places.

When he was a teenager Sylvia, a girl he met at college, tried to tell him it was just a show; but then someone claiming to be her father drove up and whisked her away, insisting that she was having one of her mental episodes, and that the family were moving to Fiji.

Ever since then, even since he married Meryl, Truman has dreamed about getting to Fiji. But like James Stewart's character in *It's a Wonderful Life*, something always seems to get in the way.

"Where is there to go?" responds his home buddy Marlon every time Truman starts getting fanciful ideas, pointing at the beautiful painted sunset. But even though the limits of the giant studio dome with its cookie-cutter streets are off limits to Truman, he tries repeatedly to reach that horizon.

Because things keep breaking through from the other side of reality. One day, it's the lighting rig that falls out of the sky on to his street. The next, a crossed wire on his radio taps into the crew's walkie-talkies alerting each other to Truman's progress down the road.

The former is explained as having fallen off an aircraft, and the latter as a temporary crossed wire with a police frequency. But Truman is having none of it.

Truman's feelings are further thrown into a spin when his father (previously "killed" in a boating accident that left Truman with a phobia about crossing water) tries to break through the crowd to get a message to him, before he is hustled away.

Just like every other time the show has failed to follow the script, the genius director Christof improvises and turns the intrusion into great melodrama.

Soon Truman is taking nothing at face value. When Meryl tries to "sell" him cocoa over the breakfast table, Truman responds: "What the hell are you talking about?" In desperation, she calls for help. "Who were you talking to?!" Truman demands threateningly. At that moment his best buddy is sent through the door with a six-pack, the usual antidote to Truman's yearning questions. "It's so unprofessional!" Meryl sobs, falling into Marlon's arms.

Still Truman doesn't put two and two together. Because rather than an **unfolding** reality where the audience learns about things at the same time as the characters, the audience remains in a superior position to Truman. All the way through, we are urging Truman on – to liberate himself, to achieve the ordinary reality that we enjoy.

In one of the most painful sequences of the film, Marlon rebuts Truman's conspiracy theory on the grounds that if everything he was saying were true, this would mean that he, Truman's best buddy, would be lying too.

As he emotionally puts this to Truman, we see Christof in the control room feeding him the lines, intercut with shots of viewers riveted by the deception.

In spite of the show's best efforts, Truman keeps getting glimpses from the other side, and tries to find a pattern that will make sense of it all.

Hot tip: creating suspense

In parallel reality, tension comes from watching the characters break through one level of reality to another; and from seeing them struggle to understand and enter into that level of reality.

Like all great characters, Truman never gives up, never stops improvising. "They" don't like "him" being "unpredictable", as he puts it, without having any idea who "they" are. He tries to catch "them" off guard, and once is rewarded when he darts unexpectedly into a building by catching a glimpse of the backstage area.

In one brilliant sequence, Truman acts out a spaceman fantasy in front of the bathroom mirror, through which we watch his wacky improvisation. Does he know he's playing to an audience, they wonder in the control room? "That one was for free," says Truman slyly to the mirror. Even though he can't see through the Matrix yet, he is beginning to take back control.

Like Phil in *Groundhog Day*, Truman is trapped within a circular story, where every day has its routine, summed up in his daily greeting to his neighbor: "Morning . . . And in case I don't see you, good afternoon, good evening and good night." But unlike Phil, who won't break out of the cycle until he learns to appreciate what's around him, Truman can't break out until he sees through the veil of artificiality that surrounds his world to the deeper truth.

Finally, Truman overcomes his (artificially created) fear of the sea to board a boat and sail it to the limits of the studio. But this is only a nod at character development. Truman doesn't change so much as a person as change the way he views the world.

The **Maverick** genius of *The Truman Show* is to take the metaphor which Truman uses: "Maybe I'm going out of my mind, but I get the feeling that the world revolves around me somehow," and to make it literally true.

Like Phil, who also believes that the world revolves around him ("I make the weather!"), it's all too easy to feel that the world revolves around us, and is acted out for our benefit. In **classic** screenwriting, this is the unspoken "given" of the protagonist's story. It's hard to believe that the world could go on without us, that we don't individually matter in the great scheme of things.

While being self-centered might be a fault in some protagonists, in Truman it is an expression not only of his own individuality, but of his instinct for the truth (that his world really does revolve around him).

Truman yearns for the **ordinary reality** that he can sense beyond the horizon. We empathize because we share this desire to expand our horizons rather than settle for second best. Truman matters not because he is the star of a hugely successful TV show, but because he is determined to follow his heart.

His struggle also reflects a truth with which the audience will empathize: that no matter how much we yearn for order and predictability (the clean, prosperous streets of Seahaven), we value freedom most.

The use of **transparency** adds poignancy to Truman's quest, because we feel that Truman is better than all the people around him who are trying to fool him. We want him to be smarter than the fake "surgeons" who struggle to improvise medical dialogue when he bursts in on them unexpectedly. We want Truman to see through them, because we'd like to believe that we too are smart enough to see through the soft soap and the hard sell. That we too would have the courage to stand up for what we believe in.

And because we want Truman to see through them all, we suspend our disbelief about whether such a show could ever be a reality (but since *The Truman Show*, reality TV has been catching up with fiction all too quickly).

Because if Truman is willing to overcome his deepest fears to expand his horizon, then so should we.

CLOSE UP: MULHOLLAND DRIVE

David Lynch's *Mulholland Drive* is the most mysterious film noir of all. It contains two consecutive parts, with characters in the second part who seem related to but different from the characters in the first, or who have been transposed into other roles.

At first it seems a mystery, but then it makes perfect sense. But not necessarily the sense of **ordinary reality**.

When we first see Betty, a naive young actress, arrive in LA, she is saying goodbye to a genial old couple with whom she has struck up a friendship on the plane. They wish her luck in fulfilling her dreams in Hollywood.

The bewitching art deco block in which her aunt's apartment – which she has been loaned – is situated is overgrown with bougainvillea. The landlady Coco is such a character she is almost a vaudeville act in herself.

But Betty does not find her aunt's apartment empty; instead, like Goldilocks in the three bears' house, she finds a beautiful, naked woman in the shower, called Rita (or at least that's the name she gives herself when she loses her memory).

Rita, as we have seen from the opening sequence, has survived a terrible car accident – which ironically saved her life, as she was about to be shot by the men driving her up Mulholland Drive.

At first Betty assumes that Rita must be a friend of her aunt's (accepting the almost fairy-tale implausibility of the scene). But when Rita explains that she has lost her memory, Betty soon delights in acting like a detective and trying to discover who Rita is, why she is carrying a large sum of money in cash – and what happened on Mulholland Drive.

Rita helps Betty prepare for an audition. When she gets there, Betty delivers an electrifyingly erotic performance which suggests that she is not entirely the naive young woman we thought her to be. It is a fore-shadowing of things to come – but not in this reality. In *Mulholland Drive*, **transparency** is only achieved when we shift to the next reality.

In a parallel storyline to Betty's, Adam, a director, is thrown off his movie when he refuses to agree to the demands of some gangsters, the shadowy financiers behind his film, to replace his leading lady. Adam not only refuses, but smashes up their limo for good measure.

His day doesn't get any better: he gets home and finds his wife in bed with the pool cleaner, and has to take refuge in a sleazy downtown hotel, where he discovers he is out of credit.

A mysterious character called the Cowboy gives him one more chance to recast the girl, or face the consequences.

The two storylines dovetail when Betty is taken by a casting director to visit Adam's set. They lock eyes for a moment, then he looks away and goes about the business of capitulating – by choosing the second-rate actress Camilla Rhodes, who in the next section of the film will be played by "Rita".

Betty and Rita's investigation takes them to the run-down apartment of Diane Selwyn, whose name Rita vaguely remembers. When they break into her apartment, they discover a girl apparently murdered in bed (at the end of the film, she'll turn into Diane). With Betty's help, Rita cuts off her long dark locks and dons a blond wig to disguise her from the killers who may be stalking her. Now they look surprisingly similar.

That night Rita and Betty go to a nightclub, where Rita keeps falling asleep and the band is pre-recorded.

Back home, Rita finds a blue key in her bag and fits it into a blue box; and then, with a word from the Cowboy telling her to wake up, we cut to Diane asleep in bed *and shift to the next level of reality.*

If it isn't obvious already, everything that has happened has been a dream, the dream which has drawn so many beautiful wannabes to the city of dreams, and left so many of them broken and wasted.

We are now brought with a jolt to the reality of Diane, a broken-down would-be actress, also played by "Betty", who wakes up looking rough, worn out and barely recognizable.

Her landlady warns her that some detectives have been looking for her. We flashback to her erotic relationship with Camilla (formerly Rita), which Camilla has been trying to break off.

In a humiliating sequence Diane, who has been given a bit part in Adam's film, is left alone watching Adam kiss Camilla, his new leading lady, on a darkened set.

Betty furiously warns Camilla that she won't give her up that easily. In the next scene, Camilla sends a car to pick up Diane for a party at Adam's house on Mulholland Drive. The car pulls over unexpectedly in a mirroring of the opening scene – or is that just Diane's conscience? – to leave her at a back entrance. At the party, Diane looks unconfident and nervous, and is humiliated by "Coco", now Adam's mother. To make matters worse, Adam and Camilla use the occasion to announce their engagement.

In the final scene of the film, we see Diane hand money over to a hit man, who says that when the job is done he will leave her a blue key. Finally we cut back to Diane, driven mad by grief for arranging Camilla's killing, blowing her own brains out.

David Lynch is a filmmaker who doesn't like to explain his films, and the pieces don't fit together like a perfect jigsaw puzzle.

But that doesn't mean that the film doesn't make sense. It does, because the film packs a terrific punch when we jump to the second level of reality: the reality of what actually happened to Betty.

If a film works on an emotional level, there's no need to make sense of every detail. If it works, it's because it *follows an emotional line*.

The first section of the film has the quality of a dream. When we remember our dreams, some details seem to have an immediate application to our lives, while the meaning of others is obscure.

Sometimes we recognize people we know, but in different people's bodies, or with the wrong names. Sometimes we put together characteristics from different people. While we are experiencing dreams, certain sequences can seem to be utterly normal and familiar; it's only when we wake up that we realize how strange they were.

Similarly, when we watch the first part of the film, we are not necessarily aware that we are watching a dream. We are carried along by the story. It is only when we awake from the dream and see the harsh reality, that those previous events make sense as the fantasy projections of Diane, a girl who must have come to Hollywood with the same hopes and dreams as Betty.

She too must have felt that her brilliant talent was overlooked by somebody who owed somebody a favor. She has watched lovers and rivals achieve undeserved success, while feeling her own confidence crumble.

If this jealousy grew and consumed you, would you kill your rival to make yourself feel better?

If you were Adam, wouldn't you believe that you could produce a work of genius, if only people would stop interfering? His betrayal of his principles by bowing to pressure to cast the wrong girl is a foreshadowing of what Betty will do, when reality is transposed in the final section of the film.

In the end, as Adam smugly says of his now ex-wife, "She got the pool cleaner and I got the pool." In this wickedly **Maverick** satire of Hollywood, Lynch suggests that those who sell their souls to the devil often prosper.

That many dreams are shattered on the road to success.

And that you have to adapt to survive.

Lynch turns the **film noir** genre on its head by showing that the real story of Hollywood is not one in which the hero always finds his way or holds on to his principles. Fame and success are as seductive as any film noir *femme fatale*.

There is a disjoint between the films churned out by Hollywood, mostly optimistic or redemptive in the tradition of classic screenwriting, and Lynch's image of the industry itself, as avaricious and cynical as it was in the days of Altman's *The Player*.

The genius of *Mulholland Drive* is to mimic this disjoint, by creating two stories, not chronological but fractured, like a block of glacial ice, into two separate sheets. Through the cracks we can still dimly see what once was perfect **transparency**.

And what about the **blue key** that Rita fits into the blue box, which then tumbles into Diane's apartment? Rita's trepidation as she sneaks into the bedroom reflects her unconscious fear that someone has betrayed her, or is going to. A fear that leaks through from the other side of the story: Diane's vengeful attempt to murder her as Camilla, an ending which takes us right back to the beginning, and the accident on Mulholland Drive, which should end the film, but instead starts it by having Rita walk into Betty's reality as if out of a dream.

This is **two-way transparency**, when both realities influence each other. It's a powerful tool for structuring two separate realities, particularly where the genre favors an **unreliable** point of view.

In Lynch's brilliant **Maverick** re-creation of **film noir**, these two realities slide up against each other, suggesting betrayal and double cross; exposing the unreliable motives of *femmes fatales* – and of Hollywood itself.

CLOSE UP: WINGS OF DESIRE

In Wim Wenders's *Wings of Desire*, which opens in a black-and-white Berlin, we swoop through the windows and into the minds of its inhabitants, hearing their thoughts and inner dialogue as they suffer the same doubts and confusions people suffer everywhere – except that in Berlin, with its dark history and divided present (this is the Berlin of the Cold War, its inhabitants still divided by the Wall), this suffering seems more acute.

Soon we realize that this omniscient view is not disinterested. It is the point of view of the angels who are everywhere, looking down on us, listening to our troubles, trying to offer us comfort across the veil of illusion that separates them from us.

Theirs is a higher, purer, wiser form of life: knowing everything and understanding all. But it is not without its curiosities: to wonder what it is like to rub your toes together, to have blackened fingers, "to be excited not only by the mind, but . . . by the line of a neck, by an ear".

For the angels cannot feel and smell, cannot rub up against life as we can. They are without substance, without feeling. And for Damiel (Bruno Ganz), this increasingly is not enough. He does not want just the disassociated view, but to know what it is to "lie through your teeth . . . to guess instead of always knowing".

The life of the mind is not enough.

But to live in life we have to accept its central contradiction: that being alive is the cause of all pain, and the cause of all pleasure too. We cannot have one without the other.

Soon Damiel is falling in love with a different kind of angel: one in human form. Marion, a trapeze artist, does her best to fly like an angel in "chicken feathers"; but she's brought down to earth when her circus season is brought to an early close and shut down for the winter. Back to being a waitress.

As she lies in her cramped caravan thinking about her future, Damiel sits by her side listening. "How should I live? Maybe that's not the question. How should I think?" she wonders. He nods encouragement. She thinks there must be something wrong with her, because she always imagines she is talking to someone else. And of course she is. But she doesn't know it. She just feels it.

Two-way transparency. It's not necessary for the **transparency** to be equal on both sides – in fact it's more effective if it isn't.

Damiel has the advantage: he sees her and sees through her, right to her soul. She only *feels* his presence, but that is the one sense that *he* cannot enjoy.

And at that moment he breaks the symmetry by taking a polished stone from her make-up table, and placing it in his pocket.

As she undresses, she longs to "be with the colors . . . neon lights in the evening sky, the red and yellow S-bahn [freeway]". Colors which he cannot see.

As his fingers caress the line of her neck, she feels the need to keep herself ready, ready for love. She knows her high-wire act is clumsy because of her "absence of desire". How can she truly fly without love?

Marion is a **Maverick** character because she longs to follow her heart, but she cannot attain what she yearns for. She cannot cross the spirit divide that separates her from him. But like all great characters, she is not defeated for long. As his departure from the room is signaled by the switch from black-and-white to color, she begins to juggle.

Lifted by his invisible presence, she has rediscovered her buoyancy, the indomitability of her spirit.

Later, as Damiel watches the circus perform, surrounded by laughing children, he meditates upon everything that we lose when we stop looking at the world in a childlike way – our sense of wonder at the beauty of it all. Now we no longer notice what is beautiful, we can not even imagine paradise, and the thought of death makes us shudder. The only enthusiasm we feel is toward our work.

It's no surprise that adults such as Phil in *Groundhog Day* or Malcolm in *The Sixth Sense* can no longer see the wonder or the mystery around them. Of all the souls in the national library, the only one able to see Damiel is a disabled boy.

A child has not yet lost the ability to see through the **veil of transparency**. Like Betty at the beginning of *Mulholland Drive*, seeing the magic all around her, a child's innocence has not yet been clouded by experience.

Maverick screenwriting often expresses the idea that, like Lester in *American Beauty* or Phil in *Groundhog Day*, we are suspended in a coma, or walking around in a dream. If only we could see life in a new way, we would appreciate all it has to offer. While **classical** screenwriting takes ordinary people and puts them in extraordinary situations, **Maverick** screenwriting suggests that extraordinary things are happening all around us all the time.

Wings of Desire speaks to a number of human longings: the feeling that somebody is out there, helping us through the long dark nights of the soul, and the desire to wake up to life, to experience it afresh.

To do that, we have to open our minds to the broader questions, the ones **Maverick** films ask:

> *"When the child was a child it was the time of these questions: why am I me, and not you? Why am I here, and not there? When did time begin, and where does space end? Isn't life under the sun just a dream?"*

These are the questions that Marion asks as she dreams of Damiel, now transformed into a mythical hero with golden armor and swanlike wings.

When Damiel meets American actor Peter Falk (in Berlin to make a film) by a roadside stand, Falk immediately knows he's there, though he cannot see him: "I wish I could just look into your eyes and tell you how good it is to be here . . . to smoke, have coffee . . . I wish you were here."

Damiel makes his decision to "enter the river" of life, to be subject to the laws of time and death at last. Like Arwen in *The Lord of the Rings*, he chooses to surrender immortality for love.

At once the world turns to color, and his hero's armor lands on his head, cutting him. He licks the blood: "It has a taste! Now I begin to understand." Everything is new and fresh to him, even the grim, icy streets. The graffiti on the Wall now seem a riot of color. He bums some change for a coffee.

Passing by Peter Falk's film set, Falk immediately recognizes him. "How long?" he asks. "Minutes, hours, days, weeks, months . . . time!" Damiel responds excitedly.

Time is now moving forward for Damiel, because like Phil at the end of *Groundhog Day*, he has finally entered the river of life.

Falk asks him how much money he got for the armor, and tells him he got ripped off. "It happens." He should know – he too was once an angel.

Being ripped off is just part of the yin and yang of life, the light and darkness, the sorrow and joy.

Falk's persona, inalienably linked with the TV detective series *Columbo*, in which he starred for so many years, gives tremendous transparency to the film. Columbo always gets his man, and is always smarter than he looks. If Columbo says this is the way it is, then that is the way it is.

He validates everything the film tells us about angels, because underneath the crumpled raincoat, he is one.

And he validates the dark reality of life, in whose shadows he has stalked many a killer through the City of Angels. Here in Berlin, death and memory stalk the still ruined city, but when Falk shows up, you can be sure that Berlin will come back to life.

Like Lynch's doubling of actors, the use of certain actors can cause a bleeding through of their other personas that can create a curious **Maverick** effect. In *Being John Malkovich*, the actor's reputation for versatility makes his true character hard to identify; and makes him the perfect candidate for the conceit of the film. (Unfortunately, most casting isn't this inventive.)

Damiel passes from one level of reality to another; there is no turning back. Life is now in color, but skin bleeds, it feels cold. He is united with his destiny.

Without time, there is no destiny. No motive. As Damiel takes the hand of his loved one, a caption reads: "To be continued".

There is no end to this story. It is a constant discovery, an improvisation. In the end, none of us can stand aloof. We have to dive in and swim.

Wenders uses an unusual **point of view** in the film. There are many swooping, gliding shots that appear to be the point of view of angels. As the camera tracks along, we discover the angels themselves in the scene, breaking the rules about a consistent point of view.

This gives us an odd sense of dislocation.

Who is doing the watching?

Aren't we all standing apart from the world at times, and at others gloriously part of it?

The photography of the black-and-white world that dominates the first part of the film has a somber poetry to it; its paucity is only revealed when we switch to color.

It is only after seeing one world in relation to another, that we learn to appreciate what we've got. *Wings of Desire* is only *It's a Wonderful Life* pushed to its **Maverick** limit. It's an **alternate** reality that makes us see our own world in a new light.

The dream within a dream

Albert Joseph Moore, "Dreamers" © Birmingham Art Gallery

> *To sleep, perchance to dream . . .*
> Shakespeare, *Hamlet*, Act III, Scene 1

There are times when you do not need to convince your audience about your new reality. You *want* them to see it for what it is – a hallucination, a mirage, a dream.

It is not the intensity of the "trip", nor how bizarre it may be, that matters, so much as its relationship to the inner life of your character.

In **absurdist** or **alternate** realities, you want to seduce the audience into believing in your world, no matter how absurd. In **dreamlike** narratives, you want them to notice the strangeness of the universe.

This strangeness could be the reflection of a disturbed mind, or it could be that society itself has become deranged. It could be the power of nature that overwhelms the human mind. Whatever the cause, this dislocation lends the story a sense of the **surreal**.

Surreality is a potent Maverick tool, but like chilli pepper, should be approached with caution: a little bit goes a long way. Too often filmmakers are mesmerized by the possibilities of fantastical imagery; but it is the *incongruity*, yet appropriateness, of the imagery used that makes surreality powerful. That's what makes Dali's lobster phone a classic.

In **Maverick** screenwriting it is the surreality of the dramatic situation, not the imagery, which is important. At the very least, the image on the screen should be an apt reflection of the character's state of mind.

Kubrick's *Dr Strangelove* is a brilliant satire on nuclear war, a subject which by rights oughtn't to be capable of being funny. Although Kubrick urged his actors to "strive for the real", they often complained that he chose their most exaggerated takes. But Kubrick understood that **surrealism** requires you to "play it straight" no matter how exaggerated your behavior may be.

Throughout the Cold War, the policy of MAD (or Mutually Assured Destruction), supposedly made nuclear war impossible. It meant that any country that launched a nuclear weapon would immediately cause mutual (and global) annihilation.

So you would have to be insane to launch a nuclear war. Just like Ripper, the rogue US general who launches his own nuclear war in *Dr Strangelove*.

The casting of Peter Sellers in three radically diverse roles – the liberal President Muffley, stiff-upper-lipped RAF Group Captain Mandrake, and unrepentant Nazi Dr Strangelove – gives the film a bizarre **transparency**.

These three characters, as different as they are, are all trying to cope with the same insane proposition, a proposition which has hypnotized and paralyzed society. MAD has distorted everyone's behavior – everyone's sense of the *normal* – whether or not they know it.

After launching his bombing missions, General Ripper shares with Mandrake his conspiracy theory that the Russians are trying to poison his "precious bodily fluids" through fluoridization of the water. This is so ludicrous that at once we know, if we had any doubts before, that he has gone completely insane. And it is not a good thing to have an insane man with his finger on the nuclear button.

This is the moment I call "**The Antagonist Revealed**". It is that moment of blinding clarity, the moment when the penny drops, and we see the villain for what he truly he is. Sometimes literally, sometimes metaphorically, it is the moment when he rips the mask off. In *The Empire Strikes Back*, this is the moment when Darth Vader tells Luke Skywalker: "I am your father." In *The Shining*, it is the moment when Jack Nicholson's wife looks at the manuscript he has been writing and realizes that, on page after page, all he has written is: "All work and no play makes Jack a dull boy."

The **Antagonist Revealed** is a chilling moment, and often a quiet one. As with all **revelation points**, its power comes not so much from a dramatic twist in the plot as from a blinding revelation which requires stillness for its full emotional impact.

What makes the "bodily fluids" scene surreal is the incongruity of the emotions on display. Ripper's sudden vulnerability and intimacy as he reveals this window into his madness is contrasted with Mandrake's British reserve and perfect manners, struggling to cope with Ripper's insanity.

In **surreality**, the rules of **subtext** are stretched to their limits. In **classic** drama the goal is to make subtext subtle, to disguise it for as long as possible.

In **Maverick** screenwriting, that subtext is likely to be more transparent. And the more transparent the subtext is, the more the character will struggle to suppress it. After all, we don't want everyone to know what we're thinking (a torment which Jim Carrey's sleazy lawyer suffers in *Liar, Liar* when he's magically prevented from lying for a day. Every time he tries to get the words out, he just can't bring himself to say them – though we know exactly what he's thinking!)

The characters' struggle to prevent the subtext from bursting out into the open is what makes such scenes funny. In the television series *Fawlty Towers*, John Cleese's hotel manager plays host to a party of Germans. "Don't mention the war!" he tells everyone on the staff; but the more he tries to resist it, the more he can't help dropping it into the conversation.

Successful use of **surreality** requires a willingness to dredge the subtext up to the surface and expose it to the full glare of the light.

When President Muffley hears about General Ripper's rogue action, he calls up the Russian premier to warn him. The scene takes on the quality of surreality when Muffley is informed that the Russian premier is drunk, and is forced to explain the situation as though the premier were a slightly quarrelsome child. The incongruity of the two most powerful men on the planet squabbling like children while the world teeters on the edge of nuclear oblivion makes the scene both funny and **surreal**.

And the ending, in which Major T. J. "King" Kong rides rodeo fashion on the back of a nuclear payload, is brilliantly surreal because it illustrates that, in spite of our advances in technology, we still act like cowboys: we haven't really moved much beyond the apes in *2001*. Our technology may have evolved – but our instincts haven't.

In pursuing the policy of MAD to its logical limit, *Dr Strangelove* reflects a world in which the insanity is so pervasive that no one can see the incongruities staring them in the face. It is the "Emperor's new clothes" syndrome, a bubble just waiting to be burst.

The insanity of the world's greatest superpower's futile struggle against a peasant army in Vietnam found its apotheosis in the equally hallucinatory *Apocalypse Now*, Francis Ford Coppola's **Maverick** epic.

In one memorably **surreal** scene, our hero Captain Willard arrives at a forward base where sniper fire is exchanged under the hallucinatory glare of night flares to the backdrop of psychedelic music and traded insults with the enemy, lurking somewhere in the jungle beyond. Willard grabs a soldier and demands: "Who's the commanding officer here?" The soldier looks at him blankly: "Ain't you?" From this point on, the command structure no longer applies; and nor do the rules of war.

Sometimes it's not only society which is insane, but nature which drives men insane. In *Aguirre, Wrath of God*, an expedition of Spanish conquistadores gets lost in search of the fabled El Dorado, a mythical golden city secluded deep in the Amazon jungle. Their military commander, Aguirre, usurps the power of the noblemen in charge. As they float downriver on a raft, he dreams of the Empire he will found, claiming all the lands they drift past as his own.

Hunger, disease and the arrows of the natives soon take their toll, and the exhausted survivors imagine they see a ship suspended in a tree. We never for a moment mistake this **surreal** moment for reality; but it reflects perfectly the survivors' feeling of being cut adrift from everything safe and familiar.

Finally Aguirre is the last man alive, issuing orders to his only remaining subjects: the monkeys who have made their home on the raft.

The power of nature is so great that it can make a mockery of men and their petty ambitions. Against its power, we can become completely impotent. It can even, as it does in *Aguirre*, turn a man's mind to madness.

In *Into the Wild* Chris, just out of college, tries to live a life free from material wants or needs, taking to the road and abandoning all family ties. He ends up in Alaska, determined to live in the wild. But he is hopelessly unprepared, and not a good hunter; after foraging for plants, he eats a dangerous herb which damages his insides and causes him to starve.

One day, as Chris is standing outside the broken-down bus he is camping in, a grizzly bear emerges from the brush. Too weak to do anything but sway dizzily, Chris remains rooted to the spot. The bear comes up to him and sniffs, then walks on by. Perhaps Chris is just too wasted to offer a tempting meal.

The **incongruity** of the powerful and utterly wild bear against Chris's vulnerability makes for a **surreal**, hallucinatory moment.

Something doesn't have to be *obviously* unreal to be **hallucinatory** (although Chris is so unwell he could have hallucinated the whole thing). It simply means that the event is so out of the ordinary that it has the quality of a **dream**.

This is often true of **traumatic** events. Anyone who has experienced the death of someone close to them will often remark upon how the subsequent hours and days feel like a dream, "unreal".

> *Facts and reality sometimes – quite often – are not enough. You need an enhancement and intensification of it, some sort of essential version of things, to make things transparent.*[52]
>
> Werner Herzog, Writer/Director

In the second half of *The Sheltering Sky* Kit, an intellectual, well-off New Yorker, finds herself alone and grief-stricken deep in the interior of Tunisia after her husband has died suddenly of a fever. She joins a bedouin camel train and enters the harem of the leader. From this point on, the film becomes a disorienting hallucination as Kit is lost in a world utterly foreign to her. She is forced at last to surrender her intellectual neurosis and immerse herself sensually into life.

Because she is stripped of everything familiar to her, of language itself, life takes on the quality of a **dream**.

This **dreamlike** illusion can be something we create to protect our own sanity. *Waltz with Bashir* is about filmmaker Ari Folman's search to remember what happened to him during the Israeli invasion of Lebanon in the 1980s. The film is rotoscoped (a technique for overlaying film with animation) to distance itself from its documentary roots, because *Waltz with Bashir* is not a documentary in the ordinary sense but an attempt to recapture the **hallucinatory** experience of combat, while illustrating at the same time the **unreliability of memory**.

Intrigued by a fellow veteran's description of his recurring dream, in which wild dogs are tearing through the streets of Jerusalem (an allusion, he believes, to the dogs he killed during the war to prevent the enemy from being alerted to his patrols), Folman realizes that he himself has almost no memory of the war and begins to wonder why.

After talking to a friend he served with, he realizes he may have been present in Beirut during the massacres in the Palestinian refugee camps. But he has no recollection of what role, if any, he played in these events.

He begins to put together the fragments of memory by interviewing fellow veterans who served with him. They share a succession of stories about the brutalization of war: the accidental killing of civilians, the shooting of child soldiers, the random destruction left in their path.

But there are also moments of terror, luck and miraculous escape that suggest other forces at work. The "waltz" in the title is inspired by an Israeli soldier who runs into the middle of a road under heavy fire, and begins a defiant dance, rattling his automatic weapon at the snipers who encircle him, seemingly invulnerable.

All young men feel invulnerable – which is why they volunteer (or in this case are conscripted) to fight. But they *are* vulnerable, and anyone who is exposed to the extreme trauma and horror of war can be damaged by it. The mind wipes out the memory in order to protect the soul. But that doesn't mean that at some point the trauma won't re-emerge.

Folman visits a psychiatrist in an attempt to understand his own lapses in memory. She tells him about a soldier who was an amateur photographer, who kept his sanity during the war by imagining that he was watching everything through the lens of a camera. Instead of being horrified by what he saw, he simply saw it as drama: "Wow! What great scenes! Shooting, artillery, wounded people, screaming . . . "

Then one day, pitifully confronting a field full of hundreds of dead and wounded horses, he could no longer keep up the illusion. "His camera broke . . . he could no longer deny reality."

Now Folman remembers where he was on that terrible night. His company was sending flares up over the camps, so the Lebanese Christian Phalangists could do their dirty work. Was he responsible for the massacre? Or does he feel doubly responsible, because of his memory of those other camps, the concentration camps that his parents survived under the Nazis? Has he become no different from those other executioners?

As if to emphasize the terrifying truth of that realization, we switch to *real* news footage as we enter the camps themselves and the full horror of the massacre is revealed, along with the heartrending grief of the survivors. Now at last we are removed from our comfortable distancing, just like the Israeli soldiers on the hills, and from the **dreamlike** animation of the rotoscoping.

There are some things too terrible to contemplate, and these can cause us to retreat into fantasy or dreams as a defense mechanism. Our minds forget, because to remember may be to learn something about ourselves that we would rather not do.

In *The Return of Martin Guerre* (later remade as the equally compelling *Sommersby*), this concept is turned on its head. During the interminable wars of the sixteenth century a farmer's wife welcomes back her husband, who's been away for some years, fighting.

He is much changed, but who wouldn't be? It is only after a certain amount of time that the jealous villagers begin to suspect that he may be a fake. The couple are arrested, and following the real Martin Guerre's dramatic reappearance at the trial, the impostor confesses the truth: after being mistaken for her husband by two childhood friends of his, he had conspired to learn as much as he could, in order to take on Guerre's identity. How we love characters who are spontaneous!

A jury must decide: did she knowingly commit adultery, or did her memory play tricks on her, and his subterfuge allay her doubts?

Maybe his good looks, and improved character, made those doubts easier to swallow? Did her mind fill in the gaps that memory threatened to break apart, or did it just reshape itself around the face of her new husband? (The impostor did better when tested about his memories of their marriage than the real Martin Guerre!) Sometimes we "remember" what is most convenient.

Using **surreality** can have a striking effect, when used not just for effect. It can lull us into a **dream** state, then deliver a powerful wake-up call when we re-enter (as we must, every time life throws us a curve-ball) "the river of life". We all have times when we need to heed this wake-up call: to be alive to life, to pay attention. At other times, we *need* to go deep within ourselves, and listen to what our dreams are telling us.

"You ever have the feeling that you're not sure if you're awake or still dreaming?" Neo asks in the opening of *The Matrix*, after he's been woken by a message on his computer screen.

Soon he meets Morpheus, the rebel leader, who asks him: "What if you were unable to wake from that dream, Neo? How would you know the difference between the dreamworld and the real world?"

This is exactly the dilemma facing the protagonist in *Waking Life*, Richard Linklater's "almost" sequel to *Slacker*. In what he knows is a dream, he has a series of fascinating conversations with thinkers and philosophers about free will, destiny and human evolutionary potential. He keeps trying to wake up, but can't. The ideas presented seem "vaguely familiar" as though others were voicing his own thoughts. They all speak to the notion that we should not accept any limitations placed upon us: "We should never simply write ourselves off and see ourselves as the victim of various forces." It's not the crayons that you're given, but what you do with them, says another.

There are those who see our huge potential once we have accepted this responsibility for our lives: "Liminal, limit, frontier, edge-zone experiences are actually now becoming the norm."

Others urge a greater appreciation of the moment: "It's like 'Holy, holy, holy,' moment by moment." Time is just our constant way of saying "no" to God's invitation to be one with eternity. But those who say "yes" will soon feel that they have "all the time in the world".

On the other hand, for those who fail to realize they are living in a dream, "The worst mistake that you can make is to think you are alive, when you're really asleep in life's waiting room." The trick is to combine rational thought with "the infinite possibilities of your dreams".

We seem to think we're limited by "the world and its confines", but really, we're just creating those limits ourselves. Once you realize you're dreaming, you have "so many options". Then you can learn to control your dreams – to have lucid dreams – which are more realistic and less bizarre than the ordinary kind; more like walking into an "alternate universe".

How do you tell whether you're dreaming? Hit a light switch. If it doesn't work, you're dreaming (our protagonist tries this and yes, he's still dreaming).

"Don't be bored. This is absolutely the most exciting time we could have possibly hoped to be alive." The opportunities are unlimited, as long as we don't glance away when passing others on the road of life. Every meeting is an opportunity for a "confrontation between souls".

(This message is particularly important for new writers, who often invent dramatic situations, but fail to exploit them to their fullest.)

In spite of the fascination of the **dream**, ultimately we don't want to be trapped in it forever. Like the protagonist, we want to wake up; and we should, because some day we "won't be able to".

Slyly, Linklater retells the story of French "New Wave" filmmaker Louis Malle's meeting with Billy Wilder during the shoot of his first Hollywood movie, his most expensive yet (it was costing two and a half million dollars). "What's it about?" asks Wilder. "Well, it's sort of a dream within a dream," Malle replies. "You just lost your two and a half million bucks," Wilder snapped back.

Don't be like those bores who want to tell you their dreams in endless detail. Use **surrealism** as an effect, when it expresses the dislocation or inner quest of your character, not just to show how clever or outrageous you are.

In Buñuel's *The Discreet Charm of the Bourgeoisie*, the characters are continually waking from each other's dreams. These dreams point up the artificiality and venality beneath the surface of their civilized veneer. Their corruption shines through the **subtext** in one great **surreal** moment after another, as they keep trying to have dinner and are interrupted.

In one scene, they finally sit down to dinner at a restaurant when they discover the owner's corpse has been laid out in the adjoining room, and the staff are all sobbing around it. In another, the friends are invited to dinner at a Bishop's house, but the chicken, when it arrives, is made of rubber. And as the curtain rises, they find themselves stranded on a stage, in front of an audience. Their lives are all show, but when they're in the spotlight on stage they have nothing to say and scurry away. First find the metaphor that sums up your characters' lives, and then make it real.

In another episode one of the characters, a corrupt diplomat, is at a smart cocktail party. Wherever he turns, he faces insulting questions about his corrupt little country. Finally, he draws a pistol and shoots one of his tormentors. As another of the characters wakes from this dream, we wonder – was it real? Or just wish-fulfillment? But why was someone else having the dream? *Because these characters feed each other's illusions.*

To create **surreality**, you have to treat the imaginary as though it were real. But you have to do more than that. It cannot simply be a cheap injection of fantasy. You have to make it fit in with the **matrix** of the story.

In Buñuel's film, the reality of these characters' lives is that, beneath the smart surface, they are up to their necks in crime and corruption; and this ugly **subtext** cannot help bursting out into bizarre but logical manifestations of surreality.

The couples never do get to enjoy their dinner, because these smug bourgeois never learn anything: which is why at the end we find them walking down an endless road, going nowhere.

Isolated by their self-centeredness, they have no idea they are even living in a dream, one they can never break out of. In their case, it is not **time** (as in *Groundhog Day*) but **illusion** which stops their lives from moving forward.

PARALLEL AND ALTERNATE REALITIES
Recap

* **Alternate** or **parallel** realities require the creation of a consistent world.

* We expect this **alternate** reality to be a reflection of our own.

* The more exotic the alternate world, and the more different from our own, the more clearly its rules need to be articulated.

* Establishing the credibility of this world is more important than plot complexity.

* If **minimalism** is ultra-reality, **alternate** reality suggests that the truth (unlike in **realism**) is not immediately apparent. It has to be searched for, and that search changes the protagonist profoundly.

* When you create an **alternate** reality, you need to find a way for the audience to connect that reality with their own needs and aspirations.

* You need to give them a "way out" – a return to normality at the end, or its replacement with a new normality.

* The more alien your **parallel** reality, the more important it is to give your characters an emotional arc.

* If **absurdism** is taken to the point where the characters can find no meaning or way to make sense of things, then your story as a whole becomes meaningless.

* **Transparency** creates ambiguity – the feeling that something may have more than one meaning. Ambiguity is tantalizing, since it suggests that more than one version of reality may make sense.

* Every scene needs some **business**. The more static and intimate the scene, the more important this business is.

* The more static your scene, the more the smallest business or gestures will be magnified.

* Actions, not words, reveal the true feelings of your characters, i.e. the **subtext**.

* The **overturn** provides a transparency that can only be enjoyed retroactively.

* In **parallel** or **altered** reality, **transparency** is between one conception of reality and another.

* **Breaking the fourth wall** is about the audience becomidng aware of the authorial voice, or by the author in some way entering into the narrative.

* Complete transparency makes the **ordinary reality** of the story less compelling.

* There are times when you want your audience to see their new reality for what it is: a hallucination, a mirage, a dream.

* It's not how bizarre your vision is that's important, but how accurately it reflects the inner life of your character.

* In **absurdist** or **alternate** realities, you want to seduce the audience into believing in your world, no matter how absurd. In **dreamlike** narratives, you want them to notice the strangeness of the universe. This dislocation lends the story a sense of the **surreal**.

* **Surreality** – a little bit goes a long way

* In **surreality**, it is the surreality of the dramatic situation, not the image that's important.

* Incongruity makes surreality powerful.

* The more **transparent** the subtext is, the more the character will struggle to suppress it.

* Use surrealism as an effect, when it expresses the dislocation or inner quest of your character..

Exercises

○ Plan a parallel reality which is exactly like our own, except in one feature. What are the consequences of this difference? Start by making them small, and then make them huge. Dramatize a short sequence explaining how your world came to be this way.

○ Imagine you're living an alternate, idealized life. Compare it with what you're actually doing. Now imagine a life which represents your worst fears – and do the exercise again. How does it change your feeling about your **ordinary** and current reality?

○ Now write *two* parallel sequences. One storyline in the first will be the projection of your heroine's fantasies, and the other her actual life; the second sequence will contrast her actual life with the one that represents the sum of all her fears. Show how these fantasies affect her present-day reality.

○ Put your character in the middle of his own dream. At what point does it become obvious to him that he is experiencing a dream? Make this moment the one that turns the scene. (**Surreality** may be appropriate here.)

○ Write a scene in which your hero suddenly becomes self-conscious, aware of themself as an actor playing in their own life story. Write a voiceover. Make sure it gives a different slant to the story told by the images in the scene.

Section 4
Point of view

© Peter Grant
Photography

9 POV to the max

I felt pretty good . . . like an amputated leg.
Raymond Chandler, Author and Screenwriter

Creating highly subjective or multiple realities

The next tool in our Maverick toolbox is **point of view**. In a play, you can adjust point of view, to a degree, by foregrounding or backgrounding action. But as a member of the audience, you never forget that you are watching actors upon a stage.

In film, you can make the audience forget they are sitting in their seat and looking up at a big screen, by making them identify with a character or point of view. By putting them in there with the action. Unlike in a play or novel, in films point of view can shift in the blink of an eye, and does so continually. But what actually happens when the point of view changes?

When we talk about somebody's **point of view**, we mean that they have their own particular take on or opinion about something. They have their own way of looking at it. So every time our **point of view** changes, there is a *subjective shift from one character to another; or from one state of mind to another.*

Classic films usually stay within one consistent point of view. The audience may be "ahead" of the hero: say, by knowing the villain's plot. We may be "with" the hero, figuring it out at the same time as he or she does.

In **Maverick** films, we tend to be a few steps behind, running to catch up. There is a mystery to be solved about the character and their motivation, a challenge to identify with their point of view. However, as long as this mystery is one we feel an urgent need to solve – as long as it is driven by an emotional desire we can relate to, as in *Memento* – these films can be as compelling as any other.

In classically structured films we may be "with" the character, or at a god-like distance; but reality is generally only open to one interpretation.

In **Maverick** films like *The Sixth Sense* or *Rashomon*, the radically different points of view which the films offer suggest multiple, irreconcilable realities. Put simply, the differences between the characters are no longer a matter of point of view, but of different versions of reality.

> *Whenever two people meet there are really six present. There is each man as he sees himself, each as the other person sees him, and each man as he really is.*[53]
>
> William James, Psychologist

Point of view and the **relativity** of reality are closely connected, because the more subjective the point of view – or the more multiple viewpoints there are – the more malleable reality becomes. In other words, a highly subjective reality is likely to be a highly skewed one, because it is limited in time and space: a narrow window on to reality. How would the world look if you had to observe it through a keyhole?

When James Stewart's character in *Rear Window* witnesses what he believes is a murder being covered up, he becomes obsessed with his own particular viewpoint on reality. Has he put all the pieces together correctly? Or has he just got an over-active imagination fueled by his being laid up with a broken leg, and the tedium of seeing everything from the same point of view every day?

Either way, the choices you make about **point of view** will dramatically influence the way the audience feels about the story.

Hot tip
Turn the mundane into the multilayered by manipulating point of view.

There are two ways you can go if you want to push POV **to the max**. You can broaden it out, so the story is told from multiple viewpoints; or you can narrow it.

In a **classic** ensemble film, each of the characters represents different values, or a different point of view. *Citizen Kane*, co-written, produced, directed and starring the boy genius Orson Welles, was one of the earliest films to push **point of view** to the limit. In *Citizen Kane*, a journalist given the assignment of getting to the bottom of wealthy newspaper magnate Kane's enigmatic death-cry, "Rosebud", interviews those who knew him. But Kane is such a mass of contradictions, none can get to the heart of who he really is nor explain the enigma of the man. Ultimately, the different viewpoints cancel each other out, leaving the reporter none the wiser.

(Some have criticized Orson Welles's inability to make his mind up about Kane's character: no doubt Welles couldn't nail the character down because, unknown to him, his co-writer Mankiewicz had based Kane largely on Welles himself.)[54]

Resignedly, the journalist concludes: "I guess Rosebud is just a piece in a jigsaw puzzle." But the truth is out there – in fact it's staring him in the face. A little sled, over which he has tossed his jacket, emblazoned with the word "Rosebud". This sled, which the boy Kane had to abandon when he was taken away from his childhood home, has come to stand for the loss of everything he loved. As the workmen clear away the remaining junk from Kane's mansion, they casually toss the sled into the flames.

After the loss of his beloved childhood home, nothing is ever enough for the enormously wealthy Kane. He accumulates more and more, but no object, no matter how priceless, can ever replace the love he has lost.

Everyone has their theory about Kane, but neither the newsreel footage which tells his life story nor the testimony of his former friends and colleagues can tell what lies in Kane's heart – nor in anyone else's. This is because, the more you multiply viewpoints, the less **transparency** you have; the surface of the subtext has been whipped up by too many cross-currents.

Manipulating **point of view** gives a particular slant on events; but it does not create **transparency**. How can it? If you have only one point of view, you have no objective viewpoint, nothing to bounce this view of reality against. And if you have multiple points of view, as in *Citizen Kane*, who's to tell which is the right one?

Kurosawa's *Rashomon* attempted to resolve this by showing four different versions of a murder. Each of the witnesses involved tells their story, each of them incompatible, and each self-serving.

Finally a woodcutter, not involved in the action and with no particular ax to grind (if you'll forgive the pun), tells the true story. Or is it? Perhaps his version is intended to create sympathy for the survivors and get them off the hook.

When you push **POV** to the max, each person's perspective not only offers a different point of view, but a different version of reality.

In **Maverick** manipulation of **point of view**, the reflecting mirrors never provide the whole picture. As in those mirrors in lifts which reflect off into infinity, one part of the picture is always obscured.

In Woody Allen's *Hannah and Her Sisters*, Hannah is the calm and collected older sister of two more needy siblings, whom she is always helping out.

In one memorable sequence, Hannah is throwing a dinner party. In the kitchen, she accuses her younger sibling Holly of writing a play which draws on private details of her and her husband Elliot's life. While her mother is delighted to be characterized as a "boozy old flirt", Hannah takes it personally and wonders how Holly could have known about conversations she had with Elliot about the possibility of adopting. Did their sister Molly tell her? Or her husband? As characters, in almost farcical style, enter and exit through the swinging door with its naval porthole, Hannah struggles to see through all the reflecting mirrors back to the origins of Holly's story

Meanwhile, in the next room, Elliot remonstrates with Lee, who assures him that their affair is now over. Hannah corners her husband in the bathroom and, pacing wildly, he tries to avoid her questions. She complains that he's been distant recently. "It's hard to love someone who gives so much and – and needs so little in return," he comments bitterly.

Hannah's unwillingness to open herself up to anyone else, to any other point of view, means that she is blind to what is in front of her. If she could only follow the thread back through the labyrinth, she would find the ugly minotaur: the truth that her husband has been having an affair with her sister.

Lying in the dark next to her husband, she finally confesses how lonely she feels. By admitting her vulnerability, she opens herself up, and he is able to hold her and tell her how much he loves her.

Having too rigid a **point of view** can blind you to what is going on all around you.

In *The Pianist*, a Jewish escapee from the Warsaw ghetto, Wladyslaw Szpilman, hides out from the Germans in a safe flat. From his window, he is forced to watch the uprising against the Nazi occupation by his fellow Polish citizens. But his **point of view** is agonizingly restricted; unable to participate, or take in the whole picture, he can only imagine the awful reality of the uprising's failure.

> *Putting the audience in the mind of the character,*
> *is, to me, the purest form of cinema.*
> Alfred Hitchcock[55]

Point of view can be widened out so broadly that every perspective offers a different version of reality; or it can be narrowed, restricting our ability to get the whole picture, and creating curiosity and suspense about what lies beyond our narrow horizon.

While a narrow point of view may in some ways be restrictive, it can also be uniquely interesting, particularly if that viewpoint is an unusual one. *The more you narrow the point of view, the stronger a slant you give to events.*

City of God, however, has a viewpoint so wide it might as well be the point of view of the whole *favela*, the crime-ridden ghetto in Brazil where the story is set. With its dizzying array of characters, the only constant is the struggle for power among the drug gangs, as each new generation turns more violent than the last.

The only one who escapes, the character whose point of view frames the beginning and end of the film, is Rocket, a teenager with an interest in photography. When his pictures of a gang are published in the local newspaper, he fears their leader will be furious at the publicity; instead, the gangster is delighted by his new-found notoriety.

Rocket escapes because he is able to stand back and observe, to see the pointless cycle of drugs, crime and violence for what it is. But in the end even he is faced with a Faustian bargain: should he publish his latest sensational photo of the body of a dead gang leader, or the one showing corrupt police letting his killer off?

He settles for the one that will further his career, and keep him out of trouble.

Rocket's ability to distance himself, like the photographer in *Waltz with Bashir*, gives him a sense of perspective. To *have perspective* means to see things in context, to place them in their proper order and give them their correct priority. You are much more likely to act pragmatically when you do this. Rocket knows where he has come from, and how lucky he is to escape; and he isn't about to start another war by himself.

This may not be heroic, but it does show a sense of *perspective*.

If, on the other hand, you can only see things from your own point of view, you are more likely to act impulsively and recklessly. Every battle becomes a major war because nothing is kept in perspective. Which is exactly how all the gang leaders in the *favela* think – apart from Benny, the only gang leader smart enough to want out, who in a moment of **absurdism** gets shot by mistake as he's leaving town for good..

Like *Waltz with Bashir*, *City of God* provides us with two very different perspectives on reality: the experience of being in the middle of the action, while simultaneously standing apart from it – like Rocket. *Wings of Desire*, on the other hand, makes its shift from one viewpoint to another in the course of the film, as the angel descends from his godlike view and becomes human, finally "entering the river" and immersing himself in life. *Mulholland Drive* also makes a single shift of point of view from fantasy to unfiltered reality.

Other **Maverick** films use a dramatic shift in perspective at the end to make us rush back and re-evaluate everything from an entirely different point of view. Films like *Jacob's Ladder*, *The Sixth Sense* and *The Usual Suspects* all pull the rug on what we thought was reality.

If you try this trick but fail to provide an alternate version of the story which is equally convincing, or if you make the current reality *too* convincing or the clues too subliminal – as they did in *Fight Club* – the audience won't be able to make the switch. They won't be able to suspend disbelief. To pull it off, you have to create an inbuilt ambivalence about the current reality: you have to create, in other words, an *unreliable narrator*, or point of view.

Hot tip

*In screenwriting, we accept the point of view
we most identify with as the equivalent of reality.*

Gosford Park, Robert Altman's reinvention (with the help of screenwriter Julian Fellowes) of the dusty country house murder-mystery genre, broadens out the perspective by using his own brand of multi-viewpoint storytelling.

In this satire on the class system, with its rigid hierarchies as much in the servants' quarters as among the lords and ladies upstairs, the genre's usual point of view is subverted.

In the **classic** Merchant Ivory costume drama *The Remains of the Day*, Anthony Hopkins's loyal butler can claim to know nothing about his master's Nazi sympathies. But in *Gosford Park*, it is the servants who know everything, not their masters. Taking the communicating stairs that keep them out of sight of the guests, servants cross the lines of class to seduce their masters, and be seduced; while a famous film actor, researching his role, disguises himself as a servant. When William McCordle, the master of the house, is revealed to have been murdered by one of his servants, any number of whom have motive, we suspect that this signals not only the end of the mystery – but ultimately, of the class system itself.

We know this because the flattening out of the **point of view** changes the emphasis of the **classic** genre murder mystery, in which there may be several suspects, but when the jigsaw pieces are put together one clear picture emerges. In *Gosford Park*, however, the fact that so many people have the motivation damns the system as a whole.

Broadening out the point of view spreads the force of antagonism, but it creates a kind of suspense as the audience scrambles from one point of view to another, trying to decide which they can trust.

Or which *thread of logic* – as in the kitchen scene in *Hannah and Her Sisters* and *Gosford Park* – can be traced back to the source.

As we've already seen, the choice of one viewpoint over another can completely alter the meaning of a story. Every screenwriter, just like Rocket at the end of *City of God,* has to make this Faustian choice. Which truth do I tell? As it is probably the most important decision you will make before you start writing your screenplay, it is best made consciously.

Ronald Harwood, the writer of *The Diving Bell and the Butterfly,* said that initially, when offered the challenge of adapting the book, he thought it un-adaptable. But when he realized that everything (or as we'll see, *almost* everything) had to be seen from the point of view of the writer, a former magazine editor with locked-in syndrome, he knew how to write the screenplay.

© Getty Images/Barry

CLOSE UP:
THE DIVING BELL AND THE BUTTERFLY

Maverick Screenwriting is not about using clever techniques for the sake of it. It is about fitting the form to the theme. Ronald Harwood's choice of a highly restrictive point of view perfectly fitted the story of someone whose own point of view is hideously restricted: Jean-Do, former editor of woman's magazine *Elle*, who is left paralyzed from head to toe after a massive stroke.

When Jean-Do first comes back to consciousness, we see through his bleary eye a coterie of doctors examining him like a piece of meat on a slab. The most senior doctor, a kindly man, explains his predicament to him. A calamity, but he is very much alive. "You call this life?" asks Jean-Do, though of course no one hears him, because he cannot speak. The doctor expresses some concern about his right eye, and pokes it with his finger. It may need to be "occluded". What does that mean?

Jean-Do's alienation from even this compassionate doctor's concern is only heightened when he finds himself alone for the first time with his two impossibly beautiful female therapists. "Am I in Heaven?" he asks. His physical therapist Marie explains that together they'll work on his tongue and his lips ("Sounds fun," he says to himself), while his speech therapist, Henriette, tells him that this is the most important job she's ever had. Such expectation makes it difficult for him to wallow in self-pity.

Before he knows it, however, he's with another doctor who is enthusing about his skiing holiday in St Moritz, and the joy of feeling "the wind in your face'. He begins to sew up Jean-Do's right eye:"Don't be scared. I've done this thousands of times."[56] He cannot hear Jean-Do's screams to make him stop, because Jean-Do cannot speak.

Three scenes in a row dramatize the poignancy of Jean-Do's perspective on his situation. In the first, he realizes that he has become a "rare case", no longer a human being in the sense that he has always known. In the second, he feels the frustration of attraction for something now out of reach, a frustration heightened by his memory of his time as editor of *Elle*, when he lived the life of a playboy. Finally, his absolute powerlessness is brought home to him when a doctor sews up his eye while blathering on about the joys of skiing.

Having a restricted point of view not only restricts what you can know about the world; in Jean-Do's case it also means that he is unable to escape the attentions of things he wants to avoid. Someone may thoughtlessly turn his TV off in the middle of a football game, or leave it on a channel that is grindingly boring. Even Marie mischievously disregards his avowals of atheism, and takes him to the priest to be blessed.

The other strange thing about Jean-Do's affliction is that, whenever he feels that the terrible isolation of locked-in syndrome makes life no longer worth living, someone arrives who seems to understand what he is going through. There is his friend Roussin, whom he gave up his seat to for a flight to Beirut. The flight was hijacked, and Roussin kidnapped. He spent four years in a cellar that he called his "tomb". He recalls how he used to run through vintages of wine to keep himself sane, and urges Jean-Do to "hold on to the human" inside him.

Even his father, at ninety-two, is a prisoner in his own apartment, and so feels he is "in the same boat". When Jean-Do tells Henriette that he wants to die, she is mortified: "How dare you. There are people who love you, to whom you matter. I hardly know you, but you matter to me already." How much does life have to be restricted, before it's no longer living? "Don't say you want to die. You're alive," she says furiously.

Though his body may be trapped, Jean-Do soon discovers that his imagination is not. Like McMurphy in *One Flew Over the Cuckoo's Nest* (see p. 247), Luis in *The Kiss of the Spider-Woman*, or Andy Dufresne in *The Shawshank Redemption*, his imagination is the butterfly that can set him free from the iron diving bell that imprisons his body.

By contrast, the effort of communicating his most basic sentiments in an endless set of blinks to Henriette highlights how effortless the process of communication is for most of us – and how much we squander it (perhaps most of all, those who edit fashion magazines!) That Jean-Do dictates an entire book in this way is a herculean effort in itself, but that this book is able to express the poetry of life when all that is left for Jean-Do is to observe and imagine, but no longer participate, is more important still.

With his book a success and his condition showing signs of improvement, Jean-Do suddenly suffers a relapse. Now as at last he is approaching death, he can remember what, amid all the bittersweet memories of his former life, he could never remember before: the events leading up to his stroke.

On this day, he had just bought himself a brand-new convertible. He says goodbye to his mistress and drives out to the country to visit his children, now living with their mother. Taking his oldest son for a drive, they have a man-to-man talk.

Now Jean-Do knows that, amid all the joys and sorrows, there was one moment at least where everything was all right with the world, when he was happy. Now he can let go.

Jean-Do's unique new perspective on life has finally allowed him to see the value in many things which before he took for granted. It has allowed him to see that no matter how extreme your situation, there is always someone who can relate to the way you feel. And that, to be a human being, your only limitation is the extent of your imagination. Those of us who are still butterflies should enjoy it while it lasts.

Harwood's choice, like the choices he made in his script for *The Pianist*, allow us to experience the world as Jean-Do does. This highly subjective point of view heightens the emotion of what might otherwise be banal scenes. As the film progresses we break out of strict POV more often, reflecting the gradual expansion of Jean-Do's world as his recovery progresses. As Jean-Do listens to his father weeping over the speakerphone, we break away from his POV and cut to Jean-Do's nearly immobile face. At moments of great emotion, even the blinking of an eye conveys so much. Life, a spirit, emotion, still beats within the locked-in body.

As we cut to these objective POVs we are surprised to find how helpless, almost childlike, he seems, after sharing for so long the sophistication and irony of his interior monologue. How many broken bodies have we walked by without imagining what flits within the mind? Those with narrow points of view, or narrow minds, often find it difficult to get any perspective. Their own pain, frustration or suffering occupies the whole of their brains, because they have no empathy for anyone else.

Jean-Do avoids this fate, which many of us would fall prey to, by remaining conscious of the absurdity of his situation, and by freeing his imagination. In this way he overcomes the narrowness of his perspective, of his **point of view**.

> *Not merely to bear the necessary . . . but to love it.*
>
> Friedrich Nietzsche, Philosopher

POINT OF VIEW
Recap

* In screenwriting, we accept the **point of view** we most identify with as the equivalent of reality.

* Every time our **point of view** changes, there is a subjective shift from one character to another, or from one state of mind to another.

* In **Maverick** films, we tend to be a few steps behind, running to catch up. There is a mystery to be solved about the character and their motivation, a challenge to identify with their point of view.

* This **mystery** should be one we feel an urgent need to solve, and be driven by an emotional desire we can relate to.

* When you push **POV to the max**, the differences between the characters are no longer a matter of point of view, but of different versions of reality.

* The more subjective the **point of view** – or the more multiple viewpoints there are – the more malleable reality becomes.

* A highly subjective reality is likely to be a highly skewed one, because it is limited in time and space: a narrow window on to reality.

* Push **POV to the max** by broadening it out, or narrowing it.

* **Broadening POV** creates multiple versions of reality. It spreads the force of antagonism, but creates a new kind of suspense as we have to choose between different versions of reality.

* **Narrowing POV** can create curiosity and suspense about what lies beyond our narrow horizon.

* The more you narrow **point of view**, the stronger a slant you give to events.

* Manipulating **point of view** gives a particular slant to events, but it does not create transparency.

* The more you multiply viewpoints, the less **transparency** you have.

* **Overturns** use a dramatic shift in perspective at the end to make us rush back and re-evaluate everything from an entirely different point of view.

* Create an inbuilt **ambivalence** about the current reality by using an **unreliable narrator** or point of view.

* Those with narrow points of view find it hard to get any perspective. Having a sense of **absurdity** can help with this.

* Never provide the full picture – always leave us some **mystery**.

Exercises

○ Write a scene between two characters. Now replay the scene from the **point of view** of the other character, showing how it takes on not only another meaning, but becomes a different version of **reality**.

○ Write a scene in which you artificially **narrow** the viewpoint of your character. Make the audience work not only to imagine what's going on beyond the narrow frame of vision, but to care as well.

○ Write a scene in which your hero experiences a moment of joy about something. Now make something happen which robs them of their joy, either because it turns out to be not what they had hoped for, or it no longer seems special or desirable. Show how this realization changes their view of everything around them.

Section 5
Technique

10

Break on
through to
the other side

Part One

Magic transference

At the opening of *Alice's Adventures in Wonderland*, Alice is sitting outside on a hot, sunny day, wondering whether it is worth the effort of making a daisy chain, when a rabbit with pink eyes runs by. "There was nothing so *very* remarkable in that," she thinks, nor is it "so *very* much out of the way" to hear it talking to itself.[57] Before she knows it, she has tumbled down a rabbit-hole.

While she is falling, she has plenty of time to look at all the cupboards and shelves as she is passing by, and even to sample a jar of orange marmalade. She imagines how brave they'll think her at home when they discover how far she's fallen, and practices the curtseys she will make when she arrives at the "antipathies".

In the sequel, *Through the Looking Glass and What Alice Found There*, Alice is a more active participant. This time she conjectures how nice it would be if she could step through the mirror to the room on the other side:

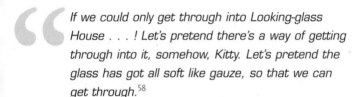

> *If we could only get through into Looking-glass House . . . ! Let's pretend there's a way of getting through into it, somehow, Kitty. Let's pretend the glass has got all soft like gauze, so that we can get through.*[58]

Before she knows it, the glass is "beginning to melt away, just like a bright silvery mist", and she hops through.

The room on the other side also has a real fire – indeed it is warmer because now no one will scold her for standing in front of it. All the rest is "as different as possible", including the pictures that seem alive, and the clock that has a face on it.

Magic transference is the process of taking us from one level of reality to another. Unless it is handled with care, you will not bring the audience along for the ride. No matter how successfully you have imagined your other world, unless you give them a smooth transition, they won't buy it.

There are a number of stages you have to go through in order to pass through the gates to the other side, just like the heroes of old. So, with a nod to Joseph Campbell's *The Hero with a Thousand Faces,*[59] here is:

Stage one: hearing the call

Before you can pass through to the other side, you have to create the desire in your hero for a change of state. In *Alice's Adventures in Wonderland*, Alice is hot and sleepy and bored. In *Through the Looking Glass*, she is finding the companionship of her kitten Dinah wearisome. As so many of us do, she imagines a life on the other side of the mirror, one where life is more satisfying and well, *alive*.

Some heroes just refuse to heed the call. These are the ones who, like Phil in *Groundhog Day*, don't realize how stuck their lives have become. They have to be placed in a pressure cooker until they're willing to confront the truth; or like the guests in *Festen*, whose car keys are stolen by the staff so they can be forced to confront the issue of sexual abuse in their ever-so civilized and rather smug family.

In *American Beauty*, disillusioned dad Lester is reluctant to take the call to watch his daughter Jane's high school cheerleader performance: after all, there's a back-to-back showing of Bond movies on cable tonight.

Others feel they have no choice but to leave. In *The Wizard of Oz* Dorothy needs to escape the grasping revenge of her neighbor Miss Almira Gulch, who threatens to have her dog Toto put down. Dorothy expresses her yearning by singing: "Somewhere Over the Rainbow" as she tries to imagine a place where dreams really do come true.

The storm that soon whips up is a magical extension of the turmoil of Dorothy's feelings, and while the others are able to take shelter in the root cellar, the feelings of a child are not always so easily grounded. As she lies back on her bed the house is caught up in a tornado and Dorothy is whirled away to Oz.

Some, like Captain Willard in *Apocalypse Now*, are ever on the alert and ready to take on a mission, even though the trauma of war has brought him close to a nervous breakdown. So badly has he lost track of reality that he assumes the Military Police who have come to give him his orders are there to arrest him. For those like Willard, for outlaws and gunfighters, the lure of "one more job" is more than they can resist. Others, like Jake in *Avatar*, on the other hand, take the mission because they've nothing left to live for. It turns out that despite his apparent unsuitability for the job he will have exactly the qualities necessary.

In *Being John Malkovich* Craig, an unemployed puppeteer, takes a job that makes good use of his dexterity: that of filing clerk. His willingness to sully his artistic talent by taking up an ordinary job shows his readiness (on the maturity scale, anyway) to begin to take control of his own destiny.

Stage two: answering the call

From the moment Phil stops being a victim of his ever-repeating circumstances in *Groundhog Day*, he begins to take control of his destiny, even if it is in all the wrong ways, like driving on the railroad tracks.

In the **classic** film this is often the case, because at the beginning of the story the hero rarely has the self-insight to understand what has been at the root of all his problems. He tries to grab the wheel of the car, only to spin it further out of control.

But the **Maverick** character, so long on the margins of society or out of sorts, has somehow always been waiting for this moment. It is a part of their wish-fulfillment. With the discovery of the portal into John Malkovich's brain, Craig has finally been given the opportunity to fulfill his dreams. Will he use this power sensibly – or will he abuse it?

While answering the call may appear to be about achieving an external goal, the true purpose is to force your character to confront something within themselves. When Willard looks at Colonel Kurtz's files – and the picture they create of the man he is supposed to kill – he realizes he is looking at someone whose career is a mirror image of his own. Someone, in other words, just like himself.

Stage three: breaking through

In social dramas, the means are often metaphorically created by shutting the doors and turning up the heat. In *Festen* this is done by the hotel staff stealing the guests' car keys. In magical or mythical dramas, the means are likely to be a passageway to another world, or a bridge. This provides the logical link, no matter how flimsy, which audiences need to make that leap.

In Alice's adventures, it's the rabbit-hole and the looking glass. In *The Lion, the Witch and the Wardrobe* it is the wardrobe, normally such a cozy and safe place to hide, that transports us to Narnia. In *Mulholland Drive* it is the blue key; in *The Wizard of Oz* it is the tornado; and in *The Matrix* it is the mirror which melts Neo.

In *Groundhog Day* it is the blizzard which keeps Phil stranded in Punxsutawney – a blizzard which he confidently assures viewers will *not* be coming their way. Phil is outraged at this betrayal by the elements. "I make the weather!" he tells the patrol officer.

At that moment, we know this is no ordinary blizzard, but a supernatural one designed to reach Phil a lesson. Yet notice how the writer keeps the door open to the possibility of a rational explanation – that Phil was just too smug or arrogant to check his facts.

In *Being John Malkovich* the passageway is the portal to John Malkovich's brain, hidden inconspicuously behind a filing cabinet. By the time Craig discovers it, we have come to take for granted so many of the oddities of his banal world, that it doesn't seem that different an order of reality.

This passage to another world often seems ordinary at first glance. If it didn't, your hero wouldn't be in such a hurry to take a leap into the unknown.

Stage four: stepping into the river

There comes a moment when the hero steps into the river – when he merges into the stream of destiny that will transform his life.

This moment is crucial. If you want to vault your audience into your new reality, you have to lay the groundwork through mood, atmosphere and foreshadowing. You have to open them up to the possibility. You have to take them there by degrees. Like a frog in a pan of water which is slowly heated till it boils to death, your audience will never notice the change until suddenly they have *shifted*.

When you move from one level of reality to another, it's important to pay attention to the *transitions*. The **transition** is the most important element in shifting levels of reality. Imagine you are trying to seduce the audience, hypnotize them, lull them to sleep, whisper them a secret, sell them something without their knowing they've been sold (an "inception", for instance).

You don't do that by beating a drum, but by helping them to enter into the dream.

In *American Beauty* Lester Burnham, an ad sales man having a mid-life crisis, is reluctantly brought along to his daughter's high-school varsity team's half-time show. Lester, who describes himself as "dead already", is suddenly brought very much alive.

> Lester, watching from the stands, picks out his daughter.
>
> His POV: Jane performs well, concentrating. Dancing awkwardly next to her is Angela. Suddenly Angela looks right at us and smiles . . . a lazy, insolent smile.
>
> Lester leans forward in his seat.
>
> His POV: we're focused on Angela now. Everything starts to SLOW DOWN . . . the MUSIC acquires an eerie ECHO . . .

Lester gets the call and enters the river all at once. As we all do in these life-changing moments, his mind goes into overdrive as it tries to keep up with the emotional impact of what it encounters. We're in slow motion now, as Lester begins to focus on Angela, to the exclusion of all else.

> We ZOOM slowly toward Lester as he watches, transfixed.
>
> His POV: Angela's awkwardness gives way to a fluid grace, and "ON BROADWAY" FADES into dreamy, hypnotic MUSIC. The light on Angela grows stronger, and the other girls DISAPPEAR entirely.

As Lester is drawn into her spell, so are we, hypnotized by the music and fluid movement.

> Lester is suddenly alone in the stands, spellbound.

Now Lester not only feels that she is dancing for him alone, but he is alone in the stands. As so often with **Maverick** distortions of reality, we *shift* from the imagination or feeling of something, to its reality.

Just as Lester only has eyes for Angela, he imagines that her attention is directed at him and no one else.

> His POV: Angela looks directly at us now, dancing only for Lester. Her movements take on a blatantly erotic edge as she starts to unzip her uniform, teasing us with an expression that's both innocent and knowing, then . . . she pulls her uniform OPEN and a profusion of RED ROSE PETALS spill forth . . . and we SMASH CUT TO:

Just as we reach the point of surreality, **ordinary** reality brings Lester back to earth with a bump.

```
INT. HIGH SCHOOL GYMNASIUM - CONTINUOUS

Angela, fully clothed, is once again
surrounded by the other girls. The HIGH
SCHOOL BAND plays its last note, the Dancing
Spartanettes strike their final pose, and
the audience APPLAUDS.
```

A few minutes later Lester is still feeling the after-shock, as he babbles away to Jane and Angela like an awkward teenager, lust short-circuiting his brain. The power of that **magic transference** is still working through him.

The tension between the banality of his conversation and the tumult of his emotions makes for a very funny scene.

So when you take the audience up to the next level, show them some respect: *pay attention to the transitions*. Wind them up before you lean into the bend; and wind them down slowly. They won't even realize that you are now driving on the wrong side of the road.

Stage five: testing the new reality

You have laid the groundwork for this transition in state by creating first an emotional need, and then the psychological readiness for shifting from one state of consciousness to another (sleepiness, the blue or the red pill, the smile of a teenage girl). Finally, you have created through mood or uncertainty a sense of the ambivalence of reality.

Then the opening appears, the crack in the wall. It still requires a certain kind of person to pass through that opening; nor would another have been able to draw the sword from the stone.

But your job as screenwriter is not done yet. In *2001* when Bowman finally gains back control of the space ship from the computer HAL, he enters a black hole that takes him through a mind-bending cosmological and alien landscape, after which time itself is dissolved; and past, present and future co-exist.

You've broken on through to the other side. Now what? Now you've got to test the new reality. You've got to verify it.

In Wings of Desire, the transition from one state to another is repre-sented by the switch from black-and-white to color. The fallen angel "tests" the blood from his bleeding head: "It has a taste!" He asks a passer-by to identify all the colors on a graffitied wall, then asks him for money for a cup of coffee, which the stranger willingly gives. What a wonderful world!

Just in case we should think this world is unrealistic, this naive former angel gets ripped off when he sells the armor which landed on his head.

Always create setbacks as well as successes when your character makes this transition. The setbacks defuse the audience's skepticism. They create a "catch" that the audience can spot and point to. When your character over-comes these setbacks, we admire them and identify with them all the more.

The Wizard of Oz marks Dorothy's transition by using one of the most elaborate and brilliant "testing" scenes in film history.

CLOSE UP: THE WIZARD OF OZ

As Dorothy emerges from her house (and from black-and-white), she looks around at the Technicolor Land of Oz in amazement. But it is not until the Good Witch Glinda emerges from a pink bubble that Dorothy utters her immortal words, "Now I know we're not in Kansas."

Glinda expresses no surprise at Dorothy's appearance. All she wants to know is: "Are you a good witch, or a bad witch?"

When Dorothy asserts that neither she nor Toto are witches, Glinda confesses to being muddled since the Munchkins told her a new witch had just dropped a house on the Wicked Witch of the East:

"There's the house – and here you are. And that's all that's left of the Wicked Witch of the East." Note the beautiful **chain of logic**. "And so what the Munchkins want to know is, are you a good witch or a bad witch?" There is no longer any doubting that Dorothy is a witch. The only question to be decided is whether she's a good or a bad one.

When Dorothy insists she is not a witch, because witches are old and ugly, Glinda reveals that *she* is a witch. Dorothy apologizes, as she's never heard of a beautiful witch before. (Notice how quickly the argument has shifted from whether we believe in the Land of Oz to whether we believe in the existence of *beautiful* rather than ugly witches.)

Despite Dorothy's protests, Belinda declares her act of destruction to be a miracle, but Dorothy launches into song:

> *It really was no miracle*
> *What happened was just this*
> *The wind began to switch*
> *The house to pitch and suddenly*
> *The hinges started to unhitch . . .*

Dorothy tries to reassert the **chain of logic** to make it sound like it was all perfectly natural, but the perfect rhymes and galloping rhythm seem forced. The lady doth protest too much. We know *that* was no ordinary tornado. She is trying to convince herself as well as us, and we don't buy it.

So now we are inclined to believe that it *was* a miracle, even though Dorothy may not actually be a witch. By disproving one small thing, we cease to notice that we have accepted the greater illusion: that we have firmly arrived in Munchkinland.

Hot tip

If you want the audience to believe the less logical
of two possibilities, provide an unconvincing argument
for what is most credible.

At this point, Dorothy is greeted by the Mayor and the important Munchkins of the land. They thank her for killing the Wicked Witch "so completely".

But before they can confirm it, they have to "verify it legally to see if she is morally, ethically, spiritually, physically, positively, absolutely, undeniably and reliably dead".

After an inspection, the Coroner assures her that she is "not only merely dead, she's really most sincerely dead", and soon it is proclaimed: "Let the news be spread, the wicked witch is dead."

If that is not enough to assure us that the Deed is Done, and Dorothy is the One That Magically Done It, she is now formally welcomed into Munchkinland by first the Lullaby League and then the Lollipop Kids. "From now you'll be history . . . you'll be a bust . . . in the hall of fame!" She has truly arrived, and so have we.

Before you have tested and confirmed your character's arrival at this new state, *you must have planted the seeds of possibility deep within their character*. Otherwise, your audience will never believe the arc you send them on. In spite of her innocence, we believe in Dorothy's ability to overcome the obstacles on the way to the Emerald City, because we have already seen her strength and resolve at home.

In *Schindler's List*, Schindler is introduced as a hedonistic, self-serving businessman on the make. He has little time for politics or ideology, and it is this independence of mind which makes it possible for him to go on the journey he does, ultimately saving hundreds of Jewish lives. In *Casablanca*, it is important to know that Rick hasn't just run a bar all his life. In the past, he fought on the side of freedom in Ethiopia and Spain. Without our knowledge of this back story, we would never believe it when he pulls a gun on Renault in the third act, and acts like he knows how to use it.

In *The Matrix*, Morpheus introduces Neo gradually to the notion that reality may not be all it seems (but of course, Neo would know that, since he spends most of his time in virtual reality anyway). Finally, he gives Neo a warning about the potential consequences of choosing the blue pill over the red one (notice that he doesn't ask him whether he wants a pill at all). *Always give your audience a false choice between two options – like the "good witch or bad witch"* – so they forget that the most obvious choice isn't on offer.

Morpheus shows Neo how the mirror melts, and his arm too, before he shows him the reality: that everything he has ever known is an illusion. He is plugged into the Matrix, one of a million human batteries feeding the Machines.

Classically, these moments of **magic transference** come near the beginning of the story; but in **Maverick** films this is not always so.

In *Mulholland Drive*, since the normal transference from **ordinary reality** to **dream reality** is reversed, the moment comes at the beginning of the third act.

In films like *Jacob's Ladder*, *The Sixth Sense* and *The Usual Suspects*, the magic transference comes with the climax. Until that moment we have been unaware that we have been living a false reality.

However, even these dramatic last-ditch reversals must give the audience time to review the logic, to turn it around in their heads.

So you've broken on through to the other side. Now what do you do? You have to get the audience to invest in that reality. You have to make them want to believe it, no matter how unlikely it is.

Part Two

Buying into unreality

> *Impossible events that are believable are better than possible ones which are not.*
>
> Aristotle, *Poetics*, c. 350 BC

In *Being John Malkovich,* Craig empathizes with his boss Dr Lester, who mistakenly believes he has a speech impediment.

Empathy is not the same as sympathy – it means understanding the way someone feels through personal experience. Craig also knows (or so *he* thinks) what it's like to be misunderstood.

Because we have created empathy for Dr Lester, we are inclined to believe him when he tells us the story of the 7½th floor. But just so we don't take it too seriously, Craig gets shown a hokey corporate video, which Maxine makes fun of. Because she's witty and sharp, and because Craig's attracted to her, we laugh along with her cynicism about corporate PR.

But we no longer question the reality of this new world. That question has been deflected. We've put it out of mind, out of sight, because Kaufman has created an empathy for the characters who accept things as they are.

We are inclined to believe the reality of the character we identify with most.

At the same time, you've got to create skeptics who question the new reality and put it to the test. Their role is to express the audience's own skepticism and defuse it. The more unattractive these skeptics are, the more we'll enjoy seeing them being discomfited. However, you should also create moments where they seem to have the upper hand, or we won't feel that our skepticism is being taken seriously.

There are several ways you can go with your hero's attitude to their new reality. They can be like Craig, and take it in their stride; or they can have harbored long-held suspicions about the false reality, like Truman in *The Truman Show* or Neo in *The Matrix*.

Or they can be like McMurphy in *One Flew Over the Cuckoo's Nest*, liberating his fellow patients by showing them the power of the imagination. When McMurphy is refused permission to have the television turned on in the ward so they can watch the World Series, he sits himself down angrily in front of the set. In the original book by Ken Kesey, McMurphy holds a silent protest. But screenwriter Bo Goldman's genius is to have McMurphy giving a running commentary on the exciting game which he imagines unfolding before him, working himself to a frenzy as it reaches its climax.

Gradually, all the patients emerge from their rooms, mesmerized by the insanity of what he's doing, but gradually getting caught up in the excitement. Finally, they whoop for joy and dance on the tables as McMurphy describes their team's home run. As we cut to the Nurse's cold expression, we know that McMurphy represents the ultimate threat to her ward: the potential to incite rebellion by freeing the minds of her patients.

Compared to the wild imagination which McMurphy exhibits in this scene, his fellow patients feel themselves to be relatively sane. This is an adjustment to their reality, and it gives them the confidence to begin to think for themselves.

When your hero is finally convinced of the new reality, he may then have to convince an even larger circle of non-believers. This sets us up for even more dramatic conflict as the hero becomes a pariah or a victim of others' ignorance (as McMurphy does, when he is given a lobotomy). This naturally creates even more empathy for our hero, and so the cycle of strengthening the new reality goes on.

CLOSE UP: RESERVOIR DOGS

Tarantino reinvented the heist genre by jumping straight into the aftermath of the heist at the beginning of *Reservoir Dogs*.

By changing the structure, he changed the question posed by the genre. The question is no longer, will they pull it off? By dropping us straight into the chaotic aftermath of a job gone wrong, the question becomes, who snitched? As a production manager I worked with liked to say: How *did* it all go "pear-shaped"?

Shrewdly, Tarantino opens with Mr Orange (Freddie) shot and bleeding to death in the back of the car. This makes the possibility that he is the informer seem remote. Surely an informer would have ensured he wasn't caught in the crossfire when it all went down?

Mr Orange's true identity as an undercover cop isn't revealed until two-thirds of the way through the film, when the identity of the snitch has become the driving imperative of the story. In the most iconic and unsettling scene of the film, Mr Blonde has just tortured a police officer whom he has taken hostage. He in turn is shot by our hero, who earns himself and the cop a reprieve. But he's bleeding to death and he knows the cops are waiting for Joe Cabot – the Mr Big of the operation – to arrive before busting in. Everything will depend on his being able to convince the others that he is not the snitch.

We now cut to a flashback sequence, Freddie's preparation for his undercover role. This sequence is held together through the device of the "commode story", an amusing anecdote about a drug deal which his police handler Holdaway tells him to learn.

At first our hero can't believe he has to memorize so many pages, but Holdaway tells him to learn what's important and make the rest his own, just like telling any funny story.

What *is* important? "The things you gotta remember are the details, cus it's the details that tell your story." As the story takes place in a men's room, he has to know all the details about the men's room. Whether they've got a hand-dryer, or paper towels. Whether there are doors on the stalls, liquid soap or "that pink granulated shit they used in high school". Whether there's hot water or not, and whether the place stinks.

"So what you gotta do is take all them details, man, and make 'em your own. And while you're doing that, what you gotta do is remember this story is about you, and how you perceived the events that went down . . ."

Tarantino, forever winking at film enthusiasts, knows exactly what he is talking about. Because these are exactly the same skills needed by the screenwriter. The professional screenwriter does not need long passages of description – she knows how to find the right detail that evokes the feeling of time and place. The right details combined with a clear **point of view** make screenwriting a concise and focused art, if not always a simple one.

Clichés and stereotypes arise when writers use generalities, picked up second-hand off the shelf. Experienced writers learn enough of the detail to give the illusion of intimate familiarity with their subject. Theirs is a skill of research, a skill that anyone can learn.

The *art* of screenwriting comes in selecting the right detail that sells the story to the audience. The things which you would only know if you had *been there*. The things that aren't necessarily obvious.

The flashback sequence starts in a diner, but soon cuts to a rooftop where Holdaway is telling Freddie that an undercover cop has to be a great actor. Freddie looks disbelievingly as he leafs through the pages. We cut to Freddie's apartment, and now Freddie is pacing in and out of frame, haltingly trying to learn the story off by heart.

By the time we cut to the next location, an empty, graffitied lot, Freddie has gained in confidence and fluency. The story about his pot-dealing days jogs along confidently without skipping a beat.

By the next cut we're in a nightclub, and now Freddie's telling the story for real, while the gang are all ears. For a moment, he's almost thrown off as Mr White asks about a minor detail – what was his drug dealer's brother arrested for? Just some traffic tickets, Freddie improvises, proving that he has made the story his own.

At the point in the story where he meets the buyer of his carry-on bag full of weed, he finds he has to go to the "boys' room". We cut from the nightclub to the men's room – but now Freddie is no longer just narrating the story, he is in it too.

In the men's room, Freddie finds four LA county sheriffs hanging out shooting the breeze, with a German Shepherd at their feet. When Freddie walks in the room they all stop talking and stare. "That's a hard situation," Mr White concurs back at the nightclub.

We cut back to the men's room, close on the German Shepherd, its jaws slobbering and teeth bared as it barks. Freddie is no longer narrating from outside the scene but from within it, as if operating on a different level of reality from the sheriffs, who don't hear him: "It's obvious he's barkin' at me." As we spin around the room, Freddie continues: "Every nerve ending, all of my senses, the blood in my veins, everything I had was screaming . . . "

Then we're in close on the sheriffs' faces as Freddie continues: "And all these sheriffs are lookin' at me and they know. They can smell it. As sure as that fuckin' dog can, they can smell it on me."

A freeze-frame of Freddie jerks into life as one of the cops tells his dog to shut up. Has Freddie been imagining that all eyes were on him? The tension grows as another cop tells the story of how he almost had to shoot a driver who was reaching for his registration. From a distance, we can see the dog still watching Freddie. We go with Freddie as he crosses to a sink, rinses his hands, and presses the blow-dryer.

It goes off like a jet engine as everything shifts to SLOW MOTION and we enter **hyperreality**, panning across the faces of the cops, all reacting to the intrusion of this outrageous noise. Here Freddie's panic and hypersensitivity push his senses into overdrive, until every detail becomes heightened and exaggerated. His hands seem to take forever to dry. The dog's barking seems like it will never end.

Yet suddenly we're back in **real time**, and the cops are kibitzing as though they've never paid him the slightest attention.

And to prove that Freddie's audience has been utterly drawn into the story, as have we, Joe Cabot gives the approving pay-off: "You knew how to handle that situation. Just shit in your pants, and dive in and swim."

The commode sequence takes us from one level of reality to another until we're no longer standing back from the story, but participating in it at the most visceral level.

The brilliance of this device is not only that it **compresses time** – instead of showing us a series of tedious scenes of Freddie preparing for his role, we get the whole process in one funny anecdote.

More importantly, it gets the audience to buy into the central tenet of the film: that Freddie is good enough in his role that neither these seasoned gangsters, nor the audience, will ever guess that it's he who is the snitch.

It's important that we believe Freddie can pull this off, so Tarantino provides us with a sequence that takes us from his first disbelief at having to memorize this shaggy-dog story, to a growing confidence in telling it, to actually being in the situation of telling the gang the story, to being *in the scene* while narrating it, and then to narrating it from within the scene.

At that moment, we're finely balanced, half in and half detached from the scene. The narration cuts out as the blow-dryer turns on. Now we're totally in the reality – and not just in it, we're vaulted into **hyperreality**. We're lost in the story, just like his audience, and we know he's pulled it off.

With Joe Cabot's approving pay-off, we enter the confirmation stage of "testing the reality". In one brilliant sequence, Tarantino takes us through all the five stages of **magic transference**, and he has also *bought us* into the reality that Freddie can successfully pass himself off as just another gangster.

Which is just as well, because after this sequence Freddie picks Mr White out in a mug shot. His boss reveals that Mr White not only butchered an undercover cop whom he discovered had been working on another job, but has killed several other cops, and their wives and children too. Now the stakes are as high as they could possibly be for Freddie. Now we are invested in the new reality, filled with a new sense of anticipation and urgency as we go into the final act.

BREAK ON THROUGH
Recap

* **Magic transference** is the process of taking us from one level of reality to another. No matter how successfully you have imagined your other world, unless you give your audience a smooth transition they won't buy it.

* Before you can pass through to the other side, you have to create the desire in your hero for a change of state.

* For the **Maverick** character, so long on the margins of society or out of sorts, this is their wish-fulfillment.

* While "answering the call" may appear to be about achieving an external goal, the true purpose is to force your character to confront something within themself.

* In magical or mythical dramas, the means are likely to be a passageway to another world, or a bridge.

* This passage to another world often seems ordinary at first glance. If it didn't, your hero wouldn't be in such a hurry to pass on through.

* If you want to vault your audience into your new reality, you have to lay the groundwork through mood, atmosphere and fore-shadowing – you have to open them up to the possibility. You have to take them there by degrees.

* Pay attention to the **transitions** when shifting levels of reality.

* First, create through mood or uncertainty, a sense of the **ambivalence** of reality.

* Then create an emotional need, and the psychological readiness for shifting from one state of consciousness to another.

* Always create setbacks as well as successes when your character makes this transition. The setbacks defuse the audience's skepticism. They create a "catch" that the audience can spot and point to. When your character overcomes these setbacks, we admire them and identify with them all the more.

* In **Maverick** films, it is not always necessary to have the **magic transference** come near the beginning of the story, where it is more easily disguised.

* We are inclined to believe the reality of the character we identify with most.

* Create skeptics who question this new reality, and whom we'll enjoy seeing proven wrong. Their role is to express the audience's own skepticism, and defuse it.

* Always plant the seeds of possibility deep within the character, or your audience will never believe the journey you send them on.

* The *art* of screenwriting comes in selecting the right detail that sells your story.

Exercise

○ Bring your character or characters into a new state of reality, paying attention to the process of **magic transference**. Have them test that reality to convince themselves – and the audience as well. Create a sceptic, either within the group, or within your hero herself. Once convinced, give your hero the challenge of convincing others.

11 Maverick dialogue

© Peter Grant Photography

All good dialogue has **subtext**, the sense that what the characters are thinking or feeling is at odds with what they are saying. In bad films, on the other hand, characters endlessly tell us how they feel. We call this "writing on the nose".

Think about how rarely you do this in real life – in moments of confession, maybe, or with those you know most intimately. But most of the time we wear a social mask, where our true feelings are concealed, so we can all rub along. We are expected to ignore our feelings about our co-workers or our boss. If we are suffering emotional turmoil in our personal lives, we keep it hidden.

We wear a social mask, because if we didn't the whole world would be a lunatic asylum. It is the task of the writer to reflect this – but also to write the things that go unsaid.

Because film is such a visual medium, every nuance of body language and gesture counts as much as any word spoken. So in writing dialogue, you are not just placing bricks, but also the mortar around them.

Many writers think that when the talking begins, the action stops, and that's the way they write dialogue. Dialogue should not be thought of as separate from the action, but part of it: a machine-gun splatter of words intended to provoke a reaction.

Every dialogue scene is 50 percent reaction. One character says something, and another reacts. It's like a game of ping-pong. If the ball's coming at you with enough impetus, you can use that energy to send it back. You need to write the *reaction*, whether it be spoken or unspoken. Every beat is a moment of action *and* reaction.

While most scenes should have an upward arc in terms of dramatic tension, within that there need to be peaks and troughs. If your dialogue scene is stuck in the doldrums, check to see whether you have too many beats registering the same intensity. It's possible to overdo passion as much as reticence. Don't make the rhythm too predictable.

It's possible that in a conversation between two people who can't communicate or listen, the rebounding of action and reaction can break down: but it's likely to be a boring scene. If one character is unresponsive or stonewalling, it's better to think of the immovable object as a powerful beast. Someone's refusal to answer, an interruption or a change of subject carry a charge that must be felt, an iceberg bobbing beneath the surface; an unexploded bomb waiting to go off. As with Bartleby, the copy clerk in Melville's short story who responds to his boss's requests to work with: "I prefer not to," sometimes refusal to do something can become a magnificent obsession.

The reason why it's important to keep the action going in dialogue scenes – even when nothing much is happening – is that without visual cues, it is difficult for the reader of your script to judge the sincerity of the lines spoken.

It is with our actions and our body language that we reveal whether our thoughts are consistent with our words, and in the visual medium of cinema actions count louder than words. Without actions to accompany the dialogue, it can be difficult for the reader to judge whether a character is confident or conflicted, impatient or impressive.

It is not for you to editorialize what your characters' inner feelings are, but to *dramatize* them. This does not mean that you are directing the actor. You are writing only action that has a narrative purpose, dramatizing only the subtext that is essential for your story. The rest is style and technique, and can be left to the actor.

If a character is shifting nervously while pledging their loyalty, there probably is some internal conflict. The audience's awareness of this conflict creates a tension. When will the conflict lurking underneath break out on to the surface?

In *The Brothers McMullen*, a wife is doing her husband's laundry when she finds a condom in his jeans. Since they haven't slept together in a while, naturally she is concerned. She goes out to the back yard to speak to him, the condom clutched in her fist. But because she never confronts him with it, the scene goes round in circles. Instead of asking: "Who is she?" and creating a dramatic triangle (you don't need to have the third person actually in the scene for this to work), the dialogue feels forced, as neither is able to say what is really on their minds. The subtext has lost its power. It has promised more than it delivered, because it has not broken surface.

Maverick dialogue goes to the other extreme, often suggesting layer upon layer of meaning in the subtext which drives the scene. In *Donnie Brasco*, there is a wonderful moment of (probably) improvised dialogue by Al Pacino, playing a middle-ranking mob guy who's trying to decide whether Johnny Depp's undercover cop, posing as a jewelry fence, is trustworthy. As Depp is driving to wherever Pacino may be taking him, Pacino asks him: "There's good money in it?" Depp does a double-take, for a moment stepping out of his role. Does he mean – as a cop, or as a fence? "What? A jewel?" Depp stutters. Pacino throws him a look – should he even have to ask? "Thank you," says Pacino sarcastically. "Oh yeah, if you know what you're doin' there is," Depp covers confidently.

Pacino's beat is: "Can I trust you? I'm going to try to catch you out." Depp stumbles, but once again lands on his feet. On the surface, what they are discussing is of little importance. The entire scene is played out through the subtext. Having survived this test, Depp is now going to have to face an even bigger one, and each test will move their relationship to a new level. A rapport is being established, but the audience are not even aware of how it is happening.

CLOSE UP: HANNAH AND HER SISTERS

In Woody Allen's film *Hannah and Her Sisters*, Hannah is meeting her younger siblings Lee and Holly at a restaurant. Hannah is unaware that Lee has started an affair with her husband Elliot. While they're waiting for Holly to arrive, Hannah – always concerned – wishes she and Elliot could fix Lee up with somebody now that she's single again. She shares her fears that Elliot seems distant, and she worries that he may be having an affair.

This awkward conversation is interrupted by the arrival of Holly, a would-be actress coming from another failed audition. She shares with Hannah her idea of ditching the acting and becoming a playwright. She just needs another loan to last her, say, a year. When

Hannah expresses skepticism about this abrupt career change, Holly gets enraged and accuses Hannah of having no faith in her. Hannah responds that she often helps her out financially, and goes out of her way to introduce her to interesting single men. "All losers!" Holly responds.

As the argument between the two sisters rumbles on, we circle the table, and all our attention is on Lee, chewed up, holding it all in. The more Holly attacks Hannah, the more guilty Lee feels. The more she is reminded of Hannah's generosity, the worse it gets. She tries several times to interrupt, finally and emotionally telling Holly to stop attacking Hannah: "She's going through a really rough time now."

A classic deflection, since it is of course herself she is thinking of.

On the surface, the **business** of the scene is the conflict between the reliable, selfless sister and the kooky, self-obsessed one. But under the surface, where all the emotional weight of the scene is, we are acutely aware of Lee's guilt for the pain she is causing Hannah.

When it finally bursts out, it does so at an inappropriate moment and at an inappropriate target: her sister Holly – when it is her own behavior she should be criticizing.

This is a classic example of a **triangular** scene. Hannah and Holly have probably had many similar arguments before, and we can see this one going on and on. But Lee's guilt forces her to take sides, shifting the balance of power in Hannah's favor. Ironically, this only convinces Hannah to give in to Holly, since it's important to her that she always appear the most selfless of them all.

Watching actors one can learn a good deal about writing dialogue. The merely good actors come with their dialogue prepared, their characterization researched and coherent in their minds. They deliver their lines perfectly, with variations as required.

The great film actor, however, does something very different. Every time the other actor feeds them a line, they listen very carefully. Even though this may be their twentieth take, they listen as though they have never heard the line before, and have to consider their response to it. They speak the dialogue as though the thought were spontaneously arising, and the thought immediately gives utterance to words.

In an interview not long before his death, Rod Steiger spoke bitterly about being on the other side of Marlon Brando's famous "I could've been a contender" monologue in *On the Waterfront*. When it came to the reverse angles, Brando left and Steiger had to deliver all *his* lines to a monotonous assistant director. If it hadn't been for that, Steiger fumed, history might have remembered his side of the dialogue a little better. Actors need a good reaction to play off.

Many acting schools play the game of "throw the ball" to train actors to learn spontaneity. A group of actors sits around in a circle. Somebody improvises a line and throws the ball randomly to someone else. Since you never know when the ball is coming to you, you cannot prepare your answer, but must answer spontaneously.

In order for an actor to do that convincingly, they need screenwriters who can write dialogue that allows them to create this illusion. Experienced screenwriters soon learn to avoid writing perfect syntax, instead mimicking the patterns of spoken speech, which follows the rhythms of breath rather than the dictates of grammar.

This style of dialogue recognizes that people interrupt each other, lose track, then double back, fail to complete their thoughts. That doesn't mean you imitate spoken speech exactly. We are far too incoherent for that. But if you are writing perfectly structured, polished speeches you are locking the actor in a gilded cage, and they will wilt and die there.

Imitate the *pattern* of real speech, not its randomness. Order is created by the constant see-sawing of action and reaction, which gives momentum to a scene. Like two fencers attacking and retreating, the tempo and intensity of conversation is raised or lowered with each new beat, as we let our emotions get the better of us, or retreat with restraint.

It is the variation in these beats, their modulation in tone and intensity, that creates texture in a scene.

As I've already indicated, dialogue cannot be separated from action or story. In order for your dialogue to sound as though it is spontaneous, it has to be freed as far as possible from the task of exposition, of telling the story.

If you have written a beat sheet, or detailed treatment, you should have worked out every twist and turn of the story before a word of dialogue is written. (If not, you may find it useful to attend my "Art of the Beat Sheet" seminar.) You should have gotten the action to drive the story. You probably won't go as far as Alfred Hitchcock, who storyboarded every shot of his films before he wrote a line of dialogue. For him the dialogue was the cherry on the cake, not what is most important.

If you know where every scene is going before you start writing your script, you free the dialogue from the burden of carrying the story. Now it becomes free to provide color, wit and emotion, to react to events rather than to prompt or describe them.

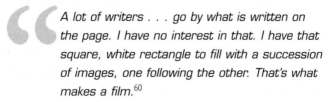

A lot of writers . . . go by what is written on the page. I have no interest in that. I have that square, white rectangle to fill with a succession of images, one following the other. That's what makes a film.[60]

Alfred Hitchcock, Writer/Director

CLOSE UP:
ETERNAL SUNSHINE OF THE SPOTLESS MIND

When Clementine meets Joel on a train in *Eternal Sunshine of the Spotless Mind*, she is pushy and bored, and he is withdrawn and reluctant to get into a conversation.

Finally she prompts him: "Aw, c'mon. Live dangerously. Take the leap and assume someone is talking to you in an otherwise empty car." He mumbles hello. She thinks she recognizes him from Barnes and Noble, where she's been a "book slave" for five years. The thought leads her to a spontaneous impulse: "You have a cell phone? I need to quit right this minute. I'll call in dead."

He might not recognize *her* because she is as spontaneous with her hair color as she is with everything else. Today it's "blue rinse", which he recognizes from the Tom Waits song. She starts inventing new names for hair colors, like "Agent Orange". She tells him her name, and says it doesn't fit her character, since she's a "vindictive little bitch, truth be told".

When Joel says she seems nice, she slaps him down, and he has to apologize. They are interrupted by the conductor, and Clementine gets in a fluster when she thinks she's lost her ticket, but she won't drop her theme: "I don't need nice. I don't need myself to be it and I don't need anyone to be it at me."

Clementine's "spontaneity" is revealed actually to be confusion and bluster – even bullying – that conceals a deep insecurity about herself. Now it is her turn to apologize, and Joel's turn to try to lift her mood. He suggests the hair colors "Old Yeller" and "Karen Black", and she responds: "You're good! We could be partners."

Finally after the insistent, needy probing of her dialogue, she has drawn him out of his shell, and through this word game he has proved they are on the same wavelength.

Nothing much has happened in this scene. Two people meet and have a conversation that seems to spontaneously leap from topic to topic. But Joel's final riposte proves that there has been a thread to the scene, there has been a story arc. He has listened and responded, and brought the conversation back on track. He has made a joke which appears spontaneous, but nevertheless is completely artful. By coming out of his shell in this way, Joel takes the first step in her direction.

The dialogue might seem inconsequential, but a connection has been made, something within each of them has shifted, and the story has moved forward.

In order for dialogue to feel spontaneous, it has to react in the moment. When dialogue anticipates, it's there to be shot down and confounded by events.

Whenever a character tells us what is going to happen, make sure that something else happens instead.

Of course, it's not always appropriate for dialogue to feel spontaneous. Sometimes it needs a rhetorical flourish. It has to be self-aware, because it's there to serve a purpose. It draws attention to itself because the occasion is formal, or because the character wants to create the illusion of formality in order to justify the authority of their actions – like Jules in *Pulp Fiction*, with his recitation of Ezekiel.

CLOSE UP: APOCALYPSE NOW

Apocalypse Now opens with Captain Willard, a special forces officer, on leave in Saigon during the Vietnam war. As we pan across the detritus of a room that looks like he's been living in it forever, we see the whiskey, the cigarettes, a revolver, the burnt photographs of his wife, overlaid with the flashbacks he is suffering: napalm lighting up the jungle.

When he jolts awake, he recalls what it was like going home at the end of his first tour:

                    WILLARD (V.O.)
          I hardly said a word to my wife, until
          I said yes to a divorce. When I was
          here, I wanted to be there. When I was
          there, all I could think of was getting
          back into the jungle. I've been here a
          week now. Waiting for a mission, getting
          softer. Every minute I stay in this room
          I get weaker. And every minute Charlie
          squats in the bush he gets stronger.
          Each time I look around the walls move
          in a little tighter.

The perfect symmetry of this speech, the careful balance, the calm and logical assessment of his situation, is belied by the images. He squats naked on the floor as though he were still living in the jungle. Then he's roaring drunk and smashing a mirror with his bare fist, smeared with blood and wrapped in a sheet, crying like a baby.

The artful rhetoric of the voiceover in fact reveals a mind that is close to psychopathy: paranoid and confused. Charlie isn't really getting stronger, and the walls aren't really getting tighter. It just feels that way. The pseudo-logic of the voiceover reveals how cut off he is from these feelings (just like the nameless narrator's voiceover in *Fight Club*).

The next morning, after being thrust under a shower by some MPs, Willard is taken to report for a mission. A Colonel Lucas asks him about some of his previous "black" missions. Willard tries to evade questions about assignments so top secret that he cannot even claim credit for them: "I'm not presently disposed to discuss these operations, sir."

Lucas presses him: did he not assassinate a tax inspector? "Sir, I am unaware of any such activity or operation – nor would I be disposed to discuss such an operation if it did in fact exist, sir."

Note how, in spite of the outpouring of pain and grief only hours before, Willard quickly slips into army jargon designed to distance him and them from the ugly reality of what they are talking about.

As they sit down for lunch, the Colonel keeps the tone light, while still suggesting an undertone of something sinister: "I don't know how you feel about this shrimp, but if you eat it, you'll never have to prove your courage in any other way . . . "

Then Lucas plays Willard a tape of a broadcast by Colonel Kurtz, who has gone AWOL in Cambodia. Kurtz's crackly voice relates his nightmare: a snail walking along the edge of a straight razor. Then later, "We must kill them. We must incinerate them. Pig after pig, cow after cow, village after village, army after army." After so much guarded language, the shocking insanity of Kurtz's broadcast cuts to the quick.

The Colonel's response at first falls back into safe jargon. Kurtz's methods have become "unsound". He has set himself up like a god among the local tribes – and here Lucas surprises us with his unguarded verdict: "and very obviously, he has gone insane".

Retreating into the security of military jargon, he explains that Willard's mission is to locate Kurtz and "terminate the colonel's command". Willard can't quite believe what he's hearing. "Terminate – the Colonel?"

A shadowy civilian, presumably CIA, who has not yet spoken, clarifies the Colonel's intent with an even greater euphemism: "Terminate with extreme prejudice". Finally, Willard is assured that: "This operation does not exist, nor will it ever exist."

Sometimes rhetoric has to be used to cover up a truth which is unspeakable.

Although dialogue should be freed as far as possible from the burden of providing exposition, there are times when the audience just need to know stuff, and there's no other way around it.

When you're in this situation, make sure you've already created in the audience a desire to know. Never have your character volunteer information, or make it easy to discover. Make sure it's dragged screaming and kicking out of them, by someone whose job it is to find out.

Avoid above all having characters who know each other intimately explain to each other things they've talked about a million times before. When people know each other well, they don't explain more, they explain less. Everything is shorthand.

Don't ever offer up exposition to the audience on a plate. They'll feel they're being fed a line. Give your exposition a dramatic arc of its own, just as Tarantino did when he turned Mr Orange's training as an undercover cop into one funny anecdote.

CLOSE UP: JFK

JFK, Oliver Stone's story about District Attorney Jim Garrison's investigation into the assassination of President Kennedy, has an enormous amount of exposition. But it is never less than a hugely exciting thriller.

One key early scene demonstrates why. Garrison is in a restaurant surrounded by his aides, listening to a briefing on Lee Harvey Oswald, the man accused of killing Kennedy, who was shot and killed before he could face trial.

It's been difficult getting information from the authorities, a female aide reports, because so much of it has been classified as top secret. What she has learned seems to be full of contradictions. Oswald joins the Marines, yet he learns Russian and professes to being a Communist. He resigns from the Marines, flies to Russia and renounces his American citizenship. Information that he gives to the Russians is believed to have led to the shooting down of an American spy plane over Russia.

Yet when Oswald returns to America, he is not arrested; he is even allowed to bring his Russian sweetheart. He becomes close to the Russian exile community, all rabid anti-Communists. Despite his well-heeled connections, he gets a job working minimum-wage stacking books at the book depository. He buys a traceable gun, which a post mortem by the FBI shows no sign of having been used that day.

These are the facts, but what is the picture they produce? Was Oswald a double agent? Or was he working for the US Secret Services all along, as Garrison proposes? It is difficult, in one viewing, to keep the threads in your head. Nor are you meant to. We are always running just behind our ability to pull them together.

All we know is that the pattern of the Government's case has been ripped apart. There it stands, full of holes: its contradictions, half-truths and exclusions revealed to the world. Stone's method is to show us many different angles, many different viewpoints. The point of view is kaleidoscopic. It stretches as wide as possible, because if the conspiracy theorists are right, this is a deception on the whole of the American people.

In this sequence, the truth is like a jigsaw constructed from different media: stills, old news footage and Super 8, mixed with fragmentary dramatizations of Oswald's private and public life, snatched moments that feel as though we are intruding or spying on him.

In utter contrast are the stilted TV interviews with his wife, where she emotionlessly "buries" him, saying that she has enough "facts" to know he killed Kennedy.

If you're going to deliver exposition, *you need to dramatize it.* This variety of sources creates a curiosity in the audience. Which of these different versions of Oswald represent the "true" one?

As the conversation goes round the table, Garrison's inclination is to follow this thread to its logical conclusion, to look for the bigger picture, to consider the ultimate possibility: that the National Security apparatus was involved in the killing of their own President.

This seems so unbelievable that it is continually challenged by a skeptic on his team, an informer who we will later discover has been planted to sabotage the investigation. For the moment, he will do to express the audience's own skepticism. Is such a conspiracy really possible?

As Garrison gradually convinces his aides that "there's no smoke without fire", we intercut with the other montage that has, almost silently, run underneath this scene. It shows unidentified hands carefully cutting out the head and shoulders of Oswald, and placing them over the body of someone holding a rifle; the composite is then superimposed over the background of Oswald's house.

As the picture comes seamlessly together, we recognize it as the image from the iconic *Life* magazine front cover that portrayed Oswald as a gun-happy loner and misfit, who killed the President out of personal motives.

The photograph, Stone would have us believe, is a fake. No matter what the inconsistent truths of Kennedy's assassination, underneath it all Stone's montage makes one thing clear. The truth is easy to fake. It is easy to fool history – as easy as faking the cover itself.

"We're through the looking glass here, people," Garrison tells his team. "White is black, and black is white. Just maybe Oswald is exactly what he said he was. A patsy." We cut finally to the finished magazine cover, a defining image of that history.

While the montage of Oswald's life provides plenty of intriguing information, it is not where the heart of the scene lies. In any case, it's too much detail for anyone to keep in their heads.

That's because this is the **business** of the scene, meant to distract us. The heart of the scene is the deception happening, almost subliminally, before our eyes as the photograph is counterfeited and turned into the Big Lie.

To deliver exposition, you have to dramatize it. Don't leave it standing naked. Create a subterfuge, a smokescreen.

In *Eyes Wide Shut* Kubrick and fellow screenwriter Frederic Raphael use a similar technique, transforming an ordinary, even hackneyed scene into one that is strange and unforgettable.

Tom Cruise's character Bill has been introduced into an erotic secret society by his old friend Nick, whom he fears is now in danger. Bill calls into Nick's hotel. The receptionist, an obviously gay man, is very taken by Bill. He tell him that Nick checked out at five o'clock that morning. Bill looks surprised, and suggests that that's a pretty early check-out. The receptionist concedes that it is, and admits that there was something unusual about his departure. His face looked bruised, and he was escorted by two large, scary men who refused to allow him to pass on a message.

The receptionist draws out this conversation as long as possible, *teasing* it out in fact. The longer he can keep Bill here, the longer he can flirt with him, and his secret motives enjoyably complicate what otherwise would be an ordinary scene about extracting information, the kind we've seen in a thousand detective movies

The scene delivers the exposition, but as reluctantly as possible, cleverly disguised by the receptionist's sexual interest. The fact that he's flirting with Tom Cruise, the ultimate pin-up, only makes it more enjoyable.

As a device, **voiceover** should be approached with caution. It's all too easy to fall into the trap of "telling not showing", and audiences are suspicious and bored by information handed to them on a plate. However, voiceover can be used to deliver exposition, as we've seen in *JFK, as long as the audience are unaware it's happening*, their attention being drawn elsewhere.

Voiceover is more powerful, however, when used to provide a slant on events. When Woody Allen wryly comments on his own behavior, he is providing a subtext to his character's behavior on the screen. He is doing it just as much as in the scene between him and Annie Hall, in which their thoughts appear in subtitles on the screen. He's doing it, only less visibly.

Voiceover that is conversational has the knack of insinuating its way into our subconscious. Sometimes this is intentional, but sometimes it can misfire, as in the opening of Clint Eastwood's *Million Dollar Baby*. As we're being introduced to boxing trainer Frankie Dunn's world, Morgan Freeman's narration fills us in with lots of back story about Frankie. It's important character background, but too much to take in at this juncture, when there are many other interesting things to explore on the screen.

As in *Apocalypse Now*, **voiceover** works best as a counterpoint to the feelings exhibited on the screen. *Fight Club* does something similar. Constantly traveling in his job as a Product Recall Specialist for an automobile company, the unnamed narrator, played by Ed Norton, is constantly called on to make cost-benefit analyses of people's death and suffering to save his company money. Norton's character insulates himself from the painful reality of a life spent ignoring human feelings with the padding provided by the contents of the Ikea catalogue. Only, he cannot sleep; and when he asks his doctor for medication because he's suffering, his doctor tells him to drop by the testicular cancer support group to learn what real suffering is like.

To Norton's surprise, when a big-breasted "juicer" (a former steroids abuser) embraces him in a bear hug, he starts crying too. Suddenly he sleeps like a baby. He becomes addicted to support groups. "Every evening I died and every evening I was born again." It all gets ruined when Marla, another "fellow traveler" starts turning up in all the same groups. "Her lie reflected my lie, and suddenly I felt nothing."

Like Willard, Norton's character is cut off from his feelings, and can only feel when playing out a role. When Marla's presence makes him self-conscious, he can no longer lose himself in the part, and is stranded: neither in one world, nor another. "When you have insomnia, you're never really asleep, and you're never really awake."

As in *Apocalypse Now*, the cool, balanced nature of the voiceover in *Fight Club* is at odds with the increasingly disturbed state of the narrator. No wonder that when Norton finally grabs Marla and confronts her, she replies: "I saw you practicing this. Is it going as well as you hoped?"

Unable to live any longer through other people's pain and suffering, the narrator opts to go even further – by starting "Fight Club", a place where men beat each other with bare knuckles in order to enjoy the experience of being fully alive.

Like voiceover, **dialogue** can also be used either as a subterfuge for what is really going on in a scene, or as a counterbalance.

As we saw in *Hannah and Her Sisters*, what is most powerful is often what goes unsaid. There are times when you want to push this to the limit, by loading the emotional weight of the scene on to the person reacting. Normally, you want to beware of writing long speeches, because the longer people are talking, the longer the action stops. Sometimes, however, you will want to break this rule to build the power of the reaction. At these times you will want to draw attention to the texture of the dialogue and its rhetorical flourish.

I call these "one-sided scenes" rather than monologues because a mono-logue implies that a character has something to say, and doesn't much care about how others are reacting. In one-sided scenes the power is with the speaker, but the longer the listener can maintain their silence, the greater their power grows.

Tarantino is a fan of such moments. Jules's calculated rendering of Ezekiel in *Pulp Fiction* is designed to create terror in his victims, while Butch's avid attention as he listens to Christopher Walken's "shaggy dog story" about the watch justifies how all-important that watch will become for him once he grows up.

Tarantino pulls the same trick in *True Romance* when Cliff, the father of Clarence, is being tortured by some mafiosi from whom Clarence stole drugs, and who want to know his whereabouts. Cliff creates a one-sided moment, using the only power left to him – the power to provoke. He launches into a long speech about how centuries ago the Sicilians cross-bred with the Moors, giving them "nigger blood". The speech is calculated to offend to the point where he knows Coccotti, the boss, will fly off the handle. Cliff has calculated that he may not be able to withstand much more torture, and the best way for him to save his son is to provoke Coccotti to kill him.

In *Schindler's List*, SS Captain Goth has fallen in love with his Jewish maid, Maria. He descends to the wine cellar where she sleeps while a dinner party goes on upstairs. As she stands shivering in her slip, he questions whether the propaganda about Jews being vermin can be true. He wants to bridge the gulf between them.

She stands shivering, knowing that the slightest word, either of rejection or encouragement, could spell death. But the longer she says nothing, the more he is encouraged to open up, projecting her responses. Finally, convinced that she has tricked him into admitting too much of his feelings, he beats her furiously.

His actions are cross-cut with two parallel storylines. First, his caressing of Maria's face is counterpointed with a singer caressing Schindler's upstairs at the party. Then Goth's feet stamping on Maria are cross-cut with a secret wedding ceremony among the Jewish prisoners. At the iconic moment, the bride and groom seal their union by stamping on a light bulb concealed within a sheet.

Even in this place of hatred, love cannot be extinguished. But Goth is denied the possibility of ever having Maria's love because of the ideology he espouses. He can take her by force if he chooses; her power comes from withholding from him the one thing that matters to him: her love. Silence is not always a sign of weakness.

Just to prove this is so, screenwriter Steven Zaillian balances this scene with another, in which Maria voices her fears, and Schindler must listen.

Stanley Kubrick was a master of the one-sided scene. In *Dr Strangelove*, the President's embarrassing phone call to the Russian premier telling him that he has mistakenly launched a nuclear war is difficult enough without knowing that the Russian leader is drunk. Will the President be able to get through to him, and if he does, what will be his reaction? The suspense is enhanced by our seeing only one side of the phone call – and by the President knowing that every word of his is being overheard by fifty generals.

In *The Shining*, Jack Nicholson's character Jack Torrance has taken a caretaking job with his wife and son in a grand hotel during the off-season. Since it's far up in the mountains, he'll be able to avoid the temptation of liquor (he's on the wagon), and write his novel. However, his behavior grows increasingly erratic, and one night he finds himself alone in the empty grand ballroom. Magically all the lights come on, and behind the previously empty bar now stands a white-coated barman, in front of a bar stocked full of drinks.

Jack looks delighted. How's his credit here, he asks. His credit's just fine, the barman responds. Jack declares him to be the best bartender from Portland, Maine to Portland, Oregon. The bartender is the perfect foil for an alcoholic: dignified, subservient, provider of credit and a sympathetic ear for a drinker's stories. Is his tone just a little sarcastic, even condescending? Jack scarcely notices as, encouraged by the bartender's obsequiousness, he launches into a story.

He explains how one day, a couple of years ago, his son had thrown all his papers on the floor. He grabbed him by the arm and yanked him up, accidentally using "a few extra foot pounds of energy per second per second", and his wife has never let him forget it.

By the time Jack has finished this speech, we know that he is a fantasist who has the potential for psychopathic violence. The presence of the dignified and restrained bartender, though imaginary, encourages him to open up.

Recently restored to Kubrick's *Spartacus* is a scene which was banned from the film as originally released. The Roman senator Crassus (Laurence Olivier) is being bathed by his slave Antoninus (Tony Curtis). He asks him whether he eats oysters. "When I have them, master." Does he eat snails? "No, master." Does he consider the eating of oysters to be moral, while the eating of snails is immoral? "No, master." Crassus tries to convince him that it is only a matter of taste, and that he himself is partial to both snails and oysters. The whole conversation has a clear sexual subtext.

The interrogation itself is as slippery as an eel, as Crassus tries to back Antoninus into a corner where, once he agrees that love between men is only a matter of taste, he can logically give in to Crassus's seduction. Antoninus ducks and dives, trying to avoid being verbally pinned down.

As Crassus emerges from his bath, he looks out over the balcony at the Roman legions marching by. "Behold," he says, "the might, the majesty, the terror of Rome . . . No man can withstand Rome. No nation can withstand her. How much less . . . a boy!" As he turns to get Antoninus's agreement, he finds the slave has disappeared – run off to join the slave rebellion. Antoninus's silence speaks more loudly than words: by his example, he has shown why thousands of slaves will stand up to Rome.[61]

As already discussed, two-handed scenes can become relentlessly circular when there is no third corner of the triangle to deflect the tension, to distract or provide relief. However, this can be a very effective technique for representing how people get trapped in a relationship.

In *The Sheltering Sky*, Port and Kit, two intellectual New Yorkers, have just arrived in Tangiers along with their traveling companion Tunner. Port (John Malkovich) begins to relate a dream he has had about a train wreck. Kit tries to silence him, telling him what a bore other people's dreams are; but we sense that there is something in the dream which reflects her fears about her troubled marriage. Tunner, the third side of their **triangle**, eggs Port on, knowing that it will annoy Kit. Kit leaves the room, and while she is away Port explains that Kit has days when "everything in the world is merely a sign for something else. A white Mercedes can't just simply be a white Mercedes, it must have a secret meaning about the whole of life . . . Nothing can just *be* what it is." When Kit comes back in, she is wearing driving goggles, as if to keep this dark subconscious symbolism at bay.

Upstairs afterwards, the two lie in their conjoining rooms and Kit asks again why Port had to tell his dream in front of Tunner. She says she doesn't trust Tunner, and worries what people back in New York might think. Port asks: "What does it mean you don't trust him? That must mean something." She replies: "Of course I mean something, it just isn't important," and shuts the door on him.

Soon after, he comes into her room. "I think I'll go for a walk. Do you want to come?" She replies, "No thanks, I'm really enjoying this room after all that sea." He repeats exactly the same question; and she responds with exactly the same answer. He repeats his question for the third time, and she laughs. The tension has been broken.

Why does he keep repeating himself? Because this is a couple for whom surface words are no longer to be trusted. Everything has to have a deeper meaning. She asks if it isn't time for him to rub her tummy; but just as they're sharing an intimate moment, he can't resist asking her again, "What do you mean about not trusting Tunner?" Their tender moment is broken, because this couple cannot resist carrying on a circular conversation.

In *In the Mood for Love*, Chow and So, two neighbors whose spouses are having an affair with each other, rehearse the conversation So will have with her husband when she confronts him about his affair. She asks him again and again, and each time he denies it. Finally, he gives in and admits it. She flounces the air angrily. Chow tells her this is not a good enough reaction, and suggests they try again.

But when she challenges him more assertively, he confesses, and she bursts into tears. Chow consoles her by reminding her that this is just a rehearsal. But she never works up the courage to challenge her husband in reality, and so the relationship between Chow and So never goes anywhere.

This couple can only role-play their emotions; they can never express them, or break free of the social restraints that suffocate them, and so their dialogue remains resolutely circular. Only in Chow's martial arts stories, which So helps him with, can his characters live truly heroic lives, and move forward.

Of course, there *is* something heroic about Chow and So's restraint; and it's the taking of this normally passive quality to its limits that makes this an exceptional **Maverick** film.

CLOSE UP: BRICK

Not all dialogue aims at **transparency**. You can go to the other extreme and make the dialogue denser, deliberately drawing attention to it. This can be for a rhetorical flourish, as in Jules's recitation of Ezekiel in *Pulp Fiction*. Or it can be an overall **Maverick** approach that deliberately dislocates the audience, asking them to suspend their disbelief about the larger improbabilities of the story.

In *Clockwork Orange*, Alex and his "droogs" speak in a private lingo that is half-street slang, half-Slavic, while engaging in their favorite pastime of violence and rape ("the old in and out"). The density of the dialogue distances us from the violence (as does Alex's joyful accompaniment of "Singin' in the Rain") and allows us to see it as high opera. Making the violence slightly unreal puts it on a par with the experimental aversion therapy, in which we must also believe in order to be convinced that Alex can be "cured". Alex's ironic **voiceover**, full of bravado, gives us the illusion of knowing what he thinks, while serving as a mask behind which he can fool everybody.

In *Brick*, a contemporary **film noir** set in a high school, the characters also speak their own lingo which is part street slang, part Dashiel Hammett. In a world in which adults are almost completely absent, this slang is a metaphor for the secret language which every generation of teenagers makes up for itself, so they cannot be understood by adults.

Unlike in *Clockwork Orange*, where the ornate language veils a threat of violence, in *Brick* the tough-guy language disguises the vulnerable teenager hiding behind it.

The strangely formal and worldly-wise language of *Brick* distances us from the reality: that these are teenagers living out a **film noir** plot, regarding life or death problems as the norm. At the same time, they also represent familiar "types". Brendan, the wounded hero, eats his lunch alone at the back of school while judging everybody. The Brain, his sidekick with oversized glasses who runs "ops", can polish off a Rubik's cube while working his brain so hard the words can hardly keep up with it:

> THE BRAIN
>
> Ask any dope rat where their junk sprang they'll say they scraped it from that who scored it from this who bought it off so, and after four or five connections the list'll always end with the Pin. But I'll betcha you got every rat in town together and said "show your hands" if any of them've actually seen the Pin, you'd get a crowd of full pockets.

The confidence with which the dialogue is delivered ensures that we don't question the likelihood of what he is saying too much.

Brendan, on the other hand, is all intensity. He warns Laura, who befriended his former girlfriend Emily, who has been murdered:

> BRENDAN
>
> I can't trust you. Brad was a sap, you weren't, you were with him and so you

```
were playing him, so you're a player.
With you behind me I'd have to tie one
eye up watching both your hands, and I
can't spare it.
```

The density of Brendan's language perfectly expresses the struggle of someone trying to find their way through a world of murky motives and double crosses, just as in all great **films noirs**. We're running behind, trying to keep up with Brendan's inexorable logic, but we're less interested in the intricacies of the plot than the emotions the characters are running. With adults – and the perspective they provide – largely absent, the usual turmoil of teenage lives is elevated to one of tortured emotions and dark complexity.

Some of the most powerful moments come after we have forgotten these are teenagers, and are startled to be reminded. Brendan goes in search of the Pin, the drug baron whom Emily mentioned before she died. He gets taken to the Pin's house, where he is badly beaten in the basement by Tug, the Pin's "muscle".

Shortly after, the Pin allows him upstairs, where they assemble in the kitchen, overseen by the Pin's (entirely oblivious) mother.

```
INT. KITCHEN — DAY
Brendan sits at a breakfast table eating
cornflakes. The kitchen is on the first
floor of the Pin's house, or rather the
Pin's mother's house. She is a soft old
lady in a pastel cotton dress, currently
bent over the fridge, mumbling.

              MOTHER
I thought we had orange juice, Brendan,
I'm sorry. How about Tang, or that's more
like soda isn't it, or not soda but it
hasn't got any juice in it, it can't be
very fortifying.
```

> BRENDAN
>
> Water's fine, ma'am, thanks.
>
> MOTHER
>
> Now just a moment, we have apple juice
> here, if you'd like that, or milk, though
> you've got that in your cornflakes, I
> don't know if drinking it as well might
> be too much.
>
> BRENDAN
>
> Apple juice sounds terrific.
>
> MOTHER
>
> It's country style.
>
> BRENDAN
>
> That's perfect.

Suddenly, they have reverted to the banality of teenage conversation in front of adults. For the moment, they are just three teenagers acting polite to Pin's mom, hoping she will leave and let them have their fun. She is rabbiting on and on, as moms seem to do when you're dying to be alone.

The boys have got more important things on their minds than cornflakes, but on the other hand, Brendan's just had a beating, so he needs the sustenance, and he munches throughout the scene. The scene continues:

> *She shuts the fridge. Tugger and the Pin*
> *sit behind her, looking comfortably bored.*
> *The Pin, a sharp black hole against the*
> *soft yellow kitchen, eats oatmeal cookies*
> *with small delicate bites.*
>
> MOTHER
>
> I'll even give it to you in a country
> glass, how'd that be? Boys?

> TUGGER
> I'm fine, Mrs M.

> PIN
> Thanks, mom.

> *The Pin kisses her on the cheek.*

> MOTHER
> Okay, well I'm going to go, um, do
> something in the other room now . . .

> *She shuffles out.*

For all the tension and embarrassment created by the situation, the Pin's mom may as well be leaving him alone with a new girlfriend. Suddenly, the spell is broken and we are back to **film noir**:

> PIN
> (*to Brendan*)
> So hows bout we take another snap at
> hearing your tale?

> BRENDAN
> I don't know. It starts out same as
> before, and this floor ain't carpeted.

> PIN
> We're cooled off.

> BRENDAN
> Yeah well, your muscle seemed plenty cool
> putting his fist in my head. I want him
> out.

> *The Pin grins thinly, uncomfortable.*

> PIN
> Looky, soldier —

> BRENDAN
> The ape blows or I clam.

The shock as we slam back into the murky world of the Pin is all the greater because we've forgotten for a moment that the stakes are high, and Brendan's bruises are real.

Brendan offers his services. The Pin responds: "I'll have my boys check your tale, and seeing how it stretches, we'll either rub or hire you." This wise-guy dialogue reflects a disturbing world-weariness reminding us that children have more sophisticated emotions than we sometimes give them credit for.

There is something quite shocking about young people who carry the burden of the world upon them. So these moments of **transparency** – when we are reminded that we are watching children – are deeply disturbing.

And if you are going to pay homage to the chewed-up feelings of **film noir**, where better to set it than in a high school, with its over-the-top emotion, rivalries and cliques?

The trick of the film and its extraordinary idiom is to distract us from the challenge of believing that teenagers live in a world of darkness and danger in which adults have no place. Of course, that *is* the way many teenagers regard their lives. But as with many **Maverick** concepts, the trick of *Brick* is to take this concept all the way.

In doing so, *Brick* elevates the teenage movie to a level of emotional complexity that reminds us why these years are often the most vital of our lives.

CLOSE UP: PRIMER

In *Brick*, the artificial language is meant to distract us from the trick that is being played on us: that these are kids, lost in a deadly **film noir**. If we can buy the dialogue, we will buy everything else.

In *Primer*, the scientific jargon used by two young entrepreneurs who develop an extraordinary new technology lends validity to an invention which appears to break the normal rules of physics. By creating a smokescreen of **dense dialogue** they increase the mystery and suspense.

What is this invention, and what is it good for? Most importantly, what effect will its discovery have on our heroes? Answering these questions, not necessarily following the **plot**, are what is important in this film.

Primer, Shane Carruth's debut, is a great example of what you can do with $7,000 if you keep your focus tight, and imply far more than you reveal – particularly if you're writing science fiction, usually the most expensive of genres.

Abe and Aaron run a small start-up research company in their garage, funded by their cash line of custom circuit boards. After a disagreement with their two partners, the two work on a "box" which creates its own energy, and accelerates time. They decide not to share this discovery with their partners; but tell them that the garage is being fumigated.

Right from the beginning, Carruth does not try to explain too much. When Aaron realizes the box seems to be creating more energy than is fed into it, he demonstrates to Abe:

> AARON
>
> It's growing with its own momentum. It's like a feedback loop and it just regulates itself, and what you do is, when it gets

```
there you bring it back . . . (He adjusts
a dial.) and there you go, it coasts.
It's stable. It stays like that.

                    ABE
So it works?
```

The brilliance of *Primer* is the mystery at its heart, and everything that it may imply. Although we may not be able to grasp the science, we can certainly understand the ethical and character issues it raises for the two young entrepreneurs. Like the discovery of the portal for Craig in *Being John Malkovich*, the mind-bending possibilities created by the box, along with its moral implications, test Abe and Aaron to their limits.

They adjourn to a restaurant for a celebratory dinner, where at first the possibilities seem endless:

```
              AARON (V.O.)
There was value in the thing clearly,
that they were certain of. But what is
the application? In a matter of hours,
they had written it to everything from
mass transit to satellite launching,
imagining devices the size of jumbo
jets. Everything would be cheaper. It
was practical and they knew it, but above
all that — beyond the positives — they
knew that the easiest way to be exploited
would be to sell something that they did
not yet understand. So they kept quiet.
```

Without telling Aaron, Abe constructs a larger box in a storage facility – large enough for a person to fit inside. He drives Aaron to the storage facility where he sees Abe's double – Abe entered the box earlier – leaving the building. Soon Abe and Aaron are using the window provided by the time machine to make money on the stock market.

However, this raises all kinds of problems about causality, which Abe and Aaron try to solve by locking themselves in a hotel room, watching football games they already know the results to, and mentally juggling their existential status. ("Are you hungry? I haven't eaten anything since later this afternoon.") However, when Aaron forgets to turn his phone off, and answers it, they have quickly to assess the consequences:

> ABE
> How do cell phones work? If there's two
> duplicate phones and I call the same
> number, do they both ring at the same
> time or is there . . . ?

> AARON
> That's not how it'll work.

> ABE
> It's a radio signal –

> AARON
> No, it's a network. The network checks
> each area. When it finds a phone it stops
> ringing. It rings the first one.

> ABE
> This one's ringing.

> AARON
> Right.

> ABE
> So the one your double has in Ruttlefield
> can't be.

> AARON
> Right. I think we broke symmetry.

> ABE
> Are you sure that's how cell phones work?

> AARON
>
> No.

> ABE
>
> Do you feel alright?

> AARON
>
> I feel fine. Do you?

They begin experiencing strange symptoms: their handwriting goes all weird, and Aaron begins to bleed from the ears:

> AARON
>
> Is that normal? This isn't normal!

> ABE
>
> For the machine?

> AARON
>
> No, for people! You think it's the machine?

Aaron and Abe's understanding of the implications runs far behind their hubris, the temptation to play God. Carruth wants to give the audience the same experience by using dialogue that continually keeps the audience at a distance, struggling to keep up with events.

Unlike in mainstream movies, the technical jargon makes few concessions to the lay audience, creating a rare sense of realism, but also a mystery, for them. Because our heroes, in spite of their superior position, are themselves improvising and taking leaps in the dark.

Primer keeps the audience on the outside, listening in on half-heard conversations, or conversations that we jump into the middle of, or that are running in a loop.

Soon, Aaron is trying out a new application of the invention for his own personal ends. He intends to go back in time to change an event that happened at a party given by Rachel Granger, the daughter of a financier Aaron and Abe are hoping will fund their project. At the party, an "ex" of Rachel's threatened her with a shotgun. Aaron wants to make sure that the next time around he will be arrested, and that Aaron will get the credit (and presumably Granger's funding).

In order to set this up, Aaron begins taping all his conversations, then climbs in the box and replays his day, staying one step ahead of the game by playing these conversations through his headphones, and giving himself a few seconds lead.

Aaron describes the feeling of power this gives him: "He had but to speak aloud the words that came into his head and those around him would fall in line." Like Phil in *Groundhog Day*, he has become godlike, directing events and turning them to his advantage.

When Abe tries to talk him out of his plan, Aaron insists: "We know everything – we're prescient."

Aaron keeps running the night of the party until he gets it right. "What the world remembers – the actuality – the last revision – is what counts, apparently . . . slowly, methodically, he reverse engineered a perfect moment."

Unlike Lester's in *American Beauty*, this "perfect moment" is not a liberation but something that drives a wedge between the partners, for whom the risks and complications are becoming overwhelming.

Soon Aaron's life is taken over by a previous version of himself; and he is forced to go abroad. In the coda, we see Aaron, in a factory warehouse, presumably in France, preparing to build a bigger box.

At the end of the film, we realize that Aaron has been providing the narration (not immediately obvious, since he refers to himself in the third person, since he is now talking about an earlier "version" of himself). This expresses perfectly the dislocation which Aaron's abuse of the laws of time and space have caused to his psyche.

Abe and Aaron are swept along by the process of discovery while at the same time standing apart from it. Like Phil, in *Groundhog Day*, emotionally their story is moving forward, no matter that they are moving backwards, or in an endless loop, in the attempt to control time and destiny. Like Craig in *Being John Malkovich*, who discovers the futility of seeking self-fulfillment by adopting someone else's identity, Aaron learns there is no point in controlling destiny if you have to give up your identity in the process.

Turn your characters' fantasies into their greatest nightmares by taking them to the limit.

> AARON
> What is your opinion on how safe this is?
>
> ABE
> Aaron, I can imagine no way in which this thing can be considered anywhere remotely close to safe.

MAVERICK DIALOGUE
Recap

* Good dialogue has **subtext**, the sense that what the characters are thinking or feeling is at odds with what they are saying.

* In bad films, characters endlessly tell us how they feel, known as "writing on the nose".

* Actions count louder than words.

* Every dialogue scene is 50 percent reaction. You need to write the reaction, whether it be spoken or unspoken.

* It's important to keep the action going in dialogue scenes – even when nothing much is happening. Without visual cues, it is difficult to judge the sincerity of the lines spoken.

* Write only action that has a narrative purpose, dramatizing the **subtext** of your story.

* Make sure the subtext breaks out to the surface.

* Avoid writing perfect speech and syntax: mimic the patterns of spoken language, which follows the rhythms of breath rather than the dictates of grammar.

* Imitate the pattern of real speech, not its randomness. Order is created by a constant see-sawing of action and reaction, which gives momentum to the scene.

* It is the variation in these beats, their modulation in tone and intensity, that creates texture in a scene.

* In order for your dialogue to sound spontaneous, it has to be freed as far as possible from the task of telling the story.

* Work out your story in detail before you write a word of dialogue.

* If you know where every scene is going before you start writing your script, you free the dialogue from the burden of carrying the story. Now it

becomes free to provide color, wit and emotion – to react to events rather than to prompt or describe them.

* Whenever a character tells us what is going to happen, make sure that something else happens instead.

* It's not always appropriate for dialogue to feel spontaneous. Sometimes it needs a rhetorical flourish. It has to be self-aware, because it's there to serve a purpose. Sometimes it acts as a subterfuge.

* Create in the audience a *desire to know*. Never have your character volunteer information, or make it easy to discover.

* When people know each other well, they don't explain more, they explain less.

* To deliver exposition, you have to dramatize it. Don't leave it standing naked. Create a subterfuge, a smokescreen.

* **Voiceover** is most powerful when not being used to feed us information but to provide a slant on events.

* **Voiceover** works best as a counterpoint to the feelings exhibited on the screen.

Exercises

○ Write a scene between two people in which one knows something about a third person that the other doesn't. Use the revelation of this knowledge to turn the scene. (Note: you are creating a **triangle**, regardless of whether the third person is in the scene or not.)

○ Write a scene in which one person is doing most of the talking while the other is simply reacting. Show how the power gradually shifts to the person reacting.

○ Write out a scene in which your hero is almost caught out in a lie, but has to improvise. Make the lie become more elaborate and far-fetched until the logic can no longer be sustained.

○ Your character is giving a formal speech or presentation. They drop their notes, or the power goes out, or they are interrupted – and now they have to improvise. Show how their true character is revealed.

○ Write a conversation between two people who know each other well, or who use a private language, or one that is unique to their trade. Have them discuss a problem in a way that allows the audience to share in the suspense, without necessarily understanding what it means.

○ Choose a favorite dialogue scene from a film you like. You are now going to rewrite the scene twice, but without, in either case, changing any of the beats in the scene. First write it at twice the length. Then rewrite it at half the length of the original. Which works better? The longer dialogue scene will tend to reduce the suspense; while the shorter version will often drain it of color. What makes the original work so well?

Section 6
Everything connects

12 The matrix

*One clear and simple theme to rule them all,
and in the darkness bind them.*[62]

© Josh Golding

Part One

Location and setting

All too often, screenwriters treat the settings of their stories as though they were empty landscapes or warehouses to be filled with people talking. Or they may paint a picture of their favorite childhood haunt, in the hope that it will be re-created down to the very last detail. Alternatively, they may feel that this is not their job, and leave it up to the director.

If they do so, they are leaving out one of the most important dimensions for a screenwriter. That doesn't mean you are given a license to paint pretty pictures or describe the wallpaper (unless you're planning to rip the wallpaper off in the next act to reveal a listening device).

In other words, **setting** doesn't exist simply to provide a space where things can happen. The right setting for a scene is one which resonates with the characters inhabiting it: either as a reflection of some aspect of themselves, or as a symbol of everything they want to kick against. Sometimes the setting will give us an insight into an unrevealed aspect of our character. This will create an interesting conflict between the image the character tries to project, and what the subtext in the setting reveals.

The lazy writer will describe a location as if punching in the numbers. If they're a party animal, there will be a cocktail bar. If they're fashionable, the furniture will be ultra-modern. Or minimalist. Or bright orange. Everything is simply a reflection of what we already know rather than revealing new layers of the onion skin.

How much more interesting if that redneck we meet in his beat-up pick-up truck turns out to have a trailer home that's meticulously neat? If the tools in his workshop are squared away and ship-shape? If he spends an obsessively long time sharpening his collection of hunting knives?

Location is there to provide an extra dimension, not just reflect what we know already about a character. It is a reflection of their hopes, dreams or frustrations. It reflects everything that we *can't* see, and that's what makes it satisfying.

It's what you *do* with the location that counts, not relying on the connotations that you think a place brings with it, all wrapped up in a cellophane package. A gothic haunted house is a cliché, but in *Psycho* it stands in eerie contrast with the bland anonymity of Bates's motel, and is a projection of the darker half of his split personality.

When Will Munny (Clint Eastwood) wakes from his long fever in *Unforgiven*, he looks around him at the frozen but awe-inspiring mountains and declares he "wouldn't normally pay no notice to high country like this, trees, but I'm sure noticing them now . . . I thought I was dying for sure." It's a sight that reflects his joy in being alive. The landscape is no longer just a pretty backdrop: it's a setting that Munny engages with as he's never done before.

In *Apocalypse Now*, Willard decides to accompany crew member "Chef" Hicks, who wants to take a short jaunt through the jungle to pick some mangoes. The jungle is primeval, dwarfing the two men beneath giant trees with roots that have to be clambered over and ferns that tower over their heads.

As they pick their way through the dense greenery, Hicks explains how in civilian life he was a *saucier*, a chef specializing in sauces. After being drafted, he joined the catering corps, and was appalled to see beautiful prime rib being boiled in giant vats. As he shakes his head over this painful memory, he notices Willard has stopped and is listening.

Willard moves forward silently, every sense alert to the sounds and movements of the jungle, while Hicks looks about him in confusion. "What is it? Charlie?" A tiger leaps out of the undergrowth straight at them – but not before Willard lets off a hail of bullets.

As they hurry back to their patrol boat the crew are already at battle stations, having heard the gunfire. As Willard and Hicks board, the young crew panic, firing off multiple rounds in every direction at the unseen enemy.

In this scene the enormous gap in preparedness between Willard, a seasoned Special Forces officer, and his unseasoned crew is brilliantly dramatized. Hicks's dream of being a *saucier* appears ludicrously out of place in this environment, a jungle so forbidding that humans seem out of scale here, as though they don't belong – just like the Americans don't belong in Vietnam, fighting a peasant army halfway across the world. Yet every day young American soldiers are beings ground up by the war machine, just like that boiled beef.

Yet Willard is an exceptional character. He knows this jungle, seems almost to merge with it, every sense alive to its nuances, alert to its millions of sounds and meanings.

The scene represents not just a scenic detour, but a brilliant exposition of character, and dramatically raises the stakes. By the end of it we know that Willard is alert to the dangers he faces, while the rest of the crew are hopelessly unprepared.

It is how we *react* to our environment that matters.

In *Dersu Uzala*, Kurosawa's only film made outside Japan, Captain Arseniev, a Russian officer, has been sent on an expedition to survey the Siberian wilderness, and has hired Dersu Uzala, a local native, to guide his company of soldiers.

One day the two of them set out alone across the frozen tundra on a recce. The horizon is limitless and flat, dazzling in the sun. As they progress, however, the normally adept guide appears troubled. The sun has melted new waterways in the ice, blocking off their advance and retreat. Finally, Dersu announces that they are lost, and that their situation is dangerous. Arseniev fires off a couple of rounds from his rifle, but gets no response.

Dersu tells the Captain that they must work quickly, gathering the marsh grass, or they will freeze to death. The thin reeds that encircle them seem as though they could scarcely offer any protection, but the two set to work with their knives. As they do so, the wind picks up and the sun begins to sink on the horizon. Suddenly, the landscape turns harsh and forbidding.

They gather the reeds in a growing pile, but now the wind is blowing up a gale, and Arseniev is forced to hurl himself on the pile while Dersu secures it with ropes. As the Captain goes in search of more rope, the howling wind and encroaching darkness make visibility almost impossible. Exhausted, he collapses, dead to the world. When he wakes, he is inside the snug that Dersu has created out of the reeds. Dersu lights a match and squeezes in with him.

This scene illustrates the second principle of setting. A good setting is one in which you use everything – and in this case, Dersu *literally* uses everything – no matter how barren the tundra at first sight might seem.

The scene is not only a brilliant piece of action in which its two characters escape seemingly certain death, it establishes the essence of what the relationship between Dersu and the Captain will become. In spite of their differences in background and education, their friendship will develop a rare intimacy and mutual dependence.

In *The Third Man* Holly Martins, a writer, has come to war-devastated Vienna on the offer of work from an old friend, Harry Lime. To his shock, he discovers that Harry has recently died, but later discovers that Harry has faked his death in order to avoid the consequences of his black-marketeering in fake pharmaceutical drugs, which has led to a number of children's deaths.

Finally Holly tracks Harry down and arranges to meet him at a funfair. The funfair is desolate and run-down. No one has any money for anything other than survival in Vienna.

As they hop into a cabin on the Ferris wheel, Harry dismisses Holly's concerns and offers to bring him in on his racket. Looking down on the tiny dots below, Harry questions whether he would really turn down money "if one of those dots stopped moving forever". When he discovers that Holly has been to the police, Harry pulls open the door and threatens to hurl Holly through it. But Holly vows to put up a fight, and Harry pretends it's all a joke and reminisces about their long friendship, a friendship in which,

Holly reminds him, he usually ended up getting caught while Harry always got away.

Throughout this scene, the compartment of the Ferris wheel takes on many associations. At one point, it is a reminder of the childhood memories they share; at another, it is a metaphor for the godlike point of view which Harry assumes, oblivious to the consequences for the tiny people below. Then it is a flimsy death trap which holds Holly one step from oblivion.

As Harry sentimentally spells out the name of the girl he has just betrayed in the condensation on the window, it becomes a symbol of the transitory nature of his affections, which can be wiped out whenever he feels the need. Finally, as they return to the ground again, having completed a circle (as befits a two-handed scene) it comes to represent their friendship, which neither can escape. They know each other too well.

In *Withnail and I*, two penniless would-be actors are struggling to survive in sixties London.

Early in the film the two return from breakfast in a café to the flat they share, still drunk and drugged from the night before. The flat is dark and dingy, but signs of its former eminence can just be made out. This was once an elegant apartment, with ornate wallpaper and portraits on the walls, perhaps belonging to some titled relative of Withnail's.

Paul McGann's character, "I", goes to fetch some coffee from the filthy kitchen. Lacking a clean cup, he pours some cold coffee into a soup bowl. Withnail demands to know why he hasn't been given soup too. McGann asks him why he doesn't do the washing up occasionally, like a normal human being. 'How dare you call me inhumane?' Withnail demands haughtily, before threatening to do the washing up. The tiny kitchenette is piled high with dirty dishes, and 'I' warns him that something may be living there. As Withnail arms himself with pliers, his greatest fear is that the 'dinner service' will be ruined.

We quickly realize that while they are living in the utmost filth and penury, Withnail is clinging to the illusion that he is superior to his circumstances. The subtle use of this formerly grand setting adds a humorous dimension to the pretensions of the character – pretensions that will be his downfall. In the end it will be "I" who moves on, taking his first step on the acting ladder.

In the opening narration of *Manhattan*, a writer struggles to find the right words to describe the city. "To him, New York meant beautiful women and street-smart guys who seemed to know all the angles." He rejects this as too corny. He decides to make it more profound: "He adored New York City. To him, it was a metaphor for the decay of contemporary culture." Too "preachy". The next opening, deriding a culture "desensitized by drugs, loud music, television, crime, garbage", is "too angry". Then: "He was as tough and romantic as the city he loved" strikes the right note. "Behind his black-rimmed glasses was the coiled sexual power of a jungle cat." Throughout all this we intercut with street scenes. At some points, these seem to chime with his words, at others to be random or to contradict them.

Finally, against a spectacular aerial view of the Dodger stadium with fireworks lighting up the sky, the writer enthuses: "New York was his town – and it always would be."

Nothing could illustrate more clearly that the city, like all locations, is a metaphor for whatever you want it to be.

The opening of *The Jazz Singer*, made in 1927, describes a New York ghetto, crowded with vendors and pushcarts. The description adds: "In the distance is seen an elevated train flashing across the background like a comet across the sky."

These words tell us everything we need to know about the working-class neighborhood it describes, a world in which prosperity and progress, though visible, remain tantalizingly out of reach.

The setting of your film is about far more than location. It's not wise to get too attached to particular locations anyway, since it's unlikely that, when your film gets made, you will get exactly what you dreamed of. The test of your screenplay is whether it can survive that transition.

I once made a film set in Thailand and Vietnam. The only problem was that neither government wanted us to film there; so we ended up having to shoot it in the Philippines. The Philippines doesn't look particularly like either of those other places, just because it's in the same part of the world. We went to a lot of trouble to ensure that the look was authentic, surreptitiously shooting documentary footage in the real countries and mixing it with footage from the Philippines. No one even noticed that the cars were driving on the wrong side of the road.

One of my favorite scenes was shot in two countries: on one side was Bangkok's worst hotel band playing Western pop songs out of tempo and out of tune – striking a discordant note for our hero, who is getting increasingly out of his depth in a culture he does not understand. He and the other actors were actually seated a thousand miles away, on a piece of scrubland where we had set up some tables, strung up some fairy lights, and adjusted the lens to deep focus. They matched perfectly. That is the magic of cinema.

One night we were setting up a scene where the two leads, a married couple, were enjoying a loving reunion at a street café. As they fed each other with noodles, a magnificent and completely unexpected fireworks display exploded in the background, "Turn over!" I cried, knowing that in the next scene we cut to, they would be making love. Every film should be alive to the possibilities that will be thrown up by your actual location.

Nevertheless, in a memo to a producer in the twenties, a studio manager barked: "A rock is a rock; a tree is a tree – shoot it in Griffiths Park!"[63] (Griffiths Park is a municipal park in Los Angeles.)

If you are determined that your scene be set against the backdrop of the Arc de Triomphe or the Empire State Building, don't be surprised if you find your production manager pulling her hair out. You also run the risk of what I call "movie tourism", making a shot just because it's an "iconic" location.

If you're going to do so, you'd better make sure that you're using it – as does *King Kong* – in a way that no one has ever done before.

In *The Day After Tomorrow*, a superstorm triggers a global deep freeze. Several of the characters take refuge in the New York Public Library, where they are forced to burn books to stay alive. Finally, the inevitable dilemma arrives: with only a few books left, should they burn one of the last remaining copies of the Gutenberg Bible?

The scene not only answers the question posed by all great dramatic situations – how far is your character prepared to go? – but also the question which should be posed by every setting: how are they going to use whatever is available in their environment in order to achieve their goal?

Hitchcock started *North by Northwest* with the notion that he wanted to have a chase across the face of the Presidents' Monument – and built the story backward from that end point. He knew that a spy story which pursued its hero across one of the most sacred icons of the United States would strike fear into the heart of its audience, for it would signal to them that far-off countries might one day pose a threat. No wonder the 9/11 terrorists chose such iconic symbols of America as their targets.

In the event Hitch was denied permission to film at the Monument – and ended up having to re-create it at considerable cost!

Never get attached to locations. A well-written film does not rely on them, anyway. Instead, it creates a network of associations that resonate with each other, connecting **character**, **plot** and **theme**, which I call the **matrix**.

Part Two
The matrix

© J. Hasson

Every city holds a million metaphors. It is up to you, the screenwriter, to decide what story your setting has to tell. To do that, you have to start thinking beyond individual locations, to creating a **matrix** that will weave together your **plot**, **character** and **theme**.

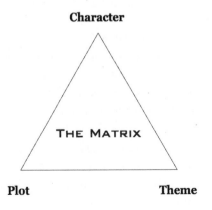

Character

THE MATRIX

Plot   **Theme**

The **matrix** combines visual and verbal metaphors into an intricate circuit in which each image connects with and illuminates the next.

To understand what I mean by this, consider the words which you use to describe your own experience of life. Do you say that things are "drifting along", or are "in a rut", or a "constant buzz"? Is your life a "roller coaster"?

Consider now how you might use **setting** to dramatize this. Should you follow *The Third Man* and set your scene in an amusement park (but remember that no one ever shot a funfair that way – or with that sort of desolate feeling – before)? Don't use setting just to remind us of what we already know.

Instead, you need to find the **images** in your world that evoke those feelings. And naturally, you're going to drive the **plot** in such a way that it forces your **character** to encounter and resonate with those images.

When you see a good movie you walk out at the end and feel: "Wow, wasn't it great the way that all hung together!" We may not know how or why, but somehow we feel that everything *connects*. Nothing was superfluous or unresolved. Everything came to have a meaning that elaborated the theme.

The longer I've been editing scripts, the more I've become convinced that stories which have too many themes don't work. They become an intellectual exercise in which two-dimensional characters stand in for ideas, and every idea jostles for space, competing for breathing room.

A **theme** represents an idea about the world: love conquers all, power corrupts, you're never too old to live your dream. Of course, how true these are depends on the circumstances and the nature of your character. A good film takes a universal theme and tests it, exploring it from every possible angle. It builds an ensemble on the same basis that you'd put together a dinner party. You want everyone to have a different opinion about whatever is being discussed, to react differently to it.

Shakespeare knew that in order to keep the public happy you had to offer a change of mood in the subplots: you had to bring on the lovers or the fool for light relief – or if you wanted to darken the mood, plotters or witches. The subplots provide a change of tone or tempo, and let in some air.

In addition, they provide a different way of looking at the protagonist – a window into his soul which the main plot cannot reveal. That's why we show the hero with his best buddy or his wife, even if the main setting is his workplace. He's not going to show who he is at work!

Most importantly, the subplots provide their own variation on the theme. If your story is about star-crossed lovers struggling against their families, have another subplot in which a couple face the tragic consequences of a similar rebellion; and maybe a second, about two elderly relatives who never dared declare their love, and have always regretted it. Now we will understand what is at stake for our protagonists.

Remember that drama is about the conflict between two powerful ideas about the world. In *Romeo and Juliet* these might be described as "people should be free to love as they choose" vs "choosing love over family is too high a price to pay". As the writer, you may have an opinion about that, but if you load the dice in favor of one point of view you will kill suspense stone dead. You need to keep the outcome in doubt to the very end. (This is probably the single most common failing of the scripts I read.)

The audience don't want to know how your story is going to turn out – so having subplots which suggest different outcomes keeps the audience guessing.

How your **main plot** turns out will decide which of these ideas – or value systems – is the ultimate victor, because that is the storyline in which we have the most investment. It tells us what, in these circumstances, holds most true: the **dominant value** of the film.

But the **subplots** have an influence too. Now, more than ever, movies have victories which come at a cost, or turn out to be worth less than we thought. We live in a complicated world, and we mistrust simple solutions. Your subplots can carry the darker reverberations which are not resolved by the main story; or the gleam of hope which reassures us that the hero's death was not in vain. They provide us with a more nuanced **matrix**.

At the end of *One Flew Over the Cuckoo's Nest*, McMurphy lies comatose after receiving a frontal lobotomy, a crude operation once used for controlling violent mental patients. He has been defeated by the system, because one person alone cannot change it. On rare occasions they can, of course – a Gandhi, a Martin Luther King, a Nelson Mandela. But they are exceptional people, and McMurphy is not.

Although McMurphy has been defeated, he has inspired the Chief to rebel. The Chief, a Native American, stands for all those who have knowingly imprisoned themselves: for years he has pretended to be deaf and dumb because he cannot cope with the outside world which has torn him from his roots. A towering giant, he has no idea of his own strength, in every sense, until McMurphy comes along. McMurphy convinces him that he is capable of anything.

Before he escapes from the institution, the Chief extinguishes McMurphy's diminished life with a pillow, to free his spirit. For McMurphy has taught him that we cannot be imprisoned as long as our spirits are free.

The conflict between freedom of spirit and the narrow-minded system is **the matrix** of the film. There is not a scene in the film which does not reflect this struggle.

I've discussed how the plot and subplots can play out variations on the theme. But that is only one dimension of a film. The others are **visual** and **verbal**. How the theme is reflected in the world around your characters and what **metaphors** they use to describe that world all link into the **matrix**. It is only when all work together simultaneously that your story is charged and fully connected.

It would be nice if you could figure out the weaving together of **plot**, **character** and **theme** in the matrix before you wrote a word of your screenplay. But in my experience it doesn't usually happen that way.

Often you will use a detail without really understanding why. When you reread what you have written, you will find that this image stands out in your story, it carries extra weight. You may find that you can draw a thread through the story, connecting this image with something else which resonates with it, repeating it – but never in the same way twice.

To uncover the deepest meaning of your story you need to think which images best apply to your characters and their preoccupations, what metaphors they use to describe their lives. After all, these characters have leapt from your subconscious because they mean something important to *you*.

The imagery of the film has to be mirrored in the action and dialogue, or it will have a decorative function only, like wallpaper. This often happens when the screenwriter has failed to create a coherent **matrix**, forcing the director to resort to **symbolism**. Symbols are things which have associations that are *external* to your story, and rarely work in films.

The **matrix** works best when it is nearly subliminal – something we catch out of the corner of our eye. **Symbols** are like neon signs, demanding our attention, while obscuring what lies beyond.

It is the interweaving of **action**, **dialogue** and **theme** which raises symbolism to the level of **metaphor**. Without it, your story is not truly cinematic.

Contrary to the notions of auterism, the **matrix** is something created by the *writer*. If you are lucky, the director will expand on it, enhance it in detail and intensity, and give it an extra visual dimension. But without the thought that you put into it, the director has nothing to build on.

Steven Zaillian's script for *Schindler's List* opens with the apparently innocent, but highly evocative lines:

> TRAIN WHEELS grinding against track,
> slowing. FOLDING TABLE LEGS scissoring
> open. The LEVER of a train door being
> pulled. NAMES on lists on clipboards.

The banality of everyday bureaucracy continues, as Jewish forced refugees alight from the train and form into orderly queues:

> HANDS straightening pens and pencils
> and ink pads and stamps.

Finally taking on a sinister tone:

> TYPEWRITER KEYS rapping a name onto a
> list. A FACE. KEYS typing another name.
> Another FACE.

And gradually we realize this list is the beginning of the process that will turn Jews into faceless numbers, to be worked to death – or worse. The details – the pens, pads and typewriter keys – tell the story of organized genocide. But they also foreshadow the salvation that is to come: Schindler's own list, which will save hundreds of Jewish lives. In *Schindler's List*, everything connects.

In *Being John Malkovich*, Craig uncomplainingly shares their apartment with Lottie's menagerie of rescued animals. They are clearly child substitutes for Lottie, who takes her chimp to a therapist to sort out its "childhood trauma".

We laugh at the transparency of Lottie's behavior, and at the absurdity of attributing human neuroses to an animal.[64] But is her fantasy really so different from Craig's, who tries to breathe life into his puppets? And is that so different from discovering a portal into John Malkovich's brain, which will allow Craig to take over Malkovich's identity? Or to Dr Lester's search for a human vessel in which to secure his immortality? Soon, even Lottie is no longer content in her own body, and is demanding "sexual reorientation surgery".

They are all part of the **matrix** which links these desires conceptually: *the dissatisfaction with who we are.* As Craig puts it: "Consciousness is a terrible curse." Lottie's tendency to treat her pets like children is only one step away from Craig's puppeteering, which is only a leap from the portal into the consciousness of John Malkovich, which is only a hop, skip and a jump from Dr Lester's search for a "human vessel" to prolong his mortality. The **matrix** links all these characters in a web of associations around identity and self-worth.

While any good screenplay should have its own **matrix**, in Maverick films a well-defined matrix can take the place of the **chain of logic**. When time or reality have been exploded, the threads of the matrix can hold the story together.

If the chain of logic is like a string of firecrackers, each one setting off the next, the **matrix** is like a spider's web: delicate, transparent, yet surprisingly powerful. It is not each individual skein which makes it so, but the crisscrossing of many threads together.

Like the warp and weft of a tapestry, the bigger picture only comes into focus when the threads are drawn together. When this is done deftly, **Maverick** films can do without the **chain of logic** altogether.

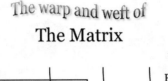

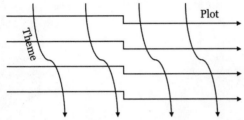

In the movie *The Matrix*, the Matrix is an illusion. If it weren't for the near perfection of that illusion, the Machines would not be able to keep the human race oppressed.

The **matrix** is like the wires connecting a circuit. Unless these wires join up, your different story strands will seem arbitrary or random. For the whole picture to be illuminated, everything must connect.

If you want your story to transcend, to aspire to the **mythic** or the **universal**, create a matrix with: "One clear and simple theme to rule them all, and in the darkness bind them."

> *There are two kinds of plots: causal and cumulative. With causal plots, things follow one after another, logically. In cumulative plots, things jump here and there, with no obvious connection, but then make cumulative sense.*
>
> Mike Leigh, Writer/Director[65]

CLOSE UP: AMERICAN BEAUTY

Face in trees

At the opening of *American Beauty*, Lester Burnham tells us that in less than a year he will be dead, but that in a way he is "dead already". In a marriage that has lost its fizz, and a job that he hates, he feels "sedated" and "in a coma". At home, his family treat him as if he "doesn't exist'. To top it all, at work some efficiency expert is evaluating who is valuable and who is "expendable".

Lester is dead to the world, his self-esteem at an all-time low.

During dinner his daughter Jane complains about the "elevator music" that her mother Caroline enjoys during dinner, poured like syrup over the table in order to create the illusion that they are a big, happy family.

For Caroline, a realtor, surface impressions are important. As her mentor Buddy puts it: "In order to be successful, one must project an image of success at all times." When she fails to sell a house, she has to pull the curtains so that nobody can see her bawl her eyes out.

How we look at ourselves and others is a central strand of the **matrix** of this film. Jane doesn't like to look at her body, which she's unhappy with. Ricky Fitts, her new teenage neighbor, likes to look at her and videos her from his bedroom window. Jane's best friend Angela, who adores being the center of attention, labels him a "freak", because he doesn't look at her even once.

Lester quits his job after fantasizing that Angela has eyes for him alone while she is dancing sexily. He starts working out, explaining to his gay neighbors that he wants to "look good naked". One night Ricky Fitts's dad, paranoid and close-minded, will misinterpret what he glimpses from his window as Ricky giving Lester fellatio.

How you look at things is important in this story – whether you just care about surface impressions or are prepared to dig a little deeper for the truth beneath things. When Angela implies that she's willing to sleep with anyone in order to get ahead, she insists "that's how things really are" (although in her case, nothing could be further from the truth).

For the paranoid Colonel Fitts, Ricky's father, surface impressions cannot be trusted. When his gay neighbors offer the new arrivals a welcoming gift, he assumes they must be selling something: they must have a hidden agenda.

Ricky copes with his father by leading a double life: he pretends to take odd jobs while actually making his money as a drug dealer, and providing his father with fake urine samples. He even pretends to hate gays too, just to keep the peace. His father is so blind to what is going on with his son that Ricky calmly tots up his drug accounts while his father rants in the driver's seat next to him. Ricky's Mom is so abused she has completely shut down, and doesn't say a word. Yet Colonel Fitts, who has repressed his own homosexuality, is the biggest liar of all – the one who struggles hardest to keep the truth hidden.

Ricky loves videoing dead or inanimate objects. One day he films a plastic bag blowing in the wind for fifteen minutes, and realizes that "there was this entire life behind things, and this incredibly benevolent force that wanted me to know there was no reason to be afraid. Ever."

Getting back in touch with this feeling of being alive is the theme that drives the film.

When Caroline catches Lester masturbating in the middle of the night, he defiantly responds that, "At least one of us has blood pumping through our veins," and describes her as a "bloodless moneygrubbing freak". When he tries to make love to her, she worries he'll spill his beer on the sofa. Lester responds furiously: "This isn't life, it's just *stuff*. And it's become more important to you than living." Their marriage, he fumes, is nothing more than "a show".

Material objects have replaced the passion between them, and in letting it happen Lester has lost sight of who he used to be.

At a work event early in the film, Lester drunkenly tells Caroline, "I'll be whoever you want me to be, honey." But after his erotic vision of Angela, Lester decides: "It's never too late to get it back."

He quits his job, gets a new one without any responsibilities at a fast food joint, buys himself a sports car, works out – and smokes pot. Lester's way of bringing himself back to life is by trying to become a teenager again, a plan which is doomed to failure.

By the end of the film, Lester will have a chance to prove whether he has finally grown up. He turns down his opportunity to seduce Angela when he learns that – contrary to the impression she likes to give – she is actually a virgin.

In letting go of his selfish object of desire, he discovers a much greater beauty in all things: "There's so much beauty in the world. Sometimes I feel like I'm seeing it all at once, and it's too much." What is this beauty that lies beneath the surface of things, and what does it have to do with the "American beauty" of the title? Over the course of the story, it comes to mean many things.

On one level "American Beauty" is the name for the roses which Caroline assiduously trains and clips, to fill her house with. These roses represent everything natural that is tamed in their white-picket suburban environment, everything artificial. Their entire lifestyle seems to aspire to the fantasy of the American Dream.

The American beauty is also Angela, that cheerleader icon of male fantasies, who unbuttons her blouse to explode a cascade of roses into Lester's brain, getting his blood pumping again and reminding him that he is still alive.

And finally, American beauty is that deeper appreciation of beauty only to be experienced in the moment, in the full knowledge of our mortality and the fleeting nature of life. All these different versions of "American beauty" form the **matrix** of the film.

How do you describe the **matrix** of a film? Everyone will have their own way of doing so. After all, the matrix is subliminal: if you put it into words, it becomes banal or "on the nose". That's why no one ever says the words of the title in *You Can Count on Me*.

So everyone will have their own way of describing the **matrix**.

Its two contrary forces cross each other at every juncture, the warp and the weft, the yin and the yang, flip sides of the same coin. Here are some ways we might describe the **matrix** in *American Beauty*:

- ○ artificiality vs real life
- ○ honesty vs living a lie
- ○ judging vs tolerance
- ○ denial vs acceptance
- ○ feeling nothing vs feeling joy
- ○ life as a living death vs life lived fully
- ○ storing up for the future vs spending it now
- ○ living every day as your last vs trying to relive your youth

These opposites are threaded through almost every dramatic situation in the film. The **matrix** of this film contrasts living life to the full, with repressing your true nature and living life artificially – living a lie.

In *American Beauty* everything connects.

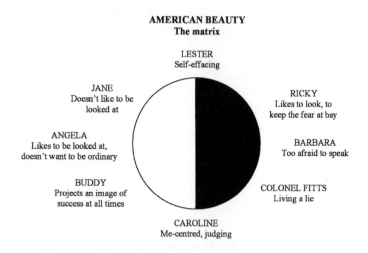

AMERICAN BEAUTY
The matrix

LESTER
Self-effacing

JANE
Doesn't like to be
looked at

RICKY
Likes to look, to
keep the fear at bay

ANGELA
Likes to be looked at,
doesn't want to be ordinary

BARBARA
Too afraid to speak

BUDDY
Projects an image of
success at all times

COLONEL FITTS
Living a lie

CAROLINE
Me-centred, judging

The opening of *2001* is set against the backdrop of an endless, barren primeval African landscape. Life is harsh and unremitting for the apes, our ancestors, who live there. Yet they live as a tribe, share their food, and groom each other. Then one day the "monolith" appears. An ape picks up a bone from a slaughtered ox, bears it down on to the skeleton of the animal, and smashes it into a thousand pieces. A tool!

Not long after, as the tribe drink at a water hole, they are approached by a rival group. The new tool is soon used to glorious effect by our ape to smash in the skull of the alpha male of the rival group. The ape throws his new-found weapon triumphantly into the air . . .

Where the ox bone transforms into a space shuttle, circling a space station like a delicate winged insect engaged in an elaborate mating ritual.

To the accompaniment of Strauss's "Blue Danube" waltz, we have been vaulted into a future far beyond man's brutal beginnings, one of effortless and elegant technological achievement.

Inside the shuttle, the sole passenger Dr Floyd dozes in business class. His pen, floating free in the air like a miniature space ship, is tucked back into his top pocket by an air hostess in anti-gravity slippers.

The interior of the space station itself is blandly anonymous, marked by familiar brand names: Howard Johnsons and Hilton. This is the business travel of the future, and the conversation between the two colleagues is businesslike and unmemorable.

Suddenly, the future seems quite ordinary.

In the next section of the film, as we join an interplanetary space ship overseen by the computer system HAL, we begin to realize that the film is deliberately keeping us at a distance from the human beings. They are strangely lacking in individual characteristics; unlike HAL, who has a distinct personality (and remains one of the great villains of science fiction history!) Every conversation opener of HAL's is ripe with subtext as we ask ourselves: is he just a machine – or does he actually have feelings?

This flouting of one of the basic precepts of screenwriting – to make us identify with our protagonists – is puzzling at first. Has mankind's ingenuity created a future in which he has somehow lost his soul?

There are two myths that lie behind all science fiction.

The first is the conflict between our desire to explore beyond the known limits of our world, and the fear of what we might find there.

The other is that, if the aliens don't get us, then maybe our own technology – artificial intelligence – will one day take over the world (as it does in *The Matrix*).

HAL comes to be the ultimate embodiment of that fear when, after a malfunction, he decides to set about destroying the crew members of the space ship to prevent further "human errors"; turning their sleek vessel of the future into a deadly trap. When the last surviving astronaut manages to regain control of the ship and deactivate the computer's hard drive, it is HAL's poignant, dying recitation of "Daisy Bell" which everyone remembers rather than the fate of HAL's victims.

Technology may be taking us into a brave new future, the film's **matrix** seems to say, but will we lose our humanity in the process?

Soon Bowman is sucked into a black hole and vanishes into a psychedelic landscape. The warping of time and space mirrors the dissolution of his personality. Bowman sees himself at several ages in succession, before dying and being reborn as a galactic baby.

The **matrix** of the film *2001* connects the dawn of human consciousness with its ultimate fate, which is the very opposite of what we might expect: our dissolution into universal consciousness. At some point in the future, the human mind may render itself obsolete.

Like *American Beauty*, *2001* travels from death to life to death to rebirth, a typical Maverick circularity (see Chapter Thirteen) which provides a perfect **matrix** of conflicting forces for the writer to explore in each story.

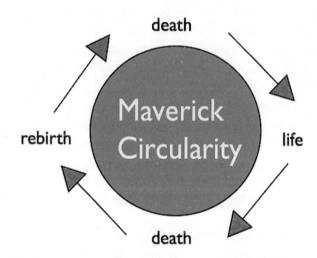

In *In the Mood for Love*, the stifled emotions of the characters are reflected in their cramped living conditions. One evening, So is caught unexpectedly in Chow's room when the landlady arrives home, hauling her drunk husband behind her.

Although So and Chow spend a lot of time together since their spouses are away so much, So doesn't feel it right that she be seen in Chow's room at night. Chow casually strolls into the kitchen, where the landlady is setting up for one of her mah-jong sessions. Do they plan to play all night? Oh no, she replies, just a game or two.

Inside Chow's cramped room the two wait it out, as the mah-jong game turns into another marathon that lasts all night and through the next day as well. Committed to being chaste, the two sit opposite each other on their single beds, the agony of their frustrated desire for each other stretching out inexorably.

The next morning, Chow has to call in sick on So's behalf, since the game is still going on; and of course the social disgrace would be all the greater if So came out now! Chow pretends to a neighbor that he's off sick as he returns from the noodle stall with some sticky rice. His neighbor looks surprised (sticky rice is rich food for delicate stomachs), and warns him not to eat it all at once!

Finally, the coast is clear. But So can't go out in her slippers, so she must borrow his wife's painfully tight shoes to creep into the hall. Even here, she must get past the landlady's mother, who wonders why she didn't see her go out to work in the morning. So has to make up a lie about going out to meet her mother (the same lie Chow's wife already used on him).

Chow and So's attempts to live according to social convention create endless complications for them – complications which their spouses, who are having an affair, easily dispense with.

The **matrix** of *In the Mood for Love* sets the emotional, physical and social bind in which the protagonists find themselves against the unstoppable power of love.

In *Festen*, there are three different levels of the story. There is the public stage – the dining room where Christian tells the gathered family about his father Helge's sexual abuse.

Beneath this, there is the kitchen where the servants, guided by the chef, conspire to keep the guests locked in by stealing their car keys. This is the level of subversion, the common role of servants: behind the scenes they are backing Christian.

Then there is the wine cellar where Helge confronts his son, deep in the basement. As the barred door is pulled shut, Christian is caught once again in the dark subconscious of his hidden fears.

His father begins solicitously. He is quite puzzled by what Christian had to say, because he doesn't remember any of it. Perhaps it is his age. Christian apologizes, puts it down to stress from work. He should forget all about it. Is he sure, his father inquires. After all, if what Christian has said is true, then they should call the police.

Suddenly Christian is a little boy again, trapped with his father. He denies what he knows to be true, even apologizes for it. He is swallowed up in the same darkness from which his sister's ghost appears to him – his twin sister who chose suicide over bringing the truth to light.

But the truth, like the hotel which Christian's family try to throw him out of, has too many doors. It will find another way back in. At the end his sister Helene, until now deeply in denial, will reveal the suicide note left by Christian's twin sister, which condemns her father utterly.

In the scene following Kit and Port's argument in *The Sheltering Sky* (discussed on pages 274–5), Port goes out alone to the gypsy camp at the bottom of the cliffs by the shore. There he sleeps with an exotic prostitute, who tries to steal his wallet. He catches her in the act, but is soon chased by other gypsies, and has to scramble up the cliffs.

Meanwhile Kit awakes sweaty-faced from a nightmare – or possibly an erotic dream. Tunner is knocking loudly at the door. Before she can answer it, Kit has to stand before the mirror and put her "face" on – a fake smile of greeting. As she opens the door, Tunner greets her with the same expression.

Tunner enters, and immediately notices that Port is not in his room. Kit lies that he went out early, but Tunner guesses correctly that he has been out all night. She tells Tunner to order "some fake croissants" and goes into Port's room to muss up his bed so that it will look like her husband has spent the night there.

Tunner invites her out shopping to purchase the mosquito net she has been wanting – yet one more thing to protect her from the world and its judgments. Everything Kit does (putting on her goggles, putting her face on in the mirror) is to prevent reality from breaking in and forcing her to confront her true emotions.

When Port shows up, looking like he has been dragged through the gutter, he is naturally surprised to find Tunner in his room, and his bed slept in. Kit fears that everything has a dark hidden meaning (Port's dream, a white Mercedes), and here Port might be forgiven for thinking so too. But, as ever for this couple, nothing is the way it seems. Kit hasn't done anything wrong, it is Port who has betrayed *her*. Tunner defuses the situation by turning Port to face a mirror: "My God, man, have you seen yourself?"

Despite all Kit's best attempts, the truth keeps breaking through. When Port dies suddenly in the next act, she will be forced to look deep within herself and confront that truth.

In *Wings of Desire*, the angel Damiel desires to come down to earth, "to feel how it is to take your shoes off under the table". Marion, the woman he has fallen in love with, is a trapeze artist whose angel's wings are only "chicken feathers". Despite her talent and beauty, she is desperately lonely.

To be an angel is to be omniscient, but passionless. Like Lester in *American Beauty*, Damiel longs to have "blood pumping through his veins". Human beings, on the other hand, aspire to soar, but so often come down to earth with a bump.

In Marion's dreams, Damiel appears as the hero Siegfried in golden armour. When Damiel finally "enters the river", this armor lands on his head, cutting him. He's delighted, savoring the taste of his own blood. He sells the armor and later Peter Falk, also a fallen angel, tells him he got ripped off. That's life. You've got to take the rough with the smooth.

In the world of angels, the Berlin Wall can be flown over; in the human world, walls are a fact. They get covered in graffiti, but as the excited Damiel discovers, even graffiti can be beautiful. Life is in color. Some colors are drab and ugly. But who would switch them for a world that is black-and-white?

Yet how many of us render our own world black-and-white by never stopping to enjoy the colors?

In *Wings of Desire* the **matrix** connects our desire to experience passion, with the inevitability of also experiencing pain. It reminds us that to be human, we cannot have one without the other.

We can, however, experience both with our eyes wide open.

THE MATRIX
Recap

* **Setting** is an untapped resource for many screenwriters.

* The right **setting** for a scene is one which resonates with the characters inhabiting it.

* **Setting** should reflect an extra dimension, not just what we already know about the character.

* **Setting** reflects everything that we *can't* see in the character, and that's what makes it satisfying.

* It's what you do with the **setting** that counts, not the connotations that come with it.

* How your characters *react* to their environment is what matters.

* The city, like all locations, is a **metaphor** for whatever you want it to be.

* The **matrix** combines visual and verbal metaphors, connecting **character**, **plot** and **theme**.

* Find the images in your world that evoke that **theme**, then drive the **plot** continually to encounter and resonate with these images.

* In a good movie, everything elaborates the **theme**.

* A good film takes one strong **theme** and explores it from every possible angle. Build your **ensemble** with this in mind.

* Use **subplots** to provide a change of tone or tempo, or another window on to the protagonist; but always to elaborate the theme.

* Having **subplots** which suggest different outcomes keeps the audience guessing.

* Drama is about the conflict between two powerful ideas. Don't load the dice in favor of either side, or you will kill the suspense.

* The **matrix** reflects not only the world around your characters, but the **metaphors** they use to describe their world.

* The **imagery** of the film has to be mirrored in the action and dialogue, or it becomes "wallpaper".

* The interweaving of **action**, **dialogue** and **image** raises symbolism to the level of **metaphor**.

* Unlike symbols, the **matrix** works best when nearly subliminal.

* In **Maverick** films a well-defined **matrix** can take the place of the chain of logic.

Exercises

○ Write a scene in which a building, landscape or room (a cathedral, a spooky house, some woods, a new school) holds an irresistible fascination for your character, but which – in spite of their best instincts – they cannot resist exploring in order to find out an important truth.

○ Write a scene in which your hero visits a location which reveals more about the character who inhabits it than is obvious at first sight.

○ Write a scene in which your hero has to use *everything* in their environment to save themselves. Make this reveal something essential about your character.

○ Write a scene in which the activity which your character is pursuing is a perfect metaphor for their state of mind.

○ Write a sequence in which *everything seems connected* by synchronicity, coincidence or fate. Show your heroine acting upon and benefiting from this awareness. (This is a form of **spontaneity**.)

13 Taking it to the limit

Apocalypse Now © Zoetrope/United Artists/Kobal Collection

Imagine being on a tropical island with the sun beating down out of an azure sky, your toes trailing through the dazzling white sand. Beside you is the partner of your dreams. Between two palm trees is strung a hammock. You lie down together and begin making love, stirred by the warm breeze. Paradise, eh?

Now imagine making love, all day every day, for ever. How long before it turns into torture?

Any pleasure when taken to extremes soon turns into its opposite. In the same way, when you pursue your concept to the limit, it often turns into the very opposite of what you expected.

Have you taken your characters to their emotional, physical and psychological limits? Because the majority of "indie" movies fail to do so, and as a result fail to make any waves. An equal percentage of mainstream movies do just the opposite. They substitute cheap effects for catharsis, and bombast for believability.

I once had a student who was writing a clever high-concept script. I asked her where the emotional content was. She said: "I don't need any – it's just entertainment!" This is a big mistake.

Without character development, and without the **matrix** of ideas, images and setting to support it, stories become random and uninvolving, or manipulative and forced.

At the same time, you have to make the audience do some work, not hand them fast food on a plate. You have to make your stories interactive – not in the fashionable sense of the gaming world, by allowing audiences to choose their own endings or to pursue alternate versions of the story. This is an abnegation of responsibility by the filmmaker, a sure sign that there is no firm hand on the tiller. It is also a misunderstanding of what it means to involve your audience in the outcome of your story.

Great stories take us on a journey outside our ordinary experience. The purpose is not to allow us to live in a fantasy or to escape from the cares of the world (although this can be an enjoyable side effect).

Louis Malle's *My Dinner with Andre* is one of the great **minimalist** films of all time. It consists of two men having a conversation over dinner, and nothing more; yet by the end we feel we have been on an epic journey. Andre Gregory, an avant-garde theatre director, tells stories about his travels around the world on a spiritual journey to wake himself out of his "trance", the state which he believes most of us to be walking around in. This culminates in a ceremony in which he is "buried alive".

Wallace Shawn, a down-to-earth New York theatre writer, counters by questioning the need to travel halfway round the world to experience "one moment of reality". "I mean, isn't New York 'real'? . . . I think if you could become fully aware of what existed in the cigar store next door . . . it would just blow your brains out!"

The purpose of great storytelling is to return us to our ordinary reality revived and refreshed, appreciating more of what is all around us, and better equipped to deal with it. Knowing that other people have had titanic struggles that dwarf our own is a comforting thought. It helps us keep things in perspective. We may not be the heroes of fantasy, but fantasy heroes can inspire us to show a little more courage in our own lives.

However, in order for them to do so we must push them to the absolute limit. We must strike the bottom note.

What made *The Lord of the Rings* such a great yarn? Was it the Orcs, the Elves, or wicked Saruman? Partly all of them. But most of us are not warriors, and we lack magical powers. This saga succeeded because the Hobbits, with their hairy feet, fondness for ale, good vittles and the evil weed, showed that true fellowship and warm hearts can overcome any amount of darkness in the world.

In my view, the trilogy fell down in only one respect: the ending. The endless leavetakings at the end of *The Two Towers* were a dead giveaway that the filmmakers did not know how to end the film. The final act shows our Hobbits returned from their adventures, ensconced in the local inn, surrounded by Shire folk, oblivious to the heroes beside them. They ended an epic saga with sentimentality, not apotheosis.

By underplaying the loss which makes the books so poignant (as the ships depart Middle Earth with the immortals aboard them), the film fails to strike the bottom note. In the book, the Hobbits discover that the Shire has not been protected from the ravages affecting the rest of Middle Earth. Tolkien, writing during the Second World War, knew well that those who refuse to stand up to evil abroad will soon find evil visiting their shores. The film, in this one respect, failed to follow the conceit to its logical conclusion.

Captain Corelli, another adaptation from a fine book,[66] also missed a trick in its ending. In this story of a doomed relationship between an Italian officer and the daughter of the doctor with whom he is billeted on an occupied Greek island during the Second World War, the lovers are eventually separated when the Italians are forced to retreat. For decades the girl mourns for him, and when he finally returns for her several decades later he feels the full force of her frustration and outrage. In the novel, before the lovers can be reunited and live into peaceful old age, however, they are overtaken by a greater tragedy.

In the film a saccharine Hollywood finale, in which the geriatric lovers putt around the island on his moped reliving their youth, was substituted for the book's tragic ending, which left countless readers sobbing on buses and subways. Whichever executives foisted this fiasco on the film should have had the confidence of a perennial tragedy which never fails to put "bums on seats", particularly in Baz Luhrmann's superb modern reworking of *Romeo and Juliet*).

Roman Polanski, a director who never fails to plumb the dark side of his own past, understood clearly that what audiences want is not necessarily to be uplifted. They want an ending that is true to the characters, and the ultimate expression of their journey. This is the meaning of catharsis – a purging of emotions, not the relieving of them, like taking an aspirin. The only truly "down" ending is one that provides no transcendence.

In the making of *Chinatown*, Polanski feuded with screenwriter Robert Towne over the ending of his script. In Towne's version, John Huston's villainous businessman, who has committed incest with his daughter and now lusts after his granddaughter, got his comeuppance in the end. In Polanski's version Huston gets away with it, having accidentally shot his daughter, leaving Jake, the private detective who has broken his pledge never to become personally involved, devastated.

"Forget it, Jake," the local cop brusquely consoles him, "it's Chinatown." For Polanski, in a world where the rich control the levers of power and the administration of justice, the good do not always win; and nor does Jake. Since the film has remained a perennial classic, we can only assume that Polanski made the right choice.

By celebrating the **anti-hero**, the Nouvelle Vague made it possible for the outsider, the criminal or the rebel, to turn defeat into a kind of victory. From Belmondo's dramatic stagger down the street as he is gunned down by police in *Breathless*, to Butch Cassidy and the Sundance Kid's defiant charge out of their hiding place into the full force of a fusillade from the Bolivian army, to Thelma and Louise's gunning of their T-Bird over the cliff edge of the Grand Canyon, the anti-hero snatches a kind of moral victory from the jaws of defeat.

Peter Fonda conceived the ending of *Easy Rider*, the iconic expression of the hippy dream, before he had written a word of the script. His image of two Harley-Davidsons blown into the air by rednecks, putting an end to their young riders' free-spirited dream, expressed everything he felt about the struggle between the generations.

What is notable about all these endings is not that they are tragic or "down" endings, but that they are transcendent. Before Belmondo expires, Patricia imitates his favorite hand gesture by brushing her finger across her lips, *à la* Bogart, and he makes her gesture of pulling a long face. This affectionate swap of their characteristics suggests that in spite of the unbearable lightness of his being, the spontaneity of his life on the run, he has finally transcended his own narcissism to connect with another human being.

For Butch Cassidy and the Sundance Kid, hiding out in Bolivia but unable to resist a return to the adrenaline rush of their outlaw life, the odds finally seem stacked against them. Wounded and overwhelmingly outnumbered, they shelter in a stable while soldiers line up in ranks on the rooftops opposite. In William Goldman's brilliant Oscar-winning script, the two buddies bicker as they have always done. Butch recommends the virtues of taking up a new life in Australia. "What about the banks?" demands the Kid. "Ripe and easy," replies Butch. "And the women?' "When you've got one, you've got the other."

All these badly wounded heroes have to do is come out shooting, grab their horses and ride out like they've done so many times before. For a moment we believe they might actually make it. They run out, guns blazing, and the frame freezes. Over it, we hear a volley that is as deafening as it is resolutely final, repeated again and again, before fading into the distance. We remain frozen on their final, defiant leap into history. Which is just the way they would have wanted it.

Twenty years on, *Thelma and Louise* pulled the same trick. The two women go on a liberating journey that turns them into outlaws. When faced with the choice of death or surrender, it's no contest at all. The final image of their '66 T-Bird flying through the air over the Grand Canyon expresses everything that is liberating – and destructive – about that journey.

At the end of *One Flew Over the Cuckoo's Nest*, McMurphy may have been crushed by the System – but he was never likely to change. Instead, he has given the Chief the courage to believe in himself. This ending may kill off the main character (the kiss of death!) but it offers us a greater prize – hope.

In *Crouching Tiger, Hidden Dragon*, the warrior monk Mu Bai has been struck by a poisoned dart from his enemy Jade Fox, whom he kills. As his reluctant protégé Jen, who has unwittingly brought Jade to their hideout, rushes off to fetch the antidote, Mu Bai confesses his love for his friend Shu Lien, whom he has known all his life, and always dreamed of settling down with. She urges him to save his last breath, to meditate and achieve enlight-enment, the goal to which his whole life has been directed. He replies that he would rather be a ghost forever walking by her side than enter the Kingdom of Heaven on his own.

Mu Bai dies before Jen can bring the antidote. She, echoing a myth that her lover Lo has told her of a man who jumped off a cliff to make his wishes come true, leaps over the side of a mountain into the clouds. Is her dream to be reunited with her lover – or to bring Mu Bai, whom she has betrayed, back to life? We will never know, but it is a leap of faith only made possible by the tragic death of our hero.

In *Apocalypse Now*, Captain Willard has been sent on a mission to assassinate Colonel Kurtz, a fellow Special Forces officer who has gone renegade, setting himself up as a godlike figure over the local natives deep in the jungles of Cambodia. After a long and arduous journey, Willard finally makes it to Kurtz's ancient citadel, with its fallen idols watching over mounds of skulls and dead bodies sacrificed in the cause of some insane ideology.

Nevertheless, Willard finds himself trapped in Hamlet-like indecision. He has never killed a fellow officer. Finally, he realizes what he has to do. Like all third-act resolutions, it has become personal. "They were going to make me a Major for this. But they didn't realize I wasn't even in their fucking army anymore."

Whatever motive your character may have set out with on their mission, in the end it always becomes personal. They may have set out with a sense of duty or obligation, or loyalty. But in the end, every protagonist must do it for themselves. They must take responsibility for their own actions.

Willard kills Kurtz and emerges on to the steps of the citadel, clutching his bloody machete, gazing down at the assembled natives, who have been engaged in the ritual sacrifice of an ox. In many Eastern myths, the king must be sacrificed in order to bring the rains and renewal to the land.[67] Will the natives, armed to the teeth, tear Willard limb from limb?

Instead they bow down before him, this foreign god, who has proved himself almighty. Will Willard assume the mantle, like so many dictators? For a moment a shadow falls across his face. At last, he tosses the machete on the ground. As a chorus, the assembled natives lay down their arms. Willard takes the hand of his last remaining crew member, and leads him to their PT boat.

Once aboard, the radio crackles, barking out orders. Willard switches it off, and cuts the boat adrift. The rain begins to fall, washing the blood and camouflage markings from his face, purifying their souls while overhead the B-52 bombers expunge the entire site off the face of the earth. Willard has done what needed to be done: he has been true to himself. And having done so, he can leave his violent past behind.

In all these stories the characters are pushed to desperate extremes in order to achieve some transcendent value. This value must be achieved regardless of whether your protagonist is victorious or defeated in the conventional sense.

In order for this to happen, your hero must have reached a state of self-awareness where the scales fall away and they see themselves as they really are. Human beings resist profound change, and the essential prerequisite is self-knowledge. Sometimes, with the **anti-hero**, this knowledge amounts to no more than knowing that they are incapable of change.

"We blew it," as Captain America says to Billy in *Easy Rider*. You cannot change society by running away from its problems.

CLOSE UP: UNFORGIVEN

In *Unforgiven*, a retired outlaw, Will Munny, is persuaded to take up a bounty killing of two cowboys who assaulted and cut up a whore. He takes on this one last job to provide for his kids whom he has brought up singlehandedly since his wife, who reformed him, died a few years before.

Ever since his wife helped him sober up, Munny has maintained that he "ain't like that anymore", and that he's just a "normal" person now. So it seems. Aging, unable to shoot straight or mount his horse, he looks to be easy prey for Little Bill, the sheriff who dispatches fearsome gunmen toting big reputations with brutal gusto.

Throughout his journey to Big Whiskey, Will is haunted by memories of his past killings. After he receives a terrible beating from Little Bill he falls into a coma, where the Angel of Death appears to him. Now at last he comes face to face with the full horror of what he has done. When he comes to, he feels reborn. He is not yet prepared to give up on his bounty mission – but from now on, he will act in the full knowledge of who he is and what he has done.

When Little Bill kills Will's best friend Ned (who took no part in the bounty killings), Munny breaks his resolution to remain sober, and takes the swig of whiskey that will make it possible for him to do what he has to do. Abandoning his young companion, who realizes he's not cut out for killing after all, Will heads into town as a storm breaks around him.

Outside the saloon, Ned's body is displayed in an open coffin to deter other mercenaries. Munny enters, shoots the bar owner, Little Bill and four armed deputies. A writer, cowering under the bodies, crawls out to question Munny about how he did it. Did he fire upon the best gunmen first? "I was always lucky when it came to killing folks," Munny replies. Little Bill, mortally wounded, stirs and reaches for his pistol, but Munny catches sight of him and knocks it away. Before Munny can deliver the *coup de grâce*, Little Bill curses him: "I'll see you in hell, Will Munny." Munny nods. Hell is where he is already, and killing is what comes naturally to him.

Before Munny emerges into the downpour outside, he warns any citizens who might be looking to become heroes that, if anyone shoots him, not only will he kill them but their wives and children too, and then he'll burn their houses down. Before he gallops away, he warns the townsfolk not to mistreat their womenfolk, or he'll come back and kill every last one of them.

In the climax, Munny is not only acting in tune with his deepest instincts, he has vindicated and even surpassed the legends of gunfighters on which the movie has poured scorn as tall tales and myths of the West. More than that, he has become an almost supernatural force, a hurricane that threatens to wipe out the town and all its inhabitants. He has ascended to another level and in doing so he has, like Willard, finally reached the catharsis necessary for him to leave this life behind.

A cursory rolling caption now ends the film, informing us that Munny subsequently brought his kids to San Francisco, where he opened a dry goods store, and began a new life.

Contemporary audiences are inclined to disbelieve neat endings, where the darkness is all eclipsed by the good. To the modern sensibility, wars are won – but at a cost. Sometimes they are lost, but they inspire others to carry on the struggle. Sometimes they are won, but the prize is worth less than we hoped for. Sometimes they are lost, but we discover that what we have already is worth more than we ever realized.

These variations reflect our sense that we live in a complicated world – and that only irony can resolve all its contradictions.

In **classic** films, how stories end up tends to be an expression of will. How strong is your character? How much have they learned?

In **Maverick** films, will counts, but it is only one of many factors that exert a powerful influence in our lives: environment, destiny, politics, coincidence, the supernatural.

In **concept-driven** films, a character is swept along by a conceit that they may or may not have control over. When that concept is pushed to the limit, it takes us to an ironic or absurd conclusion, which is often the very opposite of what we would expect.

In *Into the Wild*, a young graduate, Chris, takes to the road in an attempt to leave family ties and civilization behind him. His ultimate goal is to spend a year alone in the wild in Alaska. He fails to prepare himself adequately, however, and once there he accidentally consumes a poisonous plant which prevents his stomach from digesting food, and he begins to starve. His way back to civilization is blocked by a raging river which won't abate until the summer. As his own diary entry puts it: "Have literally become *trapped* in the wild."

Thumbing through his copy of *Doctor Zhivago*, he discovers a quote which strikes him like a bolt of lightning. He translates it as: "Happiness only real when shared." Chris has had to come all this way from civilization to discover this basic human fact. No matter how much we appreciate nature and solitude, human beings are social animals: and happiness is only real when reflected in another's eyes.

In *Aguirre, Wrath of God*, Aguirre belatedly discovers the same fact. His demented pursuit of the fictional El Dorado has killed his entire expedition and left him Emperor of a raft of monkeys.

When you take your concept to the limit, it often turns into the opposite of what you'd expect.

Taking it to the Limit

Plot-driven Drama

---➤

**taking your character to the limit:
emotionally, psychologically, physically**

Concept-driven Drama

---➤

**taking your concept to its ultimate
(often absurd or ironic) conclusion**

In *Being John Malkovich*, Craig, in the guise of John Malkovich, achieves everything he ever dreamed of as a puppeteer: fame, respect, fortune. But he loses Maxine's love, because Maxine never loved him for who he truly was. In the end he fulfills his dream of "seeing the world through someone else's eyes" by being trapped inside Maxine's and Lottie's child. His dream is turned into a nightmare as he is forced to see the world forever through someone else's eyes.

Be careful what you dream of, because the reality may not be what you expected. When you pursue your fantasies to the end of the line, they may turn into your worst nightmares.

CIRCULARITY

Same old, same old, but different

© Sybille Yates

In the modern world, at least in the West, our civilization has long focused on progress and development as a measure of humankind's innate superiority to the natural world.

Yet for millennia, life has been about the daily round, the changes of the seasons, the cycles of birth and death, and in some cultures, even rebirth to begin the round again.

We like to think that we are no longer dependent upon these natural cycles, and live frenetic lives in complete disregard of their effect upon our lives. But this does not mean that these cycles do not still act upon us, in spite of our 24/7 lifestyle. Even the debate about climate change is only about the degree of mankind's interference with these natural cycles, not whether these cycles exist. Ice ages and droughts will still come and go, regardless of man's effect on the planet.

No matter how much we focus on whether we're "getting ahead", isn't it also true that, for most of us, life is still a daily round of work and routine? Even our little daily rituals, whether we brush our teeth before we shower or afterwards, are all part of our attempts to impose order upon an uncertain world, a world where dramatic events can at any moment come crashing in upon us.

Life has a way of coming full circle, whether it's when we discover that we have become much like our parents, or our children are acting as we once did.

Maverick stories have a particular love of circularity, which is a nod to the mysterious forces that exert power over our lives, independent of our will. For them, will is often powerless in the face of destiny. And nature often determines destiny, in spite of will's frantic desire to derail it.

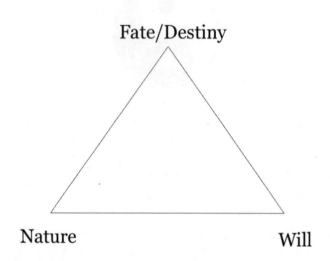

Fate/Destiny

Nature

Will

All stories use a combination of these forces, but in different proportions, according to the writer's view about which is most influential.

Nature is the state and conditions we come into the world with. Our personal qualities, our advantages and disadvantages, our social and economic circumstances. **Fate** or **destiny** are the accidents that happen in life that can either trip you up or take you closer to your goal, and **will** is the extent to which we are able to forge our own destiny.

Classic screenwriting emphasizes the **will** of the character in shaping their world (although **realism** tends to favor the influence of **nature**, and its characters are often in thrall to their social circumstances).

In **Maverick** stories, fate or destiny tends to play a larger role, and **will** is often misused or misplaced. A character pursues their goal, but other forces intervene and sweep over them. When those forces are overwhelmingly strong, it creates a **circular** story.

> *This is the excellent foppery of the world, that*
> *when we are sick in fortune . . . we make guilty of*
> *our disasters the sun, the moon, and the stars, as*
> *if we were villains by necessity, fools by heavenly*
> *compulsion.*
>
> Edmund, in Shakespeare's *King Lear*

Circular stories often give the impression of landing us back where we started, but this is only an illusion. In circular stories, the world outwardly may not seem to have changed greatly, but the hero's attitude to it has.

In Kenneth Lonergan's indie film *You Can Count on Me*, Terry pays a visit to his sister Sammy, who still lives in the small town where they grew up. Sammy and Terry were orphaned when they were children, after their parents died in a car crash. They couldn't be more different. Sammy is a solid, dependable bank worker and single mom. Terry has spent his whole life drifting around, never staying in one place or occupation for long, and is a constant worry to his sister.

At the opening of the film, he pays a visit to Sammy to borrow money for his girlfriend to have an abortion. Sammy wonders why she hasn't heard from him for many months. After beating around the bush, he finally admits he's done a little jail time after getting involved in a bar-room brawl.

Sammy is shocked, and Terry reacts furiously that he can't be spending his time worrying about how she's going to react to everything he does. As is often the case in two-handed relationships, Terry and Sammy's mutual dependence after their parents' death makes Terry feel cramped, confined. Their relationship has no third corner of a **triangle** to relieve the pressure. No matter how far he runs, Tery will always worry what Sammy might be thinking about what he's up to, and it cramps his style.

After his girlfriend's brothers make it clear to Terry that he'd better not return any time soon, Terry decides to stick around. Despite his reputation as a wild child, Terry soon shows his more loving and responsible side, becoming a father figure to Rudy, Sammy's son, and fixing things around the house.

His presence also seems to liberate the wilder side of Sammy, who embarks on a reckless affair with her married boss.

To deflect her guilt, Sammy calls in the local priest to have a chat with Terry. Even if he doesn't call it God, isn't there anything that Terry can base his life around, some anchor so that he doesn't feel like he's just drifting around without any purpose? Terry denies that this is something he feels any need for.

Without consulting Sammy, Terry decides to take Rudy to meet his feckless father, who lives in a trailer park and has never acknowledged responsibility for his son. When Rudy Sr. brutally denies any knowledge of the boy, and tries to shove them off his property, he and Terry end up in a bruising brawl. Sammy tells Terry it's time for him to be on his way.

At the end of the movie, the two are at the bus stop waiting for the bus that first brought Terry into town. Sammy is distraught, fearing that she'll never see Terry again. Thankfully, neither of the protagonists ever mouths the words that make up the title of the film, but Terry assures her that he'll write to Rudy, and come round again (like a migrating bird returning with the seasons), maybe next Christmas.

On the surface, nothing seems to have changed. Terry has screwed up again, and he's on his way once more. But something very important *has* changed. He has come to realize that this relationship, which before seemed like a shackle binding him to his sister, is the one firm anchor in his life. She will always be there for him, and he for her; and for both of them, this has at last become a positive force in their lives.

In *It's a Wonderful Life*, George Bailey (Jimmy Stewart) runs a successful savings and loan company which provides mortgages for the working poor. However, he has always dreamed of escaping his small town and becoming an adventurer like his older brother. One day, when he loses a large sum of money and it looks like he will have to sell out his business to the rapacious banker Henry Potter, George says "I wish I'd never been born!"

He gets his wish, as an angel comes down from Heaven and gives him a vision of what the town would be like without the benevolent influence of his savings and loan (now there's a scenario you'd have trouble pitching today – or maybe you should?). The town has become a den of crime and destitution, and finally George discovers what he'd never realized before: his influence on the town has been immeasurable, and the world would be a poorer place, in every sense, without him. When he returns to reality and recovers the money, he is overjoyed that his town – which before he'd always seen as boring and parochial – now seems like a wonderful place again. He's back where he was meant to be.

In *Groundhog Day*, Phil finds himself trapped in the last place in the world he wants to be. When he finally learns to appreciate life and live for the moment, time can at last move forward. He finally wakes up with Rita by his side, looks out at the beautiful snowy view and declares: "Let's move here!" Nothing has changed but Phil's attitude. At last, he can appreciate what's around him. As Dorothy learns when she returns from Oz: "There's no place like home."

In *Eternal Sunshine of the Spotless Mind*, Joel and Clementine meet on a train, unaware that they have met before. They find they have a strange affinity, and there seems to be every prospect that they will strike up a romance. However, the story then begins unwinding backwards, as we discover that these two have been lovers before, but they have both had their memories erased in a controversial therapeutic programme for deleting what is painful to recall.

In the first of Joel's memories, he stops by Clementine's workplace only to have her greet him like a stranger, then carry on canoodling with one of her co-workers. He discovers she has been through the memory erasure program, and decides to do the same himself.

As he lies unconscious being deprogrammed, the memories start flooding back, from the awkward and argumentative later stages of their relationship to the spontaneity of the early days. As these memories slip away from him, Joel starts to realize how much he loved Clementine, and tries to resist the process.

Sometimes he can interact with his memories, or break out of character while reviewing the scene; at others he is forced to watch his memories disintegrate, or fill with holes like a colander. Sometimes he can only watch helplessly, or run like a madman trying to keep up with the carpet slipping beneath him.

In spite of his best efforts to hide her away in his childhood memories, and to head "off the map", the process runs its inexorable course. So when the two run into each other on the train (both have an irresistible urge to take a train to Montauk, the place where they first met) they just "click". Joel gives her a ride to her place, where she stops to pick up a toothbrush and check her mail. In it, is a tape sent by a disgruntled employee at the clinic, where Clementine gives a full account of her relationship and her reasons for wanting her memories of him erased.

Unaware of what's on the tape, she slots it into the tape player of Joel's car, where Joel hears her giving a rundown of all his faults. Freaked out, he throws her out. Later, she stops by his apartment where he too has been sent and is listening to his tape, which she overhears, equally shocked.

In spite of their attraction to each other, this time the relationship seems impossible: they know too much. Joel begs her to stay, but she tells him that their relationship will run an inevitable course: she'll get fed up with him, and feel cramped, and want to escape, and he'll grow to hate her. For a moment, everything is poised in the balance. Then he says "Okay", accepting his fate, and embracing it. They both laugh at the irony of it all, and we know the affair will start all over again. But this time they will go into it as adults who know what they are getting into, accepting the cycles of falling in and out of love, the pain and pleasure, as inevitable. They have both grown up.

In one of the subplots Mary, the receptionist at the clinic, finally breaks down and admits her love for Dr Mierzwiak, who runs it: "I feel like I've loved you for a very long time." When the doctor's wife catches them embracing, Mierzwiak is forced to admit to Mary: "We have a history." They too have had an affair before, and he has erased her memories.

In anger, she mails the patients' tapes out to all the clinic's clients, because she has realized that love cannot be erased. Like all of our strongest instincts and deepest emotions, love is more than a series of memories.

Our deepest instincts cannot be faked. While Joel is being deprogrammed, one of the technicians views his memories about Clementine and tries to put the moves on her using Joel's lines (this gives the story yet another layer of transparency). However, he just comes across as phony.

Though the clinic may destroy the thread of time and memory, instincts are like a tide that ebbs and flows, part of the cycle of life. These instincts cannot be denied, or restrained, or faked.

In *Clockwork Orange*, Alex, a violent criminal and rapist, is given aversion therapy to cure him. He becomes an apparently ideal citizen, but is persecuted by all the people whose lives he formerly made a misery, until he jumps out of a window to try to kill himself. Since his treatment is an experimental one just brought in by the government, this is a public relations disaster, and so a minister promises to set him up in a comfortable new life.

To the strains of his beloved Beethoven – which his therapy had made unbearable to him – and eyeing up the nurse's legs, we realize that Alex's fall has caused him to regain all his original instincts. The deepest streams cannot be denied, no matter what future techniques science offers us for mind manipulation. There is nothing so powerful as instinct; but equally, nothing so shocking as the denial of our deepest instincts.

At the end of *Nineteen Eighty-Four*, our hero Winston has had all rebellion crushed within him. As he sits in a miserable dive drinking cheap gin, he looks up at the image of Big Brother screaming propaganda from the screen in front of him, with tears running down his cheeks. Now, at last, he realizes he loves Big Brother. As the tyrants of the twentieth century understood, it is not enough simply to crush rebellion, you must convince the victim that you have done it for their own good.

This denial of his own deepest instincts – he has already been forced to betray his lover – makes the ending of *Nineteen Eighty-Four* unforgettable and shocking.

Setting up a story which places your hero at odds with their deepest instincts makes for powerful drama. It creates a powerful **subtext**, which as all subtexts should, always forces its way to the surface.

Cross-currents

In **classic** structure, the hero often has to "overcome" his problems or issues in order to complete his mission. In **Maverick** screenwriting these forces, which in **classic** structure lurk within the subtext, tend to burst into the superstructure and demand our attention (as in *Liar, Liar*, when Jim Carrey's lying lawyer is "magically" forced to tell the truth for one day). Pursuing the consequences of this becomes as important as following the linear plot.

There is always a conflict between **cyclical** and **linear** time. Linear time suggests a goal, finality, achievement. Cyclical time suggests an unending dying away and resurgence. As Lester says in *American Beauty*: "Remember those posters that said, 'Today is the first day of the rest of your life'? Well that's true of every day except one . . . The day you die." As his brains are blown out, his entire life flashes before him in the second before he dies. But "that one second isn't a second at all, it stretches on for ever, like an ocean of time . . . "

At the end of *Inception*, by contrast, Cobb returns from what seems like an endless exile from his children, forced on him by his wife's suicide. To do so, he has had to perform again the very process of inception which he believes killed her, when she became convinced that "this life isn't real". He has had to go further into "the dream within a dream within a dream" than any sane man would rationally go. This time, however, the idea that he plants is one that heals, rather than hurts – a son's relationship with his father (although this unexpected benefit helps the film glide over the inception's essentially mercenary motivation, which could potentially undermine our sympathy for Cobb).

When Cobb finally buys his way back home (having achieved the obligatory emotional resolution: coming to terms with his wife's death by letting her memory go), it seems that barely a second has passed as his daughters – whose faces have forever been turned away from him – turn and smile. We are back to the beginning – but what an epic journey we've been on.

Of course, the entire mission of *Inception* is in a sense a metaphor for Cobb's emotional journey. By creating both streams in the plot, Nolan gives the film both a linear and a cyclical pattern.

Katsushika Hokusai, "The Great Wave of Kanogawa" © The Art Archive/
Claude Debussy Centre St. Germain en Laye/Gianni Dagli Orti

Using cyclical time is like creating a strong counter-current in your story. Like a great wave it periodically knocks your characters sideways, then lifts them up again on to the shore.

A great screenwriter can ride this axis like a surfer "riding the tube".

In *Jacob's Ladder*, we are given two contrary streams to guide us through the narrative. One is the story of Jacob Singer, a Vietnam veteran who has lived a diminished, unambitious life in the years since his service. At first his hallucinations seem to be part of some post-traumatic stress. Gradually, as he re-encounters his wartime buddies, he investigates and learns that they are flashbacks brought on by the terrible consequences of a powerful hallucinatory drug that the Pentagon tested on its soldiers, without their knowledge, to see if it would make them more aggressive in combat. The effects were so powerful his comrades slaughtered each other rather than the enemy.

At the same time we flashback to Jacob's former comfortable middle-class life, his marriage and the accident which destroyed it: when his son Gabe was run over and killed by a car. This is the emotional **counter-stream** to the **linear** Pentagon conspiracy plot. As with Cobb, who needs to make it back to his children in *Inception*, or Teddy (Di Caprio's alter ego, and curiously similar character) in *Shutter Island*, a detective pursuing revenge for the murder of his wife, the linear plot is constantly being overtaken by the deeper streams of the hero's emotional and psychological life.

In Scorsese's *Shutter Island*, Teddy believes he has come to this prison for the criminally insane to pursue the arsonist who killed his wife; in the end he discovers that it was he who killed his wife after she murdered their children, and that he has been an in-patient in the prison for several years. He finally accepts a lobotomy as the only way to end the pain of living with this knowledge.

Usually we prefer the truth to living with an illusion, and we awake from the dream with a clearer sense of what it means to be alive. Even the audiences who feed off Truman's life in *The Truman Show* whoop and cheer when he finally chooses reality over the varnished illusion.

(Why do we watch "reality" shows – those artificial constructs designed to create maximum conflict between human beings thrown together like rats in a lab? Because every so often, a moment or two of *reality* shines through, and makes it all worthwhile.)

When Jacob is able to come to terms with the memory of his son Gabe in *Jacob's Ladder*, he is finally able to let go of life and cross over to the other side. The entire story arc of his post-combat life has been a hallucination played out while he lies in an operating tent with his life ebbing away on the Mekong Delta.

Jake's "investigation" has, in linear terms, been a futile one: the surgeon is unable to save his life. But he has come to terms with what has happened to him, and with what awaits him on the other side. His emotional journey has been a valuable one. As Louis, the chiropractor who helps him release his locked-away feelings, explains to him:

```
                    LOUIS
        Eckhart saw Hell too; he said: the only
        thing that burns in Hell is the part of you
```

that won't let go of life, your memories,
your attachments. They burn 'em all away.
But they're not punishing you, he said.
They're freeing your soul. So, if you're
frightened of dying and holding on, you'll
see devils tearing your life away. But if
you've made your peace, then the devils are
really angels, freeing you from the earth.

In *Vertigo* and *The Sixth Sense,* the circular endings allow the protagonist to have another opportunity to experience testing events and, with the knowledge and insight they have gained, create a different and better outcome.

In *Vertigo*, Scottie has retired from the police force after causing the death of a fellow officer when he suffered an attack of vertigo on the roof of a tall building. We know that before the end of this story he will have to climb another tall building, and overcome his fear.

In fact, he has two more chances. The first time he fails to get there in time, and is left believing he has been responsible for the suicide of his client's wife. The second time, having seen through Judy (the woman who posed as the wife), he forces the truth out of her at the top of the tower, and she accidentally falls.

Sometimes we cannot overcome the circularity of events, and are left ironically or tragically ensnared by them. Hitchcock was fond of such endings – as you would be if you saw life as essentially absurd, and believed that we are all the victims of circumstance. Whether Hitchcock regarded his actors as "cattle" is apocryphal; but he certainly enjoyed treating his characters that way. They are often ordinary people, herded this way and that by force of circumstance. If they are blond, and the embodiment of innocence, all the better. He enjoyed seeing them suffer. It gave them a bigger arc.

In *The Sixth Sense*, Dr Malcolm Crowe, a child psychologist, is shot by a former patient who says the doctor failed him. When another child comes to him, complaining of the same symptoms, we know that Malcolm will get a second chance to prove himself.

The Sixth Sense showed its commercial "nous" by having the climax of the thriller storyline – will Malcolm believe the kid who says he can see ghosts in time to save a little girl's life? – dovetail with the climax of the *existential* one, the discovery that he is dead.

His need to solve the external problem and resolve his emotional and existential state deftly unites the **circular** and **linear** streams of the film.

The **cyclical** nature of these stories has the protagonist go up against his deepest instincts, resolve his inner conflict and achieve the goal of the story's **linear** plot.

© Rick Doyle/CORBIS

TAKING IT TO THE LIMIT
Recap

* Any pleasure, when taken to extremes, soon turns into its opposite. In the same way, when you pursue your concept to the limit, it often turns into the opposite of what you might expect.

* Have you taken your characters to their emotional, physical and psychological limits?

* Great stories take us on a journey outside our ordinary experience.

* The only truly "down" ending is one that provides no **transcendence**.

* The **anti-hero** turns defeat into a kind of victory.

* Whatever motive your character may have begun their mission with, in the end it always becomes personal. In the end, every protagonist must take responsibility and do it for themselves.

- In order for transcendence to be achieved, your hero must have reached a state of self-awareness where the scales fall away and they see themselves as they really are.

- Sometimes with the **anti-hero** this knowledge amounts to no more than knowing that they are incapable of change.

- Modern endings reflect our sense that we live in a complicated world – and that only irony can resolve all its contradictions.

- In **Maverick** films, **will** counts, but it is only one of many factors that exert a powerful influence in our lives: including environment, destiny, politics, coincidence, and the supernatural.

- Be careful what you dream of, because the reality may not be what you expect. When you pursue your fantasies to the end of the line, they can turn into your worst nightmares.

- Life is about the daily round, whether we know it or not.

- **Circularity** is a nod to the mysterious forces that exert power over our lives, independent of our own wills.

- **Circular** stories often give the impression of landing us back where we started, but this is only an illusion. In circular stories, the world outwardly may not seem to have changed greatly, but the hero's attitude to it has.

- Setting up a story which places your hero at odds with their deepest instincts makes for powerful drama. It creates a strong **subtext** which, as all subtexts should, always forces its way to the surface.

- **Maverick** stories take what is normally in the subtext, and thrust it into the light. Following the consequences of this becomes as important as following the **linear** plot.

- Using cyclical time is like creating a strong **counter-current** in your story. Like a great wave it periodically knocks your characters sideways, then lifts them up again.

* **Circular endings** allow the protagonist to have another opportunity to experience testing events and, with the knowledge and insight they have gained, overcome their failings and create a different and better outcome.

* Sometimes we cannot overcome the circularity of events, and are left ironically or tragically ensnared by them.

* **Circular** stories allow the protagonist to go up against her deepest instincts, resolve her inner conflict *and* achieve the goal of the story's linear plot.

Exercises

○ Write a scene in which your heroine enters a world they've never experienced before, one which takes them out of their comfort zone. This can be a physical, social or psychological test. Use it to reveal your heroine's unexpected qualities.

○ Imagine your greatest fantasy. Now imagine it turning into your worst nightmare. Write the scene in which this happens to your hero or heroine.

○ Write a series of scenes in which your hero pursues a routine activity with a friend or a lover. Show how that routine changes subtly as the relationship grows/matures/dies etc. Think of it as the Four Seasons of Love.

○ Write a series of family get-togethers over the holidays in the course of a year. Show how the relationships have changed, and match it to the seasons.

○ Write a sequence in which your hero discovers they are back where they started – this could be physically or psychologically. Make sure your ending goes for wit and irony. Show what your character has learned from the experience.

Section 7
Which structure is right for you?

14 Mashing genre

Above all, I was looking for the explosion of genres.

François Truffaut[68]

Applying **Maverick** principles to genre is a great way to make your script stand out from the crowd. There are two ways you can go about it: you can cross genres, or you can mash them.

Crossing genres means putting two or more genres together in order to reinvigorate both. *Shaun of the Dead* takes romantic comedy, that overused genre, and raises the stakes by mixing it with horror. At the same time, it gives a new comedy take on zombie horror, a genre which easily lends itself to parody.

Mashing genre means finding a new point of attack, a new way into the genre, a way of seeing it in a different light. Sometimes this means finding a new kind of hero, or a hero from another genre.

The Maverick hero

When Truffaut reinvented **film noir** in *Shoot the Pianist,* he took away the wisecracking confidence of Marlowe and substituted a hesitant, more existential hero. Charlie is a shy nightclub pianist who used to play in concert halls, but since the suicide of his wife has changed his name and withdrawn into obscurity.

When Charlie gets caught up in his hoodlum brother's problems with a gang pursuing him for money, he reluctantly becomes a man of action.

But Charlie is constrained by grief and guilt. He veers between comic inspiration, doubt and hesitancy. He tries to stand apart from the world, but is drawn back in by love and ties of blood. After it's all over, and he has lost the woman he loves for a second time, he retreats to the café, still tinkling away at the keys. Music is his only constant, in a life where fate goes in vicious circles.

Unlike Marlowe, Charlie did not choose to be a hero; he is thrown into it by chance. The randomness of everything is established in the opening scene, when Charlie's brother strikes up a conversation with an absolute stranger. The married stranger extols the virtues of sticking with and working at a relationship. This random conversation does not move the plot forward – but it does establish the theme of openness and commitment, qualities that Charlie struggles with. Tarantino watched and learned, and repeated this technique of using apparently inconsequential conversations to provide a thematic thread in his films, and Linklater took it even further when, in *Slacker*, he dispensed with story altogether.

The casualness, tentativeness or reticence of these Nouvelle Vague heroes was new; their **film noir** counterparts may have been all twisted up inside, but that wasn't about to stop them doing what had to be done. Marlowe takes on work reluctantly, and often finishes cases for personal, rather than financial reasons; but he never loses his moral compass. In spite of the fog that surrounds him, the film noir hero steps fearlessly into the darkness.

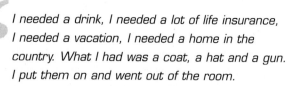

> *I needed a drink, I needed a lot of life insurance,*
> *I needed a vacation, I needed a home in the*
> *country. What I had was a coat, a hat and a gun.*
> *I put them on and went out of the room.*
>
> Raymond Chandler, *Farewell My Lovely*

The heroes of the Nouvelle Vague were less concerned about doing good, than being spontaneous. The existentialist ideas of Sartre and Camus inspired a generation into believing that being free was a moral good in itself.

As Belmondo's outlaw declares in *Pierrot le Fou*: "Life may be sad, but it's beautiful . . . I suddenly feel free. We can do whatever we want, when we want." The New Wave in Hollywood, riding on the crest of rebellion and social change, pushed the concept of the hero even further. Now a hero didn't even need to be good, as long as they were better than the society around them. Since society was corrupt, rebellion against society must be a good. For these **anti-heroes**, their frailties become as important as their strengths. Their pain is greater than their triumph. Their successes are usually short-lived.

In *Bonnie and Clyde*, directly inspired by *Shoot the Pianist*, the outlaw Clyde suffers from impotence (not just shyness, like Charlie), a problem which he is not able to overcome until he learns that he and Bonnie have become famous. The outlaw often stands not only outside society, but outside himself. He is self-consciously playing a role. *Bonnie and Clyde* reflects the shift from social and political rebel to the narcissistic hero of the media age – which reached its apotheosis in Oliver Stone's *Natural Born Killers* – from a script by Tarantino.

The **anti-heroes** took Marlowe's cynicism about the corrupt world around him, added the self-doubt of the Nouvelle Vague hero, and mixed it with an anger against society in general. Despite their faults, the faults of society were greater, and so we empathized.

Unlike ordinary heroes, **anti-heroes** rarely learn or grow. Their position is stubborn and unbending, even to the point of folly and when all the odds are against them. They are heroic – as long as we share their point of view.

From *Easy Rider* to *Alfie*, from *Taxi Driver* to *Dirty Harry* the anti-hero's arc is a short one. They don't learn anything; or they learn it too late, or they forget that they learnt it in the first place. They get bruised, but they don't give up and they don't fundamentally change.

But each of these heroes reinvented a genre by standing apart from the usual way of looking at things. They made us look at the genre afresh, and question whether its values still held true. Alfie was a cad, but in the swinging sixties, when the pill and promiscuity were in fashion, did it matter? Dirty Harry operates outside the law in order to enforce it – but who would we rather have on our side?

Brick, a contemporary reworking of **film noir**, takes the frailty of these heroes and puts it into the character of a teenager, Brendan. Like Marlowe, he gets beaten and bruised but never gives up. He never loses his loneliness either. As Emily, his ex-girlfriend, says to him: "What are you? Eating back here, not liking anybody, how are you judging anyone? I loved you a lot but I couldn't stand it, I had to get with people. I couldn't heckle life with you, I had to see what was what." *The anti-hero's alienation from society can never be healed.*

By **crossing** the genre of film noir with the high-school drama, we are reminded that young people experience profound emotions and are capable of deep moral thought. We are also reminded why they need to be protected from the harsh realities of life.

Genre can be reinvented by changing the **motivation** or the **context** of the protagonist. *City of God* takes the ethos of the gangster movie and puts the guns in the hands of children, who can't even begin to understand the value of the lives they so casually take away.

Crossing genre is about taking a character from one genre and placing them in another. They land in our story, confounding our expectations of how the hero should behave.

Hot Fuzz, the follow-up by the *Shaun of the Dead* team, took the fusty fish-out-of-water genre, the village mystery, and gave it a spin by substituting a different kind of protagonist. Instead of the usual naive but determined outsider who arrives to probe into the villagers' secret affairs (*Wicker Man*), Angel is a high-adrenaline city cop who's been posted to the sticks for making his less gung-ho colleagues look bad. Initially bored after clearing up all the local, hitherto unnoticed crimes in short order, he's suddenly faced by a series of murders which the locals put down to "accidents".

The insertion of a different, more powerful protagonist (from the crime action genre) allows the filmmakers to raise the force of antagonism within the village (ending with a long, well over-the-top shoot-out involving most of the residents). It allows them to raise the stakes in a way that is absurdly out of character with this normally genteel, rural genre, which makes it very funny indeed. In a way, *Shaun of the Dead* does the opposite. Simon Pegg's untogether boyfriend is the last person you'd want defending you from zombies; except that in the end, he turns out to be the very best.

Mashing genre

Mashing genre, on the other hand, is about *shifting focus*.

As Robert Benton, co-writer of the groundbreaking *Bonnie and Clyde* put it: "The thing that mattered in *Bonnie and Clyde*, although in some senses it's a genre film, were the things which the New Wave stressed, the specifics that made people unlike what you thought people would be like, and the fact that the important scenes happened before or just after they would normally have occurred."[69]

Reservoir Dogs takes the heist genre and changes its meaning by throwing us straight into its aftermath. How and why things went wrong, and whether the bonds between the characters will hold, becomes the focus of the drama. In the stag-night comedy *Hangover*, the missing groom's friends attempt to retrace their steps after a wild stag night, in order to find him in time for the wedding. Their trip becomes a mystery, not only concerning his whereabouts, but about what each of them may learn about themselves.

Inception also takes the heist story, but reconceives it as the implanting of an idea into the mind of someone. We all are familiar with the theft of things which belong to us – but what about the theft of our thoughts? *Inception* may seem like science fiction, and yet we know that the power of persuasion and influence, from advertising and media, has its effect on us every day.

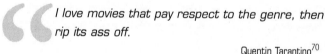

> *I love movies that pay respect to the genre, then rip its ass off.*
>
> Quentin Tarantino[70]

By *changing the focus* of the genre, putting the emphasis on aspects which are normally ignored or marginalized – such as the pain and suffering caused by violence or criminality – you can make your audience look at genre in a whole new light.

Million Dollar Baby, the story of a female boxer taken on by a reluctant veteran male coach, took a genre with a familiar story arc – the triumph of the underdog – and gave it a tragic twist that forced us to look at the effects of violence on the body as well as the soul (in doing so, Clint showed us that he had moved on from the character of *Dirty Harry*).

In Butch's storyline, *Pulp Fiction* took the "crooked sports" genre and transformed the boxing cheat into an **anti-hero**. In *On the Waterfront* Marlon Brando, a fighter forced to throw a fight that ended his career, may have redeemed himself by turning snitch, even though it went against everything in his nature.[71] Butch requires no such justifications. When Butch is told to throw a fight, he not only wins the fight but *kills* his opponent, and double-crosses his boss at the same time. (He is redeemed anyway, but not in the way we would expect!)

Some films **cross** genre, and **mash** it too – such as *Before the Devil Knows You're Dead.*

CLOSE UP:
BEFORE THE DEVIL KNOWS YOU'RE DEAD

In *Before the Devil Knows You're Dead* Andy, a louche, disaffected insurance broker, enlists his feckless younger brother Hank's assistance in "knocking off"a store.

Before he makes his pitch, Andy challenges Hank: "You used to have the world by the balls. Now what's happened to you . . . ? Well, let's see if you still have some cojones." "I've got them when I need them," Hank replies. Unknown to Andy, Hank is having an affair with his wife.

"It's insured, so it's a victimless crime," Andy tells him. "So, it's safe, nobody gets hurt, everybody wins. It's perfect." Andy refuses to give him any details until Hank declares himself in. Finally Hank, behind with his child payments to his ex-wife, agrees. Andy explains that it's a "mom and pop operation", and outlines the layout, which he explains Hank will be familiar with. Gradually it dawns on Hank that Andy is talking about their parents' jewelry store.

The whole idea of this "victimless" crime suddenly seems horrifying. There are certain rules, even among thieves. The first is that you do not steal from your own.

On the one hand, Andy's plan is logical and well thought out. On the other, it breaks a fundamental taboo. Even Hank recoils: "You can't do that."

In the end, the hold-up goes badly wrong because Andy can't handle the responsibility himself, and gets Bobby, a friend, to go in for him. Instead of the elderly weekend assistant, their mother is behind

---

the counter, and resists. She shoots her assailant before being shot herself, and is rushed to the hospital, where she lingers in a coma, brain dead, for some days until her life support is turned off.

The structure of the film plays with time in the same way as *Reservoir Dogs*, **mashing** genre by throwing us straight into the mayhem of the job gone wrong and its consequences (the linear story), then backtracking and intercutting with the story of how it all came about. Eventually the streams join and the film moves forward, as the consequences push the characters and their relationships **to the limit**.

This structure shifts our attention from the issue of the linear plot – "Will they get away with this?" (increasingly unlikely) – to the **Maverick** question: "How could they have done it?" How could two ordinary guys have done something so desperately wrong?

In an earlier version of the script, the two leading characters weren't actually brothers. As director Sidney Lumet put it: "I didn't want to have an exploitative picture and the way to avoid that . . . was to ratchet up its intensity. Anything that would increase the emotional risk."[72] **Crossing** the heist movie with family melodrama added a new emotional intensity to the heist story, while breathing new life into that old chestnut, sibling rivalry. The stakes for this sibling rivalry are as high as they could possibly be.

Tarantino's fetishizing of drug-taking and violence in *Pulp Fiction* rendered it unreal, easy to distance ourselves from. Instead he *shifted focus*: to the banal details of his characters' lives, which were treated more realistically, and taken more seriously. That made it easier for us to empathize. The exaggerated reality of *Pulp Fiction* took lives lived beyond the pale and dared us to see them as normal and ordinary.

Lumet, on the other hand, like all **realists**, takes ordinary lives and reveals their exceptional qualities, pushing them to extraordinary acts. Ethan Hawke (Hank) described – perhaps with Tarantino in mind – why he decided to take the role: "Sometimes people can take anger and darkness and try to make it cool, and when you do that . . . it's not real. [Lumet] wouldn't try to 'sell' these characters, there wouldn't be a lot of close-ups of burning cigarettes."[73]

These brothers aren't hardened criminals. Far from taking events in their stride, they begin to unravel under the pressure. Andy's firm's discovery of his embezzlement, and Hank's blackmail by a criminal associate of Bobby (who is killed in the hold-up), pile the pressure on and raise the stakes.

Soon Andy is talking Hank into helping him rob and kill his drug dealer in order to pay off Hank's blackmailer – whom he also kills, just to be on the safe side. It's only when Andy threatens to kill Bobby's wife that Hank says "enough".

The **shift of focus** from "what went wrong' to 'how could they do this", turns our attention away from the crime – with its genre expectations – to the family melodrama at the heart of the story. Unlike the traditional heist movie, where the failure of the job builds tension between an ensemble of loosely related characters, in Lumet's **crossing** of genres these complications are driven deep into the family's soul.

We learn that Andy always felt unloved by his father, in spite of being stronger and smarter than his younger brother. He was never as "cute" as Hank, and when you're cute your parents will forgive a lot. Hank both desires the approval of his older brother and wants to punish him for outshining him, even if only secretly, by sleeping with his wife.

However, the real inspiration in this **mixing** of genres comes in giving the detecting role to their father, Charles. Unsatisfied with the police investigation, Charles begins to investigate for himself, visiting a fence who reveals to him that Andy recently approached him about selling some jewels. Charles realizes his eldest son was behind the plan which led to his wife's murder.

When Andy turns his gun on his brother, revealing that he knows about Hank's affair with his wife, Hank begs Andy to shoot him.

"That's a good idea," Andy agrees. Before he can kill Hank, he is shot by Bobby's wife.

We might not believe the story could drive the tensions created by the heist any further into the heart of this family. But we have not taken it **to the limit** yet.

As Andy is lying in hospital, he confesses all to his father, begging his forgiveness. In response, Charles smothers him with a pillow, a taboo even more shocking than the one breached by his sons.

This double tragedy raises the film to a **mythic** level, matching (for melodrama) anything in the drama of the ancient Greeks.

Before the Devil Knows You're Dead takes the heist genre and drives it into family melodrama, giving the melodrama a deadlier and edgier hue. At the same time, the family melodrama invests the heist story with an intimacy which the genre often lacks, since in the **classic** heist the characters are usually strangers.

When you **cross** genre, each genre informs the other. This creates a **transparency**, not only from one genre to another, but also from one **level of reality** to another. When you **mash** genre, it changes what we think is important, and puts our focus elsewhere. This gives us a different **point of view** on the story.

In screenwriting, **time**, **point of view** and **reality** are all interwoven. Change one and you change all the others. Chaos theory tells us that unusual consequences develop from even small deviations in the pattern. When a butterfly flaps its wings on one side of the world, the ripple may create a wind that causes a tsunami on the other.

It is the job of the **Maverick** screenwriter to observe these small changes in the pattern – these cracks in reality – and follow where they lead.

It is up to you to catch the butterfly on the wing, and capture eternity in an hour.

> *To see a world in a Grain of Sand*
> *And a Heaven in a Wild Flower,*
> *Hold Infinity in the palm of your hand,*
> *And eternity in an hour.*

William Blake, Poet

MASHING GENRE
Recap

* **Crossing** genre means putting two or more genres together to invigorate them both.

* **Mashing** genre means finding a new point of attack, a new way into the genre.

* Sometimes this means finding a new kind of hero, or a hero from another genre.

* You can reinvent a genre by having a hero who stands apart from the normal way of seeing things.

* The anti-hero's alienation from society can never be healed.

* Genre can be reinvented by changing the motivation or the context of the protagonist.

* **Crossing** genre is often about taking a character from one genre and placing them in another.

* The insertion of a more powerful protagonist allows the screenwriter to raise the force of antagonism to match it. A weaker protagonist, on the other hand, creates bathos and undermines the pretensions of the antagonist.

* **Mashing** genre is about shifting focus.

* **Realism** takes ordinary lives and pushes them to the limit, revealing their exceptional qualities.

- **Exaggerated** reality takes exceptional characters and tries to convince us that they are normal and ordinary.

- When you **cross** genre, each genre informs the other.

- This creates a **transparency**, not only from one genre to another, but also from one **level of reality** to another.

- When you **mash** genre, it changes what we think is important, and puts our focus elsewhere. This gives us a different **point of view** on the story.

- In screenwriting **time**, **point of view** and **reality** are all interwoven.

Exercises

- Write a sequence which starts in one genre and crosses into another. How does each genre inform the other?

- **Mash** your genre by *shifting focus* to some element of the story which is normally marginalized or part of the background.

- Take a **classic** genre – now **mash** it so the question is no longer "How will it all end?" but "How did we get here?" How does it change our expectation about the story?

- Brainstorm the most unlikely combination of genres, and come up with a storyline that works.

- Find a genre that's out of fashion, and bring it back to life by giving it a contemporary twist.

- Now go back and rewrite all the exercises in this book, from a different **point of view**.

Notes

1 Goldman, William, *Adventures in the Screen Trade*. London: Abacus, 1996.

2 Interviewed in Froug, William, *Zen and the Art of Screenwriting*. Los Angeles: Silman James Press, 1996, pp. 54–5.

3 Konow, David, "Christopher McQuarrie", *Creative Screenwriting*, September/October 2000.

4 Brooker, Charlie, "A Glance at the Cinema Listings Proves Hollywood's Imagination Has Crashed", *Guardian*, 3 August 2003.

5 W. H. Auden, "Writing", part 1, *The Dyer's Hand*, 1962.

6 Bauer, Erik, and Konow, David, interview with Oliver Stone, *Creative Screenwriting*, July/August 2001.

7 David, Larry, Bonus Q&A "The US Comedy Arts Festival in Aspen", *Curb Your Enthusiasm: The Complete Third Season*, HBO Video, 2004.

8 Metz, Christian, "The Cinema: Language or Language System? Film Language: A Semiotics of the Cinema", p. 69, quoted in Monaco, James, *The New Wave*. New York: Oxford University Press, 1976, p. 129.

9 Luhr, William, *Raymond Chandler and Film*. Tallahassee: Florida State University Press, 1991, p. 13.

10 'The French New Wave', *Cinéma! Cinéma!*. London: Channel 4, 1992.

11 Ibid.

12 Steppenwolf, "Born to be Wild", RCA , 1968.

13 'Stanley Kubrick and Joseph Heller: A Conversation', in Castle, Alison, ed., *The Stanley Kubrick Archives*. London: Taschen, 2005, p. 365.

14 Fonda, Peter, *Don't Tell Dad: A Memoir*. New York: Simon & Schuster, 1998, p. 241.

15 So-called because the fate of the studio's fortunes rests on the performance of a few big-budget productions.

16 *Quentin Tarantino Talks to Kirsty Wark*, BBC2, 2003.

17 Cathcart, Thomas, and Klein, Daniel, *Plato and a Platypus Walk into a Bar*. London: Penguin, 2007, p. 46.

18 Buñuel, Luis, *A Walk Among the Shadows*, Studio Canal Video, 2005.

19 A style of formating that emphasizes readability and simplicity over technical details like scene numbering. The style arose from the practice of writing scripts "on spec", or uncommissioned. The writer takes the risk of being paid no money up front, in the hopes of a bigger payout when the script is sold.

20 Truffaut, François, *Hitchcock.* New York: Simon & Schuster, 1967, p. 17.

21 Tarkovsky, Andrei, trans. Kitty Hunter-Blair, *Sculpting in Time: Reflections on the Cinema.* Austin: University of Texas Press, 1987.

22 Springsteen, Bruce, "Livin' in the Future", Columbia Records, 2007.

23 This dialogue differs from the published version.

24 Both quotes from Linklater, Richard, *Slacker.* New York: St Martin's Press, 1992, p. 10.

25 Ibid.

26 "The Weight of Time" documentary, *Groundhog Day*, DVD, Columbia Tristar, 2003.

27 Arendt, Hannah, *Eichmann in Jerusalem: A Report on the Banality of Evil.* London: Penguin, 2006.

28 Nietzsche, Friedrich, *Thus Spake Zarathustra* (1883).

29 Nolan, Christopher, *Director's Commentary: Memento*, 3-Disc Special Edition DVD, Pathe, 2000.

30 Biskind, Peter, *Down and Dirty Pictures: Miramax, Sundance and the Rise of Independent Film.* New York: Simon & Schuster, 2005, p. 189.

31 *Quentin Tarantino: Hollywood's Boy Wonder,* dir. David Thompson, London, BBC, 1994.

32 Baxter, John, *Stanley Kubrick: A Biography.* London: HarperCollins, p. 356.

33 Quoted in McCabe, Colin, *Godard: A Portrait of the Artist at Seventy.* London: Macmillan, 2005, p. 326.

34 Bauer, Erik, "Quentin Tarantino", *Creative Screenwriting,* January/February 1998.

35 Quoted in Wilmington, Michael, "Through the Eyes of a Critic", *Chicago Tribune,* 17 May 1998.

36 Bauer, Erik, and Konow, David, "Interview with Oliver Stone", *Creative Screenwriting,* July/August 2001.

37 Sartre, Jean-Paul, *Nausea.* Harmondsworth: Penguin, 1938.

38 Cadwalladr, Carole, "Woody Allen: My Wife Hasn't Seen Most of My Films", *Guardian,* 13 March 2011.

39 Preston-Robertson, Bill, *The Coen Brothers, Art Zone*, BBC2, 2000.

40 Phillips, Gene D., "Dr. Strangelove, or: How I Learned to Stop Worrying and Start Loving the Bomb", *The Stanley Kubrick Archives*. London: Taschen, 2005, p. 346.

41 Ibid., p. 348.

42 Kubrick MS, Kubrick archives, by kind permission of the Stanley Kubrick Archive at the University of the Arts, London, Ref. SK/11/1/21.

43 Linklater, Richard, "Vertical Narrative", in *Slacker*. New York: St Martin's Press, 1992, p. 10.

44 Ibid.

45 Crowe, Cameron, *Conversations with Wilder*. New York: Knopf, 1999, p. 357.

46 Raphael, Frederic, *Eyes Wide Open: A Memoir of Stanley Kubrick and Eyes Wide Shut*. London: Phoenix, 2000.

47 Konow, David, "Christopher McQuarrie", *Creative Screenwriting*, September/October 2000.

48 Truffaut, François, *Hitchcock*. New York: Simon & Schuster, 1967, p. 163.

49 Macdonald, Kevin, *Emeric Pressburger: The Life and Death of a Screenwriter*. London: Faber, 1994, p. 240.

50 Beauvoir, Simone de, *The Ethics of Ambiguity*. Secaucus, NJ: Citadel Press, 1949, p. 129.

51 Robert Mckee, known for his charismatic screenwriting seminars and groundbreaking book *Story* (London: Methuen, 1999).

52 Yentob, Alan, *Werner Herzog: Beyond Reason, Imagine*, BBC, 2008.

53 Quoted in Perry, Ralph Barton, *The Thought and Characters of William James*, 1899, Vol. 2, ch. 91.

54 Simon Callow, in his otherwise excellent biography, *Orson Welles: The Road to Xanadu*, is particularly harsh in this regard.

55 Interviewed by Bogdanovich, Peter, in *Who the Devil Made It*. New York: Ballantine, 1998, p. 544.

56 My translations.

57 Carroll, Lewis, *Alice's Adventures in Wonderland* (1865).

58 Carroll, Lewis, *Through the Looking-glass and What Alice Found There* (1871).

59 Campbell, Joseph, *The Hero with a Thousand Faces*. New York: Princeton/Bollingen, 1973.

60 Gottlieb, Sidney, *Alfred Hitchcock: Interviews*. American Film Institute, 1972, p. 90.

61 For Hollywood insiders, this statement would have had even greater resonance. Penned (or "inked" as *Variety* would say) by Dalton Trumbo, Hollywood's most famous blacklisted writer, it was the first film he had written permitted to bear his name for over a decade. Following his refusal to give evidence about his Communist beliefs, he was sent to prison for contempt of court for eleven months. After that, he was only able to work through "fronts" – other writers who presented his work as their own. *Spartacus* is filled with Trumbo's hidden (and entirely justified) vitriol against his persecutors.

62 Inspired by the legend, "One ring to rule them all, and in the darkness bind them", in Tolkien, J. R. R., *The Lord of the Rings*. London: HarperCollins, 1994.

63 The Stern Brothers, quoted in *The Man in Lincoln's Nose*, compiled by Corey, Melinda and Ochoa, George. New York: Simon & Schuster, 1990, p. 175.

64 Of course, Kaufman ensures that this offhand remark isn't just a good gag but also a set-up, by having the chimp, emboldened by its own childhood memory of capture, come to Lottie's rescue after Craig has tied her up.

65 *Front Row*, BBC Radio 4.

66 Bernières, Louis de, *Captain Corelli's Mandolin*. London: Secker & Warburg, 1994.

67 See Campbell, Joseph, *"Masks of God"*, Vol. 2: Oriental Mythology. New York, London: Arkana, 1991.

68 "Questions à l'auteur", *Cinema 61*, January 1961, quoted in Monaco, James, *The New Wave*. New York: Oxford University Press, 1976, p. 41.

69 "The French New Wave", *Cinéma! Cinéma!*, London: Channel 4, 1992.

70 *Front Row*, BBC Radio 4, 2009.

71 There was, of course, a subtext. The director Elia Kazan had recently testified to Congress about the Communist affiliations of fellow artists, and the film attempts to justify his action.

72 Interviewed on *Charlie Rose*, PBS, USA, 2007.

73 Ibid.

Index